The Composition
of Aristotle's
Athenaion Politeia

The Composition
of Aristotle's
Athenaion Politeia

Observation and Explanation

JOHN J. KEANEY

NEW YORK   OXFORD
OXFORD UNIVERSITY PRESS
1992

Oxford University Press

Oxford   New York   Toronto
Delhi   Bombay   Calcutta   Madras   Karachi
Kuala Lumpur   Singapore   Hong Kong   Tokyo
Nairobi   Dar es Salaam   Cape Town
Melbourne   Auckland

and associated companies in
Berlin   Ibadan

Library of Congress Cataloging-in-Publication Data
Keaney, John J.
The composition of Aristotle's Athenaion politeia: observation
and explanation / John J. Keaney.
p. cm.   Includes bibliographical references and index.
ISBN 0-19-507032-1
1. Aristotle. Athēnaiōn politeia.   I. Title.
JC71.A41K43   1992   320.938'5—dc20
91-26295

9 8 7 6 5 4 3 2 1

Printed in the United States of America
on acid-free paper

Memoriae matris Bridget

e
per le graziose
Edwina M.
Anne M.
Laura C.

Preface

During the gestation of this book, portions of it were delivered as lectures or colloquia at McGill University, Rutgers University and, on several occasions, at my own university. I am grateful for the reactions of these audiences. Particular gratitude is owed to the members of an informal (i.e., not-for-credit) colloquium with graduate students at Princeton in the fall term of 1989, in which most of the contents were exposed to critical discussion: for their participation I thank C. Champion, R. Ganiban, A. Lardinois, L. Maurizio, K. McCarthy of the Department of Classics, and S. Monoson of the Department of Politics.

Nearly all of the Greek has been translated, and for this I have used (with minor modifications) the renderings of M. Dilts (Heracleides Lembos), P.J. Rhodes (for the Ἀθηναίων πολιτεία), and T. Saunders (Plato, *Laws* and Aristotle, *Politics*). See Bibliography.

The dedication records four generations.

Princeton   J.J.K.
August 1991

Contents

Introduction

Aristotle's Ἀθηναίων πολιτεία (Ἀθπολ, *AP*), since its discovery a century ago, has been treated as an historical document and much utilized by students of ancient history. This approach continues to create difficulties. Some have believed that the work is so poor as history that it must have been the product of a mind inferior to Aristotle's: another version of this belief is that the work is so different from the rest of what remains from Aristotle's voluminous output, the *corpus Aristotelicum*, that it must have been composed by someone else. At least partially because of the dominance of the "historical" approach, the work has been largely ignored by students of ancient philosophy.[1] It is, clearly, not illegitimate to use the Ἀθπολ as an historical source—sometimes it is a *fons unicus*—nor would anyone deny that it and other πολιτεῖαι have some necessary[2] connection with Aristotle's political philosophy, but to make conclusions about authorship or about the nature of the work based on criteria of Greek historiography or of Aristotle's philosophy is to ignore a third possibility, namely that the Ἀθπολ was neither intended to be a piece of historical writing nor was it entirely conceived to be ancillary to other works, whether the *Politics* or some other project.[3] I rather propose to examine the work in and for itself, without the hindrance of these scholarly blinkers, by means of a literary approach.[4] Perhaps I may be permitted here to give a brief example of this approach.

I will argue that a major thesis of the *AP* is that the people (δῆμος) ultimately gains political control by appropriating to itself powers which originally belonged to three other organs of the state, the College of Archons, the Council of the Areopagus (= the Areopagus) and the Council of the Five Hundred (= ἡ βουλή). Now, Aristotle never articulates this thesis in so many words: the closest he comes to that is his statement in chapter 9 on the connection of control of judicial decision and control of political power, and his statement in chapter 41 on the fact that the people have achieved control over everything by means of assembly decrees and strength in the popular law courts. Details of the overall process are presented piecemeal: in chapter 3, Aristotle contrasts the earlier judicial power of the archons with their lack of such power in the fourth century, and in chapter 25 he says that certain powers of the Areopagus have been taken away and given partly to the people (= assembly), partly to the law courts. We have no way of knowing to what kind of powers he refers, unless we are aware of an allusion in his language, through which we learn that the powers are judicial. The allusion to chapter 3 encourages another look at the reference to the archons there, and we note that the only powers to be identified are judicial. The statement of chapter 41 contains a reference to the βουλή, and this reference is fleshed out in chapter 45, in which Aristotle's theme is the limitation upon the judicial powers of the βουλή. All of this is reflected in the quadripartite structure I put on the work (I = beginning to chapter 3, II = 5–41, III = 42–62, IV = 62–end), for the limitation on the archons is mentioned in I, that on the Areopagus in II, that on the βουλή in III; and IV, though in form a long excursus, is integrally connected with what precedes it, since it describes how the people operate in the law courts.

I set out the methodology and some initial applications of it in chapters 2, 3, and 4; chapters 5 and 6 deal with two related structures which inform the whole of the ᾿Αθπολ. The content of the remaining chapters will, I trust, be self-explanatory.

I began this introduction with the possessive form of Aristotle. This may be thought to reflect a naive act of faith in his authorship, but I hope, in the first chapter, to have grounded that belief in rational argument. *Incipiamus igitur.*

NOTES

1. Not uncharacteristic is the remark of I. Düring in his big book on *Aristoteles: Darstellung und Interpretation seines Denkens* (Heidelberg 1966) 477: Die Problematik der ᾿Αθηναίων πολιτεία gehört zur Geschichtsforschung und daher nicht in den Rahmen dieses Buches (the problematic of the *Athpol* belongs to historical research and therefore not within the boundaries of this book).

2. Necessary in the sense that some parts of the *Politics* (e.g., book 5) could not have been written without the collection of historical data exemplified in the πολιτεῖαι.

3. At the end of the *Nichomachean Ethics* (1181B17–23) Aristotle promises that he will use the collected *politeiai* (πολιτεῖαι συνηγμέναι) in forming best-state theory, but he never fulfilled the promise.

4. In broad outline, no one has attempted a literary analysis since Kaibel in his *Stil und Text* of 1893. While there are points of contact between our approaches in the sense that I sometimes attempt to take his conclusions somewhat further (e.g., chiastic structure, the vocabulary of δῆμος and πλῆθος), he was concerned with smaller sections of the text (the larger part of his work [pp. 117–272] is a linguistic *Commentar*) in which he was determined to say something about every chapter). With one exception (ch. 41), I deal with interconnected themes and structures spread mostly, but not entirely, over the narrative portion of the work.

The Composition
of Aristotle's
Athenaion Politeia

1

The Origin and Authorship
of the *Politeiai*

When we consider the questions of the origin and authorship of the *politeiai*, it is useful to begin by reminding ourselves of the genre with which we are dealing. One set of general terms of a genre have been defined by Jacoby.[1] Ancient works with the word πολιτεία in their titles were one of three types: the philosophical *politeia,* the best example of which is Plato's work; the political *politeia,* like the 'Αθηναίων πολιτεία wrongly ascribed to Xenophon,[2] and the scientific *politeia*. This last was the invention of Aristotle and in Greek antiquity did not survive him. As we will see, Jacoby's schematization is of very limited value: it does not account for all the examples of Aristotle's πολιτεῖαι (note 5 below); and, more generally, although it is possible to describe the 'Αθπολ in terms of a (sub)genre, the utility of this kind of characterization is not very high.

There is only one extant example of the (sub)genre, the 'Αθηναίων πολιτεία, preserved partially on one papyrus (Berlin Inv. Nr. 5009) and more fully on another (London British Library Nr. 131), the beginning of which is missing and the end of which is mutilated.[3] In practical terms, then, the knowledge of and statements we make of the *politeiai* are based upon the text of the *AP* (papyri + *testimonia*) and fragmentary quotations of other of the *politeiai*. Given these conditions, generalizations about features common to the *AP* and the other *politeiai* must be made and received with caution.

The limitations of such knowledge may best be clarified by posing two questions: what made up the contents of the genre, and how typical of the genre was the 'Αθπολ? Absent other πολιτεῖαι, we cannot, of course, begin to give an adequate answer to these questions, but there are indications that this notion of genre may not be too helpful. Jacoby thought that the scientific *politeia* was concerned with how the fourth-century constitution came to be and thus entailed an historical narrative. This would seem a minimal requirement of content, and yet we know of at least one case in which special circumstances dictated that there be no narrative beginning,[4] and there may have been other cases in which there was no description of a contemporary πολιτεία.[5]

There is a related aspect to the second question in that special circumstances resulting in specific approaches in the 'Αθπολ will have been absent for other πολιτεῖαι. These circumstances are both general and particular. For the first, for example, we know the extent to which knowledge of Athenian law was necessary to reconstruct Solon's πολιτεία. When faced with the problem of reconstructing other πολιτεῖαι (e.g., that of Lycia), Aristotle did not have this kind of evidence for, as we are told by the excerptor of the πολιτεῖαι, the Lycians νόμοις οὐ χρῶνται[6] (they don't employ laws). Again, Aristotle urged (among others) two theses, that political degeneration at Athens began with Pericles, and that the figure of Theramenes was to be compared with the figure of Solon. Both theses could not be duplicated in any other πολιτεία, and source material to be used for similar theses may have been lacking.

Other generic implications may be worth brief exploration. If one were to ask a different but related question, what genre does the ᾿Αθπολ most closely resemble, I suppose that the the the answer would have to be history. But this answer would be unsatisfactory, for several reasons. It is not only because "Aristoteles kein geschichtlicher Forscher ist,"[7] nor because the ᾿Αθπολ is not granted even a mention in Renate Zoepffel's monograph on Aristotle and history.[8] It is partially because "history" is too broad a rubric. If we limit its scope and refer to "constitutional history," we are closer to what we find in the ᾿Αθπολ, but there remain some of its contents which do not seem comfortably to fit even within that rubric.

We can consider this aspect of the question from two other viewpoints: the first is Aristotle's relation to his sources, the second the relation of the ᾿Αθπολ to the political and other writings of the first generation of the Peripatos.[9]

It is all but certain that chs. 42–69 were Aristotle's innovation and not drawn from any single source. They depend on observation and documentary research.[10] In contrast, for facts chs. 1–41 are almost entirely dependent on historical sources. But existence of a plurality of sources again raises an interesting question. It is clear that the chronological skeleton of the ᾿Αθπολ was provided by Attidographers, the writers of Athenian local histories, ᾿Ατθίδες. It is also clear that representatives of this genre will have provided many of the historical details. In fact, while it is plausible to conceive that Aristotle could have gotten all of his details from this genre alone, it is clear that he did not. On one level, he used Herodotus and Thucydides directly.[11] He also used Atthidographers who themselves will have drawn their accounts from Herodotus and Thucydides: why this plurality of sources?[12] Sometimes Aristotle used a later source to correct an earlier one.[13] At other times, it seems as if his account were influenced only by the earlier source: this presumably means that the later source did not offer a variant.

A different reason for a plurality of sources is relevant: it is that Aristotle was a wide reader.[14] Hitherto, we have been considering only historiographical works as sources of facts. If we widen Aristotle's net to include works less "objective" than ᾿Ατθίδες, we may ask why he used things so diverse as the essay on Athenian demagogues by the opinionated Theopompus and the *Apology* and *Gorgias* of Plato. It was certainly not to recover facts of history.[15]

If I have seemed overly to stress the importance of sources in discussing generic qualities of the ᾿Αθπολ, it is because hardly any statement about the work can ignore their importance. To use one analogy, it is the historical data mediated through secondary sources which form the matter or material cause of which the written πολιτεία is the form or formal cause. If it is true that works like these were exploited by Aristotle, it makes the contents of the ᾿ΑθποΛ take on a rather different appearance from what they would have if they were limited to the mainstream of historiography. There is no all-embracing answer to this question, on generic or any other grounds, and I will deal with specific questions and specific answers.

AUTHORSHIP: THE ANCIENT EVIDENCE

When the London papyrus was discovered,[16] a new chapter in the history of classical scholarship began. As was to be expected, one of the foci of analysis was the question of authorship,[17] but arguments against Aristotelian authorship were neither good nor persuasive, and giants like Wilamowitz and Kaibel did not involve themselves in that skirmish.

In 1952, however, the question took on new urgency. In a statement which was to become highly influential, especially in British scholarship, Hignett (29) wrote:

> The historical survey in the *Athenaion Politeia* resembles a careful essay written by a modern research student who brings to his task much industry but no judgment. Anyone who disregards the ancient attribution to Aristotle and decides for himself on the internal evidence of the treatise is bound to conclude that it was written by one of Aristotle's pupils. Presumably the ancients attributed it to Aristotle because it was one of the *Politeiai*, constitutional histories of particular states, issued by his school.

The textual bases of Hignett's claim are reducible to discrepancies between the *Politics* and the *AP;* the conclusion Hignett drew from these I have attempted to refute elsewhere.[18] For now, it is relevant to note the assumptions implicit in such phrases as "the modern research student," "one of Aristotle's pupils," and "issued by his school." I deal with these assumptions later in this chapter.

The skeptical position of Hignett has been reinforced by the similar stand taken by the author of what will be for many years the standard commentary on the *AP,* P. J. Rhodes:

> The case in favor of Aristotelian authorship depends upon the attribution of antiquity; but this is a weak foundation unless one is prepared to believe that Aristotle himself wrote all the 158 *politeiai* and all the other works attributed to him.[19]

There are implications to these remarks which have gone unnoticed. The evidence of antiquity, external to the text, points to Aristotle not only as the author of the *AP* (that was not a separate question[20]) but as the author of all the *politeiai*. Whatever may be held about the *AP* today, I doubt whether anyone would unhesitatingly support the latter attribution. A partial reason for this reluctance may be the very unanimity of the evidence. But unanimity does not here rest upon a monolithic base, and-it is useful to examine how variously weighted unanimity is, when it is applied to the works attributed to Aristotle. Such attribution may be unanimous in one (or more) of four ways: (1) a work is known only from a catalog item, whether it be that preserved by Diogenes Laertius (a) or that by Hesychius (b); (2) a work may be known as a catalog item and by citation; (3) a work may be known as a catalog item, by citation and from a preserved fragment; (4) finally, besides these criteria, a work may be preserved in papyri and/or in medieval manuscripts.

Examples of (1a) are Περὶ φιλίας (no. 24)[21] and of (1b) Περὶ τῶν Σόλωνος ἀξόνων ε' (no. 50). An example of (2) is Τὰ ἐκ τοῦ Τιμαίου καὶ τῶν Ἀρχυτείων α', referred to by Simplicius in *de Caelo: Comm. in Arist. graeca* 7.379.16. (3) is represented by Εὔδημος ἢ περὶ ψυχῆς (no. 13) cited by Plutarch, *vitDion* 22.3 and partially preserved in fragments 37–48R. The fourth category is exemplified by the *Poetics*, Πραγματεία τέχνης ποιητικῆς (no. 83), cited in the *Vita Marciana* 4 (Düring 97) of Aristotle, and the text of which is based upon Greek, Latin, Syriac, and Arabic manuscripts.

The point of this analysis is not to show that the *AP* and the *politeiai* fall comfortably into this group[22] but to make two observations. The first is that the catalog preserved by Diogenes Laertius contains very few works not certainly by Aristotle,[23] and the authenticity of a work listed therein is almost guaranteed.

The second observation is that the kind of "unanimous attribution" that we find for the *politeiai* is unique. By this I mean that our knowledge of these works comes to us in five different and independent channels. The first is the reference to the collection (ἐκ τῶν συνηγμένων πολιτειῶν) in *NE* 10.1181B17. The second is the item in the catalog preserved by Diogenes Laertius (no. 143): πολιτεῖαι πόλεων δυοῖν δέουσαι ϱξ', κατ' εἴδη δημοκρατικαὶ καὶ ὀλιγαρχικαὶ καὶ ἀριστοκρατικαὶ καὶ τυραννικαί. (constitutions of 158 states, by classification democratic, oligarchic, aristocratic, and tyrannical). If Moraux is correct, the author of this catalog was the scholarch of the Peripatos, Ariston of Ceus, of the last quarter of the third century B.C.[24]

The third channel is the citations of the *politeiai* as Aristotle's in the preserved fragments. It is a possible, but not a necessary, assumption that most references of this kind can be traced back to the (cataloging? and) dissemination of the *politeiai* through the library at Alexandria.[25] Another assumption can be granted, viz., that Alexandrian attribution to Aristotle cannot mean much in terms of authorship, unless it could be shown that the *politeiai* received the same kind of historical and stylistic analysis to which, for example, the texts of the Attic orators were subjected.[26] Evidence for bibliographic activity on the *politeiai* at any period is extremely slight.[27]

A fourth channel is the attack on Aristotle and Theophrastus—an attack dateable within the latter's lifetime—by the historian Timaeus of Tauromenium.

Τίμαιος δ' ὁ Ταυρομενίτης ἐν τῇ ἐνάτῃ τῶν Ἱστοριῶν "οὐκ ἦν" φησί "πάτριον τοῖς Ἕλλησι ὑπὸ ἀργυρωνήτων τὸ παλαιὸν διακονεῖσθαι," γράφων οὕτως· "καθόλου δὲ ᾐτιῶντο τὸν Ἀριστοτέλη δημαρτηκέναι τῶν

Λοκρικῶν ἐθῶν· οὐδὲ γὰρ κεκτῆσθαι νόμον εἶναι τοῖς Λοκροῖς, ὁμοίως δὲ οὐδὲ Φωκεῦσιν, οὔτε θεραπαίνας οὔτε οἰκέτας + πλὴν ἐγγὺς τῶν χρόνων, ἀλλὰ πρώτη τῇ Φιλομήλου γυναικὶ τοῦ καταλαβόντος Δελφοὺς δύο θεραπαίνας ἀκολουθῆσαι. παραπλησίως δὲ καὶ Μνάσωνα τὸν Ἀριστοτέλους ἑταῖρον χιλίους οἰκέτας κτησάμενον, διαβληθῆναι παρὰ τοῖς Φωκεῦσιν, ὡς τοσούτους τῶν πολιτῶν τὴν ἀναγκαίαν τροφὴν ἀφῃρημένον· εἰθίσθαι γὰρ ἐν ταῖς οἰκειασκαῖς διακονεῖν τοὺς νεωτέρους τοῖς πρεσβυτέροις." (Athenaeus 264CD = 566 F 11 (a) J)

In the ninth book of his *Histories,* Timaeus of Tauromenium says: "It was not an inherited custom for the Greeks of old to be served by purchased servants." He writes as follows: "people accused Aristotle of being mistaken about Locrian habits. For it was not customary for the people of Locri, as similarly it was not for the people of Phocis, to possess servants of either sex, . . . but two female servants first attended the wife of the Philomelus who captured Delphi. Similarly, Mnason, the companion of Aristotle who possessed 10,000 slaves, was extremely disliked by the Phocians on the grounds that he had deprived that number of citizens of the necessities of life: for it was their custom for the younger to be servants to the older in households."

Similarly, Polybius says: Ἐμοὶ δὲ συμβαίνει καὶ παραβεβληκέναι πλεόνακις εἰς τὴν τῶν Λοκρῶν πόλιν καὶ παρεσχῆσθαι χρείας αὐτοῖς ἀναγκαίας . . . (12.5.1)

οὐκ ὤκνησα καὶ λεγείν καὶ γράφειν ὅτι τὴν ὑπ᾽ Ἀριστοτέλους παραδιδομένην ἱστορίαν περὶ τῆς ἀποικίας ἀληθινωτέραν εἶναι τῆς ὑπὸ Τιμαίου λεγομένης. σύνοιδα γὰρ τοῖς ἀνθρώποις ὁμολογοῦσιν ὅτι παραδόσιμος αὐτοῖς ἐστιν αὕτη περὶ τῆς ἀποικίας ἡ φήμη παρὰ πατέρων, ἥν Ἀριστοτέλης, εἴρηκεν, οὐ Τίμαιος. (12.5.4–5)

πλὴν ταῦτα μὲν ἡμῖν ὑπὲρ Ἀριστοτέλους εἰρήσθω πῶς καὶ τίσι προσέχων τοιαύτην ἐποιήσατο τὴν περὶ τῶν Λοκρῶν ἐξήγησιν. (12.7.2)

οὐ μὴν ἀλλὰ προφανῶς ἐν τούτοις ἐψευσμένος, μεταβὰς ἐπὶ τοὺς ἐν Ἰταλία Λοκροὺς πρῶτον μέν φησι τήν τε πολιτείαν καὶ τὰ λοιπὰ φιλάνθρωπα τοῖς Λοκροῖς ἀμφοτέροις . . . Ἀριστοτέλη καὶ Θεόφραστον καταψεῦσθαι τῆς πόλεως. (12.11.5 = F 12 J)

It happens that I have visited the city of the Locrians several times and have provided them with very useful services.

I have not hesitated both to say and to write that the report of the colony handed down by Aristotle is truer than that given by Timaeus. For I know that the people agree that they have an oral account of the colony handed down from their ancestors: and this is the one Aristotle used, not Timaeus.

However, let this much be said in Aristotle's behalf, how and relying on what he produced a narrative like this on the Locrians.

Moreover, having been clearly caught lying in these matters, he crossed over to the Locrians in Italy: first he said that the constitution and other things in both Locri were civilized . . . that Aristotle and Theophrastus attacked the city falsely.

What is important in this polemic is not the personal attacks—like those of the Epicureans[28]—upon Aristotle and his friends nor even the question as to whether Aristotle or Timaeus was correct in the account of the foundation of Epizephurian Locri in southern Italy.[29] It is the fact that a Λοκρῶν Πολιτεία is early attributed to Aristotle,[30] that this πολιτεία was in some kind of circulation outside Aristotle's school in the generation after his death, that Aristotle and Theophrastus are the only scholars attacked,[31] and that the account therein was based on oral tradition.

The final channel is the testimony of Philodemus:[32]

τί δὲ δὴ μετέπεσε τῆς ⟨φιλοσοφίας καὶ τῆς πόρ)ρω προτροπῆς τῶν νεωτέρων καὶ δεινῆς ἐπειρᾶτο νεμέσεως καὶ δυσμενείας εἴτε τῶν ἀφ᾽
Ἰσοκράτους εἴτ᾽ ἐνίων ἄλλων σοφιστῶν; πῶς δ᾽ οὐχὶ θαυμασμὸν ἐνέφυσε
μέγαν τῆς δυνάμεως, ἐξ οὗ τε ἀπεπήδα τῆς οἰκείας πραγματείας καὶ διὰ
ταῦτ᾽ ἐφωρᾶτο τούς τε νόμους συνάγων ἅμα τῷ μαθητῇ καὶ τὰς τοσαύτας
πολιτείας καὶ τὰ περὶ τῶν τόπων δικαιώματα καὶ τὰ πρὸς τοὺς καιροὺς
καὶ πᾶν ὅσον τῆς τοιαύτης ἐστὶ ⟨πραγματείας κτλ.

Why did he shift from philosophy and the further encouragement of the young and leave himself open to terrible anger and hostility whether from the pupils of Isocrates or from some other sophists? How did he not instill great admiration for his (rhetorical) power from the time when he leapt away from his proper activity and in this way was caught, in conjunction with his pupil (sc., Theophrastus), collecting the laws and the great number of *politeiai* and the claims about places and responses to opportunities[33] and the whole body of work related to this kind of activity.

The critique goes back to the early generations of Epicureans,[34] and it is characterized by accuracy of detail in three areas, insofar as those details can be controlled. These areas are chronology, terminology, and attribution.

One of the segments of philosophy from which Aristotle fell away was ἡ προτροπὴ τῶν νεωτέρων: this is clearly a reference to one of Aristotle's earliest and most famous works, the *Protrepticus*. Philodemus uses the verb συνάγειν to refer to Aristotle's activity: this is the same verb used by Aristotle himself of the *politeiai* in the *NE*. It is correct to draw attention to the large number of *politeiai*. The works mentioned are accurately entitled and accurately attributed, the first and fourth always to Theophrastus, the second and third always to Aristotle.[35]

This evidence is variegated, mostly early, and shows, at a minimum, that two and only two scholars, Aristotle and Theophrastus, were involved in this activity. To say that the fact of variegation in the evidence and the implications of this have been slighted by all scholars who have concerned themselves with the origin and authorship of the *politeiai* would be an exaggeration: in fact, they have been ignored. Instead, scholars have preferred to operate within a set of assumptions, several of which may not have been relevant to conditions in the Peripatos.[36]

These assumptions have included the following:

1. the *termini* for the composition of the *AP* are 329/8 and 322;[37]
2. the *politeiai* were produced during Aristotle's second stay at Athens;[38]
3. the *politeiai* form one set of a group of documentary works characteristic of Aristotle's second stay at Athens;
4. because of the large number of *politeiai,* it is not conceivable that Aristotle produced them all himself: collaboration was needed.
5. the *AP* may be taken as typical of the *politeiai.*[39]

It is easy to see how the first four of these assumptions are linked. If (1) is correct, it may be legitimate to reduce the time span of (2) from fourteen to eight years. If that is done, (4) is almost entailed, for reasons of chronology if no other. It is equally easy to see how important (1) is to this concatenation. If (1) is removed, the other assumptions are necessarily affected, if not destroyed. Now, on the basis of discrepancies between the text of the *AP* used by some ancient lexicographers and the text contained in the London papyrus, it was long ago argued that two versions of the work circulated in antiquity.[40] With further evidence and argumentation on the same basis,[41] it became clear that a first edition of the work was written sometime between 334 and 331.[42] One immediate effect of this redating is to widen the period during which work was being done on the *politeiai* and perhaps to diminish the need to assume (a great deal of) collaboration.[43]

Now is perhaps the best point at which to address more precisely the whole notion of collaboration, a notion which no participant in the discussion has elected to define. I will attempt to do this through three avenues. First, I will set up some theoretical models of cooperation. Second, I will examine known instances of collaborative activity to see how well or poorly they match these models. Finally, I will focus on one Peripatetic of the first generation, Phainias, whose oeuvre would seem to make him a prime candidate for collaboration in political writings.

Initially, two types of collaboration may be envisaged. For the first, a student or students will have provided Aristotle with information about a specific πόλις from book knowledge, from a visit to the place, or from personal knowledge of the place; Aristotle will have taken this information and turned it into a *politeia.*[44] Alternatively, a pupil will have amassed the information and himself will have turned it into a *politeia:* the similarity in the finished products will have caused them all to be attributed to Aristotle. If these are the correct alternatives,[45] I suggest that the first is more consistent with the available evidence. The discussion will focus on two aspects of the matter: (1) what is known about one historically attested instance of collaboration; and (2) what is known about the activity of those of Aristotle's pupils who had an interest in political history.

(1) Apart from the information provided by Philodemus about the activity of Aristotle and Theophrastus, the single other example of Aristotle associated with someone else in the production of a specific work is the list of Pythian victors authored by Aristotle and his nephew Callisthenes. It is known to us through an inscription:[46]

συνέταξαν πίνακ-
α τῶν ἀπ' αἰῶνος νεν-
ικηκότων τὰ Πύθια
καὶ τῶν ἐξ ἀρχῆς τὸ-
ν ἀγῶνα κατασκευασ-
σάντων, ἐπαινέσαι
'Αριστοτέλην καὶ Κ-
αλλισθένην καὶ στ-
εφανῶσαι, ἀναθεῖν-
αι δὲ τὸν πίνακα το-
ὺς ταμίας ἐν τῷ ἱε-
ρῷ μεταγεγραμμένο-
ν εἰς στήλας

[composed a complete list of those who were victorious at the Pythian games and those who established the contest from the beginning. To praise Aristotle and Callisthenes and to garland them, the treasurers are to set up in the temple the list transcribed onto *stelai*]

The details of the literary and historical contexts of this inscription are as follows:

1. Callisthenes, the nephew of Aristotle, wrote a monograph on the Sacred War (356–346), of which one fragment is preserved (124 F 1 Jacoby).
2. Diogenes' catalog (no. 131) lists a Πυθιονῖκαι α' In Hesychius' catalog there is a note attached: ἐν ᾧ Μεναίχμον ἐνίκησεν. This list will be the πίναξ of the inscription.
3. Diogenes also lists a Πυθικὸς α' and a Πυθιονικῶν ἔλεγχοι (nos. 134–35).
4. In 335, Callisthenes left the mainland to join Alexander in Asia.
5. The πίναξ was inscribed sometime between 339 and 327.[47]
6. Aristotle returned to Athens in 335/4.

Items 4 and 6 suggest that Aristotle worked on the πίναξ while in Delphi and finished it before he returned to Athens. This last is not a necessary conclusion, but it finds some support in a recent epigraphical discovery.[48] Daochus, a *hieromnemon* at Delphi—first in 336—had a monument erected in honor of an ancestor, Agias, a Thessalian pancratiast. The inscription recording the victories of Agias is identical with another found in Pharsalus, with one exception: the latter records five Pythian victories—πεντάκις ἐν Νεμέοις, τόσα Πύθια—while the former has only three—τρὶς Πύθια. It was Miller who discovered that the Delphic inscription originally read τόσα. Given the date of the inscription, "almost certainly in the period between 336 and 332," and the fact that the date of the correction is very near to that of the original, it is almost an inescapable conclusion that the correction was based on Aristotle's πίναξ.

(2) Although the nature of the collaboration is unclear, the fact of collaboration is indisputable and in sharp contrast to the type of evidence attached to names mentioned in the same context by Brink, for example: Dicaearchus,

Clytus, and Phainias. Clytus (490 *FGrH*) wrote a Περὶ Μιλήτου of which two fragments survive: these are insufficient to establish what, if any, focus this book had or to show any connection with a Μιλησίων πολιτεία.[49]

Of more potential interest is the oeuvre of Phainias of Eresos because only in his case do we have adequate evidence to deal with: this consists of three titles and nine untitled fragments of a historical or biographical content, eight of which have to do with Solon and Themistocles. The titles are Περὶ τῶν ἐν Σικελίᾳ τυράννων *(On Tyrants in Sicily)*, Τυράννων ἀναιρέσεις ἐκ τιμωρίας *(Tyrants eliminated through Revenge)*, and Πρυτάνεις Ἐρεσίων *(Chief Magistrates of Eresos)*. The first two titles show that the major focus of these works was not on πόλεις. The second work may have been conceived as a continuation of a theme already established by Aristotle.[50] To what extent any of these works were documentary or relied on documentary sources cannot be known, but in the second of them Phainias is using secondary sources like Theopompus (F 11 W) and citing Hippys of Rhegion (F 12). The Πρυτάνεις Ἐρεσίων was a chronographical history: theoretically, it (like an *Atthis*) could have served as preliminary to an Ἐρεσίων πολιτεία, but no such a title is attested, and Eresos is nowhere mentioned by Aristotle.

Phainias' citation of secondary sources and the parallel with the *Politics* suggest that the first two works were drawing on material already collected. The suggestion is consistent with the first of the only two immediately relevant historical fragments and is supported by the second. In F 21, Phainias rejects a chronological relationship between Solon and Peisistratus which apparently had been put forward by Heraclides Ponticus (F 148 W). The basis of the rejection was a chronology from which it was known in what year Peisistratus began to rule and in which year Solon died. Another relationship between the two was already rejected by Aristotle on precisely the same basis.[51] In F 20, Phainias says that Solon solved the economic crisis facing Athens by using deceit toward both parties in the *stasis,* promising redistribution of land to the poor and confirmation of debts to the rich. This is a view of Solon totally at odds with that of the *AP,* and Aristotle is there so careful to defend Solon's reputation that he probably would have mentioned this view, had he known of it. Phainias' view represents a revisionist, not to say sensationalist, rewriting of history, much in the spirit of Τὰ πολιτικὰ τὰ πρὸς τοὺς καιρούς of his fellow citizen, Theophrastus, and perhaps even containing an allusion to Aristotle's more orthodox view.[52]

Some initial conclusions seem justified at this stage. (1) Explicit evidence for collaboration is restricted to two sets of instances, between Aristotle and Theophrastus and between Aristotle and Callisthenes. (2) This evidence is unknown to two of the later traditions, the Peripatetic and the Alexandrian: this does not mean that these two channels have diminished probative value on the question of authorship; it only means that they are not exhaustive. (3) No extant evidence about any of the people in the Peripatos who wrote in these areas suggests collaboration involving them.

On the other hand, the limitations of the evidence should be recognized. The first limitation is that we have names only if they are connected with written work. That is to say, individuals become visible only when they are connected to a finished product. With this evidence, nothing can be said about collaboration which was anonymous and occurred at a stage prior to the finished product. Of explicit evidence about such collaboration there is no trace: there is only what may be inferred about the processes involving Aristotle and Theophrastus on the one hand and Aristotle and Callisthenes on the other. Further and wider inference may, theoretically, be justified simply because we know that a body of written work was produced and this depended on a collection of historical material, howsoever this was gathered. In fact, however, we have so little information about the content of other *politeiai* that such inference would ultimately prove futile. I prefer to turn to an aspect of the matter for which the evidence is rather more solid.

THE AUTHORSHIP OF THE *AP*

It is agreed, although some of the formulations have nothing to support them, that the *AP* is a product of Aristotle's school during the second stay at Athens. It may be agreed that the work was written by Aristotle himself or by a pupil himself or produced in some kind of collaboration. How can we tell? In an ultimate sense, we cannot, but in that denial we run the risk of doing something which would be found totally unacceptable in any other area of study of the ancient world, namely rejecting *tout court* all the ancient evidence we have on the subject.

The ordinary criteria for deciding the authenticity of a work of ancient Greek prose are (1) chronology, (2) content, and (3) language. Here, (1) does not apply, for the *AP* was written within the bounds of Aristotle's second stay at Athens. (2) there is nothing in the content of the work which is so inconsistent with the (agreed-to-be) genuine works of Aristotle as to rule out Aristotle's authorship.

(3) Linguistic evidence is complicated. It is evident that words which are basic to Aristotle's philosophical vocabulary are absent from the *AP*. For example, as Rhodes (8) correctly states: "The words τέλος and φύσις are not used at all with teleological implications in *A.P.*," but that statement becomes irrelevant to the question of authorship, once it is realized that in the *Politics* Aristotle never uses these words of any historical constitution. Again, the statement (Rhodes 39) that: "many favourite terms of Aristotle are absent [sc., from the *AP*], such as εὐλαβεῖσθαι, ἐφίεσθαι, ὀρέγεσθαι, ὑπολαμβάνειν;" has no force, unless we are supplied with contexts in which these words and only these words would have been used.

It may be more promising, on the other hand, to work from a positive approach and consider the desirability of accounting for a phenomenon which Rhodes (39) acknowledges, namely the presence in the 'Αθπολ of "expressions which are distinctly Aristotelian." That phenomenon should receive more precise analysis, and I will attempt this by focusing on some expressions common to the Αθπολ and the works of Aristotle and assessing their rarity or absence in other authors. When this is done, it will be clear that there is not total justification in Rhodes' (40) doubt "that further stylometric tests would enable us to determine whether Aristotle himself was the author of *A.P.*"

Two aspects of diction are relevant: vocabulary and phraseology. I have already[53] pointed to two of these: the first is a penchant, shared by Aristotle and the author of the ᾿Αθπολ, for coining verbs with two prefixes; I used the example of words beginning with προ-. This feature would not have been outside the capacity of a pupil, if he were sufficiently prolific and dealt with a sufficient number of technical or semitechnical subjects. Theophrastus qualifies on both counts, and the verbs προανατέλλειν, προεκλύειν, προεκπηδᾶν, προεκτρέχειν, and perhaps προεκπίπτειν seem to have been coined by him.

The second example was of narrower compass, the almost unique way in which Aristotle used a common word, γνώριμοι, with reference to a political elite. With two exceptions, this usage is confined to the *AP* and to the *Politics*.[54] It is possible that an attentive pupil could have picked up this nuance from Aristotle's lectures or from conversation.

Decisions based on phraseology can be more firmly based. I will not lay great stress on a small phenomenon like the phrase τῷ ὕστερον ἔτει (34.2), in which ὕστερον is a functional equivalent of ὑστέρῳ,[55] and which has one parallel in classical prose, *HA* 545A27: τὰ τῷ ὕστερον ἔτει γεννώμενα.[56] Stress must be placed rather on the incidence of other, semantically and functionally related, phrases. Again, the evidence is set out in three stages, and concerns closure patterns.

1. 16.1 · ἡ μὲν οὖν Πεισιστράτου τυραννὶς ἐξ ἀρχῆς τε κατέστη το-
   ῦτον τὸν τρόπον . . . (that is how Peisistratus' tyranny was established from the beginning). Cf. also 26.1 and 35.1. This is one version of a closure pattern involving the use of μὲν οὖν and τοῦτον + τὸν τρόπον. Aristotle used it twenty-six times outside the ᾿Αθπολ; it was used once in Greek prose before him,[57] and Theophrastus did not use it.
2. A second version is μὲν οὖν . . . τὸν τρόπον τοῦτον. This is not found in the ᾿Αθπολ nor in classical prose, but it occurs sixteen times in the *Corpus Aristotelium* and is used once by Theophrastos (*HP* 1.1.5).
3. A third version is the most popular for Aristotle and is illustrated by four passages:
   3.5: τὰ μὲν οὖν περὶ τὰς ἀρχὰς τοῦτον εἶχε τὸν τρόπον,
   9.1: τὰ μὲν οὖν περὶ τὰς ἀρχὰς τοῦτον εἶχε τὸν τρόπον,
   43.1: τὰ μὲν οὖν περὶ τὴν τῶν πολιτῶν ἐγγραφὴν καὶ τοὺς ἐφήβους τοῦτον ἔχει τὸν τρόπον,
   60.1: τὰ μὲν οὖν περὶ τοὺς θ' ἄρχοντας τοῦτον ἔχει τὸν τρόπον.

In this formula, the stable elements initially to be isolated are μὲν οὖν, the placement of the verb, and τοῦτον τὸν τρόπον. The position of the first is determined by the rules of the language, the positions of the second and third are theoretically free, but certain positions are preferred by Aristotle, and, once again, we may set out smaller amd larger parallels in three sets (in all cases the end of the formula is τοῦτον ἔχει τὸν τρόπον):

(a) τὰ μὲν οὖν : 8x total, 5x in the *Historia Animalium (HA)*;

(b) περὶ μὲν οὖν: 16x total, 14x in the *HA*;

(c) τὰ μὲν οὖν περὶ: 13x total, 12x in the *HA*.

Some initial observations: first, this closure formula is used only by Aristotle; it is not used by Theophrastus and does not occur in the *spuria* of the *corpus Aristotelicum*. Second, when ἔχει + τοῦτον τὸν τρόπον are found in a different order, it is, with one exception,[58] never in a closure. Third, especially remarkable is the incidence of the formula in the *HA*.[59]

What conclusions should be drawn from these observations? We do not, perhaps, have the comparative evidence to say that Aristotle's penchant for τὰ μὲν οὖν, περὶ μὲν οὖν, τὰ περὶ μὲν οὖν . . . τοῦτον ἔχει τὸν τρόπον is a kind of signature distinctive of his style,[60] but the fact remains that the evidence exists to make some such distinctions between Aristotle and Theophrastus, the single pupil of Aristotle whose remains make the comparison possible. Table 1-1 offers some examples of closure patterns and the numbers of times (×) used:

Table1-1

	Aristotle	Theophrastus
ἀρκεῖ/ἀρκείτω τὰ εἰρημένα	0x	5x
ἱκανῶς εἴρηται	8x	4x
ἱκανῶς + εἰρήσθω	1x	17x
τοσαῦτ(α) + εἰρήσθω	18x	1x

On the basis of this evidence, I see no other conclusion except that Aristotle himself was the author of the ᾿Αθπολ, and the coincidence of the use of one closure pattern in the *HA* and in the ᾿Αθπολ is final proof that both works are to be dated to the latter part of the 330s.[61]

NOTES

1. *Atthis* 212.

2. The ascription doubtless was made by a cataloger who found the essay in a batch of manuscripts containing genuine works of Xenophon: cf. E. G. Turner, *Greek Papyri: An Introduction* (Princeton 1968) 103.

3. Much of the content of this part of the work can confidently be supplied from later writers who quote it.

4. This is the Arcadian League, founded in the 360s. Cf. F 483 R = Harpocration M 43, s.v. Μύριοι ἐν Μεγάλη πόλει· . . . διείλεκται δὲ περὶ αὐτῶν καὶ ᾿Αριστοτέλης ἐν τῇ κοινῇ ᾿Αρκάδων πολιτείᾳ, ἀρχόμενος τοῦ βιβλίου (The Thousand in Megalopolis . . . these were discussed also by Aristotle in the *Federated Constitution of Arcadia*.) Presumably, the lexicographer noted that the descriptive content of the beginning of this πολιτεία was dissimilar to the narrative content of others.

5. Prof. M. Hatzopoulos reminds me that some of the cities represented by πολιτεία titles will have had no independent πολιτεία when Aristotle was writing, viz., after they had been conquered by Philip II.

6. Her[acleides], *Exc.* 43 Dilts.

7. Wilamowitz, *AA* 1.373: cf. also *Greek Historical Writing* (Oxford 1908) 18: "he was no historian." By this Wilamowitz meant that "the ascertaining of historical truth was [not] an end to him." I would qualify this to say that it was not an ultimate end for Aristotle.

8. R. Zoepffel, *Historia und Geschichte bei Aristoteles* = *Abhl.Heidelb.Akad.* (Heidelberg 1975).

9. I treat this in "The Cultural Origin of the 'Αθπολ."

10. For the latter, cf. the reference to a Solonian law at 47.1 and the reference to the στῆλαι πρὸς ταῖς συμμαχίαις καὶ προξενίαις καὶ πολιτείαις (pillars connected with alliances, appointments of *proxeni*, and grants of citizenship) at 54.3. Note the comment of Rhodes (603) on the sparsity of argument in the descriptive sections.

11. Indeed, the only historical source he names is Herodotus (14.4).

12. The question is complicated by the fact that we are almost entirely ignorant of how and to what extent the Atthidographers used earlier historians.

13. Cf. P. Harding, "Atthis and Politeia," *Historia* 26 (1977) 148–60.

14. 'Αναγνώστης (reader) was one of Plato's nicknames for him: cf. Düring 98, 132, 152.

15. For the *Apology*, see Keaney 1979[2]; for the *Gorgias*, chapter 12, "Aristotle and Theramenes."

16. For details of the discovery, see Rhodes 1–5.

17. Sandys[2] xlix–lxv has a fairly superficial discussion of the issues raised around the question.

18. Keaney 1980.51–56.

19. Rhodes 61–62, on which see Keaney 1982.456–57.

20. There is apparent objection to this statement in Cicero, *Ep. ad Atticum* 2.2: Πελληναίων in manibus tenebam et hercule magnum acervum Dicaearchi mihi ante pedes extruxeram. . . . Κορινθίων et 'Αθηναιών puto me Romae habere. (I have the "Pellene" in my hand and a goodly heap of Dicaearchus piled up in fron to me. . . . I think I have the "Corinth" and the "Athens" in Rome [tr. Shackleton Bailey]). This would be invaluable evidence for collaboration in the production of πολιτεῖαι if it could be taken at face value (as it is e.g., by Shackleton Bailey *ad loc.*). Since all three works are attested for Aristotle (Pell., F 567 R; Cor. Her., *Exc.* 19 D), Cicero or his bookseller has made a mistake.

21. The numeration is that of Düring 41–50, 83–99 and Moraux 22–27.

22. (1) Diog. Laert. no. 143 (below), (2) Aristotle, *NE* 10.1181B17, Philodemus (below), fragments 381–611 R, (4) London papyrus.

23. The reason for Plutarch's (*vitArist* 27.2) doubts about the authenticity of the Περὶ εὐγενείας is unknown: he may be reflecting a discussion in Andronicus, the cataloger and editor of Aristotle's works of the first century B.C.: cf. Moraux 36. The question of the item 'Ιατρικά αβ' (no. 110) is more complicated. According to Galen (*Corp. Med. Graec.* 5.9.1), αἱ τῆς 'Ιατρικῆς συναγωγῆς βίβλοι are ascribed (ἐπιγραφόμεναι) to Aristotle but are agreed to be by Menon, his pupil. If the two works are the same, we have the single instance of a work known to be by someone else attributed to Aristotle in this list: this possibility does not seem to affect the credibility of the rest of the list, for the 'Ιατρικά, along with the other indisputably non-Aristotelian

work, the Φυσιογνωμικόν α' (no. 109) seem to be later interpolations therein: Moraux 186–89.

24. In Keaney 1963², I have attempted to support Moraux' conclusion with two further arguments: (1) that the order of the πολιτεῖαι in Diogenes' list reflects the order of treatment of these constitutional forms in *Politics* 4 (the same order at *Rhet.* 1.1365B27–28) and (2) that the absence of the biological works from the list is inconsistent with the knowledge of these works by contemporary Alexandrian scholars and argues against an Alexandrian origin for the list. Düring 476 n. 297, replied to the first argument with the suggestion that an Alexandrian pinacographer may have gotten this arrangement from the Peripatos. That is possible: he did not get it from the *Politics*, knowledge of which seems to have been almost nonexistent in Alexandria. Cf. Newman 2.ix–xx and A. Dreizehnter, *Aristoteles Politica* (Munich 1970) xvi–xix. Only one papyrus fragment has been found: E. G. Turner, "Two Greek Papyri," *WS* 79 (1966) 186–91. Düring chose not to reply to the second argument.

25. It is by now clear that two editions of the *AP* circulated in antiquity (Keaney 1970² 326–37; Rhodes 51–58). Given the fact that the earlier edition was the one used by the lexicographer Harpocration (who had Alexandrian connections), it is possible that this was the one more widely disseminated through Alexandria, but we have too little knowledge of that subject.

26. Cf. K. J. Dover, *Lysias and the* Corpus Lysiacum (Berkeley and Los Angeles 1968) 1–27.

27. It is restricted to two items. The second-century lexicographer Harpocration cites the κοιναὶ πολιτεῖαι of Arcadia (M 14: Μύριοι ἐν Μεγάλῃ πόλει) and Thessaly (T 7: Τετραρχία). The fact that only Harpocration uses this form of reference might suggest that he invented the term κοινὴ πολιτεία to distinguish constitutions of federated states, were it not for a curious bit of later evidence. In his *Bibliotheca*, cod. 161, Photius reports that one Sopater—perhaps to be identified with the fourth-century rhetor—wrote excerpts of the *politeiai* of Thessaly, Achaea, Paros, Lycia and Ceus. Of these, Thessaly, Achaea, and Lycia would have had κοιναὶ πολιτεῖαι for they were federations. The three cities of Ceus—Ioulis, Carthaea, Caresus—were joined in a federation earlier in the fourth century, and that arrangement may still have been in effect when Aristotle was writing. The latest discussions are by J. Cargil, *The Second Athenian League* (Berkeley and Los Angeles 1981) 134–36 and E. Ruschenbusch, "I G XII 5 609: Eine Burgerliste von Julis und Koresia auf Keos," *ZPE* 48 (1952) 175–88; P. Brun, "L'île de Keos et ses cités au ive siècle av. JC," *ZPE* 86 (1989) 121–38. The presence of Paros in this context is anomalous, but it may be that the other four *politeiai* represent a (library's?) subdivision of the collection.

28. On both, see Düring 376–78; 375–78.

29. For discussion, see F. W. Walbank, *A Historical Commentary on Polybius* 2 (Oxford 1967) 331–53.

30. The existence of this work is otherwise attested by a scholiast to Pindar and by Clement of Alexandria (F 548 R). Many, if not all, of the *politeiai* will have included foundation legends (cp. Plutarch's term for them: κτίσεις [*Moral.* 1093C]). It is not known to which work of Theophrastus reference is made: the obvious possibilities are listed by Walbank 330. A judicial practice of Locri was discussed in the Vatican fragment to be assigned to Theophrastus' *Laws* (side A, lines 53–59: Keaney 1974.192–93).

31. Mnason became a victim presumably because he was a tyrant (of Eritrea).

32. *Rhetorica* 2. p. 57 Sudhaus.

33. This is mistranslated by Düring (306) as "the laws enacted at critical times." The fuller title was Πολιτικὰ τὰ πρὸς τοὺς καιρούς.

34. This is the single reported Epicurean criticism of Aristotle which is taken seriously by D. Sedley, "Epicurus and His Professional Rivals," *Etudes sur l'épicuréisme antique = Cahiers de Philologie* 1 (Lille 1976) 119–59.

35. The works mentioned are based largely on documentary sources (πρὸς τοὺς καιρούς may have been an exception), but other documentary works (e.g., the *Didascaliae, List of Pythian Victors*) were not mentioned, presumably because they were nonpolitical in content. An apparently surprising omission is the *Politics:* the omission is most probably to be accounted for in that it was a work not known outside the school.

36. Cf. especially Jaeger 327, W. D. Ross, "The Development of Aristotle's Thought," *PRBA* 43 (1957) 63–78 and K. O. Brink, "Peripatos," *RE* Suppltb. 7.917–19. It is one of the ironies of history that two of the literary dates cardinal in Jaeger's seminal theory of the development of Aristotle were wrong: these are the dates of the composition of the Ἀθπολ and of the inscribing of the list of *Pythian Victors* (cf. D. M. Lewis, "An Aristotle Publication-Date," *CR* n.s. 8 [1958] 108).

37. The first because of the mention of the archon of that year (*AP* 54.7; the second because the official mentioned as being sent to Samos (62.2) was not sent after that year.

38. Düring, *Aristoteles* 51 revives the suggestion that some of the πολιτεῖαι were collected before Aristotle and Theophrastus returned to Athens.

39. Cf. the statement of Jaeger 327 that the *AP* forms "the first book of the collection": whence this mistake arose I have tried to show in Keaney 1969.

40. References in Keaney 1970.[2] 332 n. 29.

41. Keaney 1970[2]; Rhodes 51–58.

42. This statement depends upon one fact and one assumption. The fact is that Aristotle used Androtion's history of Athens, the *Atthis,* which was completed while he was in exile, ca. 340. The assumption is that this work was not available to Aristotle until he returned to Athens in 335/4.

43. There is no hard evidence to date any *politeia* before 335/4 and after 322. In fact, there is only one indication of date in all of the fragments. The single fragment of the Κυρηναίων πολιτεία has a reference to gold coinage, and this does not appear to have been introduced into Cyrene before ca. 340: cf. Rhodes 58 n. 20.

44. There is another obvious option, viz., that the πολιτεῖαι were the products of a restricted group or circle with a special interest in the subject. Again, there is no positive evidence for this, especially in the—admittedly scanty—biographical tradition. We know that some of these scholars knew each others' work (cf. below on use of the same material by Theophrastus and Dicaearchus; Phainias' possible knowledge of *Politics* and *AP*), but knowledge does not entail collaboration.

45. There is occasionally introduced into the discussion an analogous phenomenon: the well attested intellectual histories including Menon and the history of medicine, Eudemus and the history of mathematics, Theophrastus and the history of scientific philosophy, Dicaearchus on the history of civilization; Cf. Brink 919, Düring, *RE* Suppltb. 11. Although these are cited to support the notion of collaborative efforts with the *politeiai,* I do not see that they do so. Here (as is not the case with the πολιτεῖαι) we are dealing with named individuals who left their impress on an identified body of work.

46. I print the text of the most recent edition: J. Bousquet: "Delphes et les 'Pythioniques' d'Aristote," *REG* 97 (1984) 374–80.

47. *Fouilles de Delphes* III.5.58, line 42.

48. S. G. Miller, "The Date of the First Pythiad," *CSCA* 11 (1978) 127–58, esp. 140–44.

49. This is unattested but almost certainly one of the sources of Parthenius (F 556 R).

50. *Pol.* 5.1311A31ff. Note 1311A35: τιμωρίας χάριν. In other words, this work would have stood in a similar relation to the *Politics,* as did part of Theophrastus' work preserved in the Vatican B fragment.

51. Cf. *AP* 17.2: οὐ γὰρ ἐνδέχεται ταῖς ἡλικίαις, ἐάν τις ἀναλογίζηται τὸν ἑκατέρου βίον καὶ ἐφ' οὗ ἀπέθανεν ἄρχοντος. (the chronology does not allow it, if you reckon up the life of each man and the archonship in which each died.)

52. Compare Phainias' Σόλωνα χρησάμενον ἀπάτῃ πρὸς ἀμφοτέροις ἐπὶ σωτηρίᾳ τῆς πόλεως (using deceit toward both sides for the safety of the city) with *AP* 6.3: ἀμφοτέροις ἀπεχθέσθαι καὶ περὶ πλείονος ποιήσασθαι τὸ καλὸν καὶ τὴν τῆς πόλεως σωτηρίαν ἢ τὴν αὑτοῦ πλεονεξίαν (accepted the hatred of both sides and set a higher value on honor and on the safety of the city than on his own advantage).

53. Keaney 1982.456–57.

54. Xenophon, *Hell.* 2.7.6, of the aristocracy at Samos, and the *Hellenica Oxyrhynchia* VI.2, of Athens (the text is restored but the restoration is certain: I owe this reference to a reader for the Press). In the *Politics,* mostly to the "historical" books: 26x in book 5, 7x in 6, 7x in 4, 2x in 3, 1x in 2 (1274A19), with reference to Athens; 0x in 1, 7 and 8; 8x in the 'Αθπολ. This suffices to negate the claim of H. Richards, *CR* 5 (1891) 273 that he could find in the *AP* "no word that has a distinct Aristotelian stamp."

55. Chambers in his apparatus suggests ὑστέρῳ.

56. The words are within a *locus vexatus,* but there is no clear need to emend them

57. [Dem.] 43.75, dated to 370–365.

58. This is *PA* 695B1: τὰ μὲν οὖν τῶν ὀρνίθων μόρια τὸν τρόπον ἔχει τοῦτον. There are two apparent exceptions, but they are only apparent. At *Pol.* 1322B6–7, both Ross and Dreizehnter print ταύτην τὴν ἀρχὴν ἔχει τὸν τρόπον τοῦτον, the reading of MSS ABCDEH, the family which editors rightly prefer. The "normal" order, however, is in MPS, and I suspect this is right. A similar situation obtains with *HA* 623B4: περὶ μὲν οὖν τούτων τῶν ζῴων τοῦτον ἔχει τὸν τρόπον, where Dittmeyer prints the "normal," Louis the "abnormal," order, each with MS support. Cf. *HA* 513A15 and *PA* 671B17.

59. Significantly, it it is found in every book of the *HA* except 7 and 10. 10 is certainly, and 7 is possibly, spurious. On the other hand, it is found thrice in book 8, chs. 21–30, which some have thought to be spurious (603A30; 605A2; 605B7).

60. I find that I have been preceded in this methodology by L. Spengel, "Aristotelische Studien III," *Abhandl . . . königlich. Bayer. Akademie der Wissenschaften* 11.3 (1868) 53–128, at 70, who used περὶ μὲν οὖν . . . and τὰ μὲν οὖν περὶ . . . as *usitatae dicendi rationes* in support of the authenticity of *Pol.* 2.12.

61. The position of Jaeger 329–30 that the biological works, like the other scientific treatises, were the products of Aristotle's second period at Athens, after 335/4, has not been tenable since 1948, when H. D. P. Lee, "Place-Names and the Date of Aristotle's Biological Works," *CQ* 42 (1948) 61–67, showed that much of the biological *research* was carried out before Aristotle returned to Athens. Lee's conclusions have been unsuccessfully challenged by F. Solmsen, "The Fishes of Lesbos and Their Alleged Significance for the Development of Aristotle," *Hermes* 106 (1978) 467–84. More recently, D. M. Balme "The Place of Biology in Aristotle's Philosophy," in A. Gotthelf and J. G. Lenox, eds., *Philosophical Issues in Aristotle's Biology* (Cambridge 1987) 9–20

has shown, in a preliminary way, that much of the *HA* consists of revisions of material in the other biological works. The relevance of this observation is that it is precisely the *HA*, among the biological works, which contains the preponderance of place-names, and the present form of the work will be a combination of the rewriting and incorporating the results of research, apparently as soon as Aristotle returned to Athens.

2

The "Cultural" Origin
of the πολιτεῖαι

We have seen that, while there is some validity in Jacoby's use of the term "scientific" πολιτεία, as a genre label that term does not seem particularly helpful in accounting for much of the content of the Ἀθπολ. There is another approach to genre which consists of treating the Ἀθπολ as a species of *Kulturgeschichte*. The initial justification for this approach will be the use of similar language in works of Aristotle and in other works which more clearly belong to the genre of cultural history.

At *Poetics* 1449A9–16 Aristotle summarizes the development of tragedy as a genre:

> γενομένη δ' οὖν ἀπ' ἀρχῆς αὐτοσχεδιαστικῆς— καὶ αὕτη καὶ ἡ κωμῳδία— καὶ ἡ μὲν ἀπὸ τῶν ἐξαρχόντων τὸν διθύραμβον, ἡ δὲ ἀπὸ τὰ φαλλικὰ ἃ ἔτι καὶ νῦν ἐν πολλαῖς τῶν πόλεων νομιζόμενα —κατὰ μικρὸν ηὐξήθη προαγόντων ὅσον ἐγίγνετο φανερὸν αὐτῆς· καὶ πολλὰς μεταβολὰς μεταβαλοῦσα ἡ τραγῳδία ἐπαύσατο ἐπεὶ ἔσχε τὴν αὐτῆς φύσιν.

> beginning from improvisation—both tragedy and comedy, and the one from those who led off the dithyramb, the other from those [who led off] the phallic songs which even now remain practiced in many of the cities—it grew little by little with [individuals] advancing each element of it which came to light. And, having undergone many changes, it stopped [growing], when it achieved its own nature.

In his commentary on this passage,[1] Else drew up a list of other passages in Aristotle from which he constructed a pattern:

> *de Caelo* 271Bll–13: τούτου δ' αἴτιον ὅτι ἡ ἀρχὴ δυνάμει μείζων ἢ μεγέθει, διόπερ τὸ ἐν ἀρχῇ μικρὸν ἐν τῇ τελευτῇ γίνεται παμμέγεθες.

> the reason for this is that a principle is greater in potentiality than in extent: therefore, what in the beginning is small in the end is very large;

> *Metaphysics* 982B12–15: διὰ γὰρ τὸ θαυμάζειν οἱ ἄνθρωποι οἱ νῦν καὶ τὸ πρῶτον ἤρξαντο φιλοσοφεῖν, ἐξ ἀρχῆς μὲν τὰ πρόχειρα τῶν ἀτόπων θαυμάσαντες, εἶτα κατὰ μικρὸν προϊόντες καὶ περὶ τῶν μειζόνων διαπορήσαντες,

it was because of wonder that human beings now and in the beginning began to philosophize, in the beginning wondering about strange things near at hand, then, progressing in this way, little by little posed difficulties about larger things,

Metaphysics 993B3: ἐκ πάντων δὲ συναθροιζομένων γίγνεσθαί τι μέγεθος·

from all things gathered together, something sizeable comes into existence,

Sophistical Refutations 183B17–34: τῶν γὰρ εὑρισκομένων τὰ μὲν παρ᾽ ἑτέρων ληφθέντα πρότερον πεπονημένα κατὰ μέρος ἐπιδέδωκεν ὑπὸ τῶν παραλαβόντων ὕστερον· τὰ δ᾽ ἐξ ὑπαρχῆς εὑρισκόμενα μικρὰν τὸ πρῶτον ἐπίδοσιν λαμβάνειν εἴωθε, χρησιμωτέραν μέντοι πολλῷ τῆς ὕστερον ἐκ τούτων αὐξήσεως. μέγιστον γὰρ ἴσως ἀρχὴ παντός, ὥσπερ λέγεται, διὸ καὶ χαλεπώτατον. ὅσῳ γὰρ κράτιστον τῇ δυνάμει τοσούτῳ μικρότατον ὂν χαλεπώτατον ὀφθῆναι. ταύτης δὲ εὑρημένης ῥᾷον τὸ προστιθέναι καὶ συναύξειν τὸ λοιπόν ἐστιν· ὅπερ καὶ περὶ τοὺς ῥητορικοὺς λόγους συμβέβηκε, σχεδὸν δὲ καὶ περὶ τὰς ἄλλας πάσας τέχνας. οἱ μὲν γὰρ τὰς ἀρχὰς εὑρόντες παντελῶς ἐπὶ *μικρόν τι προήγαγον*· οἱ δὲ νῦν εὐδοκιμοῦντες παρὰ πολλῶν οἷον ἐκ διαδοχῆς κατὰ μέρος *προαγαγόντων* οὕτως *ηὐξήκασι*.[2]

of all discoveries, some are taken over from others, first elaborated, and experience a step-by-step improvement at the hands of those who take them over. Others, immediately upon discovery, frequently make a small advance at first, progress which is far more useful than the development later to come from them. For perhaps, as the saying goes, the beginning of everything is most important: for this reason, it is also the most difficult. To the extent that it is most powerful in its potential, to that extent is it most difficult to perceive, being very small in size. When the beginning has been discovered, it is easier to add to and make to grow the rest. This is what has happened with rhetoric, and pretty much with all other cultural skills. Those who discovered their beginnings on the whole advanced them only a little: its currently famed practitioners, taking it over from many predecessors in a kind of succession, have brought it forward step by step and and made it as complete as it is today.[3]

Pol. 2.1274A9–11: καὶ τοῦτον δὴ τὸν τρόπον ἕκαστος τῶν δημαγωγῶν *προήγαγεν αὔξων* εἰς τὴν *νῦν* δημοκρατίαν.

and in this manner each of the popular leaders brought forward the democracy, making it grow into its current size.

᾽Αθπολ. 3.3: διὸ καὶ νεωστὶ γέγονεν ἡ ἀρχὴ μεγάλη, τοῖς ἐπιθέτοις αὐξηθεῖσα ·

this is why the office [of archon] has recently become important, having increased its size by additional functions.

Else (153) commented, "these passages reveal clearly that we are in the presence of a pattern, a sequence which Aristotle believed was a standard one for all the arts: a very modest beginning (ἀρχή), small and unimpressive to the eye but pregnant with possibilities ('big δυνάμει'): then a long, gradual (κατὰ μικρόν) development (προάγειν) and expansion (αὐξάνειν), based on what went before; and finally the attainment of 'something sizable' (τι μέγεθος), a result that amounts to something.''

In the 'Αθπολ and *Politics,* elements of this pattern are applied to the political history of Athens in small and larger compasses. Besides the reference to archonship, Aristotle notes the motive of Cleisthenes at 1319B21: οἷς Κλεισθένης τε 'Αθήνησιν ἐχρήσατο βουλόμενος *αὐξῆσαι* τὴν δημοκρατίαν (wishing to increase the democracy) .

In the 'Αθπολ the pattern is central:[4]

Exc. Her. 1: 'Αθηναῖοι τὸ μὲν *ἐξ ἀρχῆς* ἐχρῶντο βασιλείᾳ.[5] (the Athenians had a monarchy from the beginning)

Plut. *vitThes* 25.1: ἔτι δὲ μᾶλλον *αὐξῆσαι* τὴν πόλιν βουλόμενος (wishing to increase the city still more) [sc., Theseus]. [If this comes from the lost beginning of the 'Αθπολ, it will be a paratext of 23.1]

41.2: the constitution of Solon, ἀφ᾿ *ἧς ἀρχὴ* δημοκρατίας ἐγένετο.
(a change which brought about the origin of democracy)

23.1: τότε μὲν οὖν μέχρι τούτου *προῆλθεν* ἡ πόλις, ἅμα τῇ δημοκρατίᾳ *κατὰ μικρὸν αὐξανομένη*.[6] (up to this point there had been gradual change.)

25.1: ἔτη δὲ ἑπτακαίδεκα μάλιστα μετὰ τὰ Μηδικὰ διέμεινεν ἡ πολιτεία προεστώτων τῶν 'Αρεοπαγιτῶν καίπερ *ὑποφερομένη κατὰ μικρόν. αὐξανομένου* δὲ τοῦ *πλήθους*.[7] (for about seventeen years after the Persian Wars the constitution in which the Areopagus was dominant persisted, although it graduallly declined.)

41.2: ἦν δὲ *τῶν μεταβολῶν* ἑνδεκάτη . . . (the eleventh change)

3.5: ἔτι *καὶ νῦν* γὰρ τῆς τοῦ βασιλέως γυναικὸς ἡ σύμμειξις ἐνταῦθα γίγνεται τῷ Διονύσῳ καὶ ὁ γάμος.[8] (even now the rital encounter and marriage of the *basileus'* wife and Dionysus takes place there.)

7.1: *ὅθεν ἔτι καὶ νῦν* οὕτως ὀμνύουσι. (and so even today they continue to swear this.)

8.1: *ὅθεν ἔτι* διαμένει ταῖς φυλαῖς. . . . ὁ περὶ τῶν ταμιῶν νόμος, ᾧ χρώμενοι διτελοῦσιν *ἔτι καὶ νῦν*.[9] (it is still the practice for each of the tribes. . . . the law on the treasurers, which remains in use even today.)

22.2: τὸν ὅρκον ἐποίησαν ὃν *ἔτι καὶ νῦν* ὀμνύουσιν.[10] (the oath which it still swears today.)

The language shows that Else's pattern is operative, but it will be seen that Aristotle has manipulated it in various and unique ways. First, the phenomenon of development is not applied to a single, separable entity but, in order, to δημοκρατία (ἀρχή), πόλις and δημοκρατία (αὔξησις) and πλῆθος (αὔξησις). Second, αὔξησις is interrupted by the regime under the leadership of the Areopagus. Third, there are two, not one, patterns of movement: the one forward, so to speak, and interrupted; the second backward, that of the Areopagus. These are tied together by the repetition of κατὰ μικρόν. Another repetition, of αὐξαν-, restarts the forward movement. Fourth, the formulaic ἔτι καὶ νῦν is endowed with a new function.

1. First, the shifting referents of the pattern show that the process is both quantitative and qualitative. The beginning of the pattern—as well as the first occurrence of the word δημοκρατία—shows that we are dealing with a structural unit enclosed within the boundaries of the pattern. This unit begins with Solon and ends with the reestablishment of democracy at the end of the fifth century. That aspect of the pattern which emphasizes the importance of beginning is reflected in the fact that the chapters introductory to (2–3) and devoted to (5–13) Solon and his reforms comprise about 30 percent of the narrative. The end of the process is realized at 41.2:

> μέχρι τῆς νῦν ἀεὶ προσεπιλαμβάνουσα τῷ πλήθει τὴν ἐξουσίαν. ἁπάντων γὰρ αὐτὸς αὑτὸν πεποίηκεν ὁ δῆμος κύριον, καὶ πάντα διοικεῖται ψηφίσμασιν καὶ δικαστηρίοις, ἐν οἷς ὁ δῆμός ἐστιν ὁ κρατῶν

> the constitution has continued to that in force today, continually increasing the power of the masses. The people have made themselves masters of everything, and control all things by means of decrees and jury courts, in which the sovereign power resides with the people; even the jurisdiction of the council has been transferred to the people

The initial anaphora (ἁπάντων–πάντα) and the content of this passage are foreshadowed—in style and in content—in the summary of the most important (μεγάλα)[11] measures of Solon (9.1):

> τρίτον δέ, ᾧ μάλιστά φασιν ἰσχυκέναι τὸ πλῆθος, ἡ εἰς τὸ δικαστήριον ἔφεσις· κύριος γὰρ ὢν ὁ δῆμος τῆς ψήφου κύριος γίγνεται τῆς πολιτείας

> and the third, the one which is said particularly to have contributed to the power of the masses, the right of appeal to the jury court—for when the people are masters of the vote they are masters of the state.

Again, chapter 9 comes directly in the middle of the Solonian account, with four chapters preceding and four following.

2–3. Second and third, there is a heavy focus on the council of the Areopagus, and this is paralleled in other ways: (1) in the list of constitutional changes in chapter 41, the leadership of the Areopagites is precisely in the middle, with five changes preceding and five following. (2) in the course of political development, the *demos* appropriates to itself some of the powers of three organs; the chronological series is archons, Council of the Areopagus, Council of Five Hundred. (3) apart from technical usage[12] the word μέχρι occurs thrice; at 2.2, μέχρι Σόλωνος, before the discussion of Solon; at 23.1, μέχρι τούτου, before the discussion of the Areopagus; at 41.2, μέχρι τῆς νῦν, before the discussion of the fourth-century democracy. The first and third of these signals are of obvious importance, and so must be the second. The structural centrality of the Areopagus[13] and the way the pattern works suggest that its leadership came at a time crucial to the history of the Athenian constitution: a time in which future development could go in one of two directions, toward that of continued leadership of the Areopagus or toward that of radical democracy.[14] The fact that the pattern is used at all makes it clear which alternative will be followed.

4. Fourth, ἔτι καὶ νῦν was used long before Aristotle to express two ideas: (1) to point out the stable continuity of an institution from past to present[15] or (2) to show the antiquity of a practice in a context in which, by contrast, some parts of the world have gone beyond others.[16] Aristotle uses the phrase in sense (2) in our passage from the *Poetics* (1449A12), in sense (1) in the ᾽Αθπολ. At 3.5, however, he gives it a new twist. Not only does it show the continuity of an institution, it is used also to make an argument, and the continuity becomes a σημεῖον for the identity of the place of original residence of the king archon.

DIFFERENCES IN THE USES OF THE PATTERN

So far I have tried to show that, while the basic elements of the pattern are unchanged, Aristotle can use different parts of it differently. It may be worth-while now to show how his use of it as a whole differs in the ᾽Αθπολ.

It has been noted in another context[17] that the words φύσις and τέλος in their teleological senses are absent from the ᾽Αθπολ. Yet Wilamowitz[18] wrote "die ἐσχάτη δημοκρατία erfüllte immer mehr ihre φύσις in der sprache der Politik zu reden" (final democracy more and more fulfilled its φύσις, to speak in the language of the *Politics*). The statement is misleading in more ways than one.[19] For Aristotle, democracy is a παρέκβασις or a πολιτεία παρεκβεβηκυῖα, a deviation form. Although it may be said that every society comes into being and perdures by nature, φύσει, this is not true of every society characterized by a particular political arrangement. Insofar as political forms may be good (kingship, aristocracy, polity) or bad (tyranny, oligarchy, democracy), only the first three are κατὰ φύσιν in Aristotle's moral world; the last three are παρὰ φύσιν.

Now there are two senses in which the history of the Athenian constitution may be seen as a progression. The first is as a chronological construct, simply because it is described as a series of events taking place over time. There is another sense, as Aristotle saw and described this process, in which the progression is (to some extent) goal-directed, toward a specific end, a form of government in which the decrees of the assembly and the decisions of the law courts were authoritative. But there is no important sense in which the process could be described as a natural process, and this is the way in which the process and the pattern differ from those in the *Poetics*.[20]

The lack of "nature" in the process also characterizes the use of the pattern in the *Met* and *SophRef*. Its place is taken by theoretical intelligence *(Met)* or craft-intelligence *(SophRef)*. From both points of view, and by comparison with some aspects of the use of cultural material in Theophrastus and Dicaearchus, it is interesting to observe one feature of ᾽Αθπολ's narrative.

At chapter 9, Aristotle sums up the most significant features of Solon's reforms, and we may focus on one sentence. Aristotle says that some people think that Solon made his laws deliberately unclear so that the resolution of disputes would be in the control of the people. He responds:

οὐ μὴν εἰκός, ἀλλὰ διὰ τὸ μὴ δύνασθαι καθόλου περιλαβεῖν τὸ βέλτιστον· οὐ γὰρ δίκαιον ἐκ τῶν νῦν γιγνομένων ἀλλ᾽ ἐκ τῆς ἄλλης πολιτείας θεωρεῖν τὴν ἐκείνου βούλησιν.

however, it is not likely that he was unclear for that reason, but rather because it is impossible to define what is best in general terms. It is not right to estimate his intentions from present-day practice: one should judge from the rest of his political programme.

At *Pol.* 2.1274A11–15, after establishing the strength of the law courts and the leadership of the demagogues εἰς τὴν νῦν δημοκρατίαν, Aristotle says:

φαίνεται δ᾽ οὐ κατὰ τὴν Σόλωνος γενέσθαι τοῦτο προαίρεσιν, ἀλλὰ μᾶλλον ἀπὸ συμπτώματος (τῆς ναυαρχίας γὰρ ἐν τοῖς Μηδικοῖς ὁ δῆμος αἴτιος γενομένος ἐφρονηματίσθη καὶ δημαγωγοὺς ἔλαβε φαύλους ἀντιπολιτευομένων τῶν ἐπιεικῶν)

but it seems that all this took place not according to Solon's intention but as a result of circumstances. For the Athenian sea-power in the Persian wars was due to the Athenian people; this gave them a great opinion of themselves and they chose inferior men as popular leaders when respectable men pursued policies not to their liking.[21]

What Aristotle is stating, in other words, is that even if Solon could have controlled the outcome of events almost two centuries into the future, he did not have the desire to control them in the way in which they eventually turned out.[22]

That said, it remains to remark one striking feature. This is that the vocabulary of intention is curiously lacking from the narrative on Solon. Apart from βούλησις, the only words of volition used are in noninstitutional contexts and refer to his neutral position (11.1: βουλόμενος; 11.2: μεθ᾽ ὁποτέρων . . . εἵλετο) There is a slight contrast with Peisistratus whose first described measure is accompanied by a statement of purpose: τοῦτο δ᾽ ἐποίει δυοῖν χάριν (16.3). The contrast with Cleisthenes is sharper. His innovative activity is divided into two chapters. In 21, the measures are set out in four parts, each accompanied by a purpose clause:[23]

1. ten tribes, ἀναμεῖξαι βουλόμενος, ὅπως μετάσχωσι πλείους τῆς πολιτείας· (wanting to mix them up so that more men would have a share in the running of the state)
2. not twelve tribes, ὅπως αὐτῷ μὴ συμβαίνῃ μερίζειν κατὰ τὰς προϋπαρχούσας τριττῦς· (to avoid allocating them according to the already existing thirds)
3. three trittys in each tribe, ὅπως ἑκάστη μετέχῃ πάντων τῶν τόπων. (that each tribe should have a share in all the regions)
4. fellow-demesmen, ἵνα μὴ πατρόθεν προσαγορεύοντες ἐξελέγχωσιν

τοὺς νεοπολίτας. (so that they should not use their fathers' names and make it obvious who were the new citizens).

The focus of chapter 22 is ostracism,[24] one institution among the new laws made by Cleisthenes στοχαζόμενον τοῦ πλήθους (aiming at the masses). The last mention of Cleisthenes is in the notice of the first victim of ostracism, Hipparchus, δι' ὃν καὶ μάλιστα τὸν νόμον ἔθηκεν ὁ Κλεισθένης, ἐξελάσαι βουλόμενος αὐτόν (against whom especially Cleisthenes had the law made, since he wished to exile him).

This distinction in motivation between Solon and Cleisthenes[25]—the main purpose of which is to acknowledge but minimize the role of Solon in the development of democracy[26]—allowed Aristotle to make a fine distinction. At 22.1 he says that after the reforms of Cleisthenes[27] δημοτικωτέρα πολὺ τῆς Σόλωνος ἐγένετο ἡ πολιτεία (the constitution was much more democratic than that of Solon); at 41.2 he describes the *politeia* of Cleisthenes as δημοτικωτέρα τῆς Σόλωνος. Does the use of the comparatives imply a belief that the constitution of Solon could be described as δημοτική?[28] The answer is no, for reasons positive and negative. At 29.3 Cleitophon moves a search of the ancestral laws which Cleisthenes made when he set up the democracy (ὅτε καθίστη τὴν δημοκρατίαν). Aristotle's comment on this is ὡς οὐ δημοτικὴν ἀλλὰ παραπλησίαν οὖσαν τὴν Κλεισθένους πολιτείαν τῇ Σόλωνος (it being his assumption that the constitution of Cleisthenes was not democratic but similar to that of Solon). On the negative side, it is legitimate to talk about elements in a constitution which are δημοτικά without applying that term to the constitution itself, and this is what Aristotle does at 9.1 (δημοτικώτατα) and 10.1 (δημοτικά).[29]

The result of this is that Aristotle's analysis is able to recognize Solon's contribution to the development of Athenian democracy and at the same time to reaffirm the fifth-century view of democracy as of Cleisthenic origin.[30]

THE PERIPATETIC CONTEXT

A major effort was devoted to various aspects of cultural history by several members of the first generation of Aristotle's school. While the subject matter of some of these may not have lent themselves easily to this pattern,[31] there is ample evidence that elements of it were used in two influential works, Dicaearchus' Βίος Ἑλλάδος and Theophrastus' Περὶ εὐσεβείας. Neither treatise was particularly extensive, the first comprising three books, the second one.

Dicaearchus treated the anthropological origins of civilization, and it is possible to get some idea of how he went about this from two longish fragments, one in Varro, *Rerum rusticarum* 2.1.3–5 (F 48 W), the other in Porphyry, Περὶ ἀποχῆς ἐμψύχων 4.2 (F 49). Each writer used the Βίος Ἑλλάδος in ways which reflected his own purposes, and the agricultural interests of Varro turn out to make his borrowing more useful than the moralizing approach of Porphyry. Varro says that he will speak *de origine* (2.1.1) in which *origo* will have translated ἀρχή. The development of civilization was looked at from two points of view. The first was comprehensive: necesse est humanae uitae *a summa memoria gradatim descendisse ad nostram aetatem* (it is a necessity that from the remotest antiquity of human life they have come down step by step to our age [2.1.3: tr. Hooper]): the italicized words could be a version of ἀπ' ἀρχῆς κατὰ μικρὸν προελθεῖν μέχρι τοῦ νῦν. Secondly, each stage of transition within the overall development was examined, from the summus gradus naturalis (the most distant stage, the state of nature) to the secunda uita pastoricia (the second, the pastoral [2.1.4]) and, finally, tertio denique gradu a uita pastoriali ad agri culturam descenderunt, in qua ex duobus gradibus superioribus retinuerant multa, et quo descenderant, ibi *processerant longe, dum ad nos peruenerit* (then by a third stage humans came from the pastoral life to that of the tiller of the soil: in this they retained much of the former two stages, and after reaching it they went far before reaching our stage [2.1.5]). The numbered series recalls the numbered μεταβολαί in *AP* 41, but *gradus* would not seem the readiest translation of μεταβολή. The italicized words could represent προῆλθον πολύν χρόνον.[32] Finally, as the text continues, the difference between more- or less-developed parts of the Mediterranean world is signaled by the presence of wild flocks *etiam nunc* (even now) = ἔτι καὶ νῦν.

Most of the remains of Theophrastus' Περὶ εὐσεβείας[33] are from the same work of Porphyry and concern the development of religious sacrifice. Again, a double process can be discerned, (1) a general history of that development and (2) discussions of sacrificial continuity and idiosyncracy in different societies. I focus on the most obvious parallels to the πολιτεῖαι and the Βίος Ἑλλάδος.

In his general treatment, Theophrastus seems to have demarcated each stage of development by calling attention to its beginning:

I 5.1 ἤρξατο πρῶτον· (first began): sacrificial element, grass:
II 5.6 μετὰ τὴν ἐξ ἀρχῆς: πόαν (after the primeval grass): leaves[34]
III 6.1 καρποῦ πρώτου . . . φανέντος (the fruit of Demeter first appeared): barley
    6.1 ἀπ' ἀρχῆς (from the beginning)
    6.1 ὕστερον. (later)

Characteristic of Theophrastus' approach seems to have been his observation of the continuity of certain practices into his own day.

> I 5.6: τὴν δὲ ἀρχαιότητα τῶν εἰρημένων θυμιαμάτων κατίδοι τις ἂν ἐπιβλέψας, ὅτι πολλοὶ καὶ νῦν ἔτι θύουσι συγκεκομμένα τῶν εὐωδῶν ξύλων τινά.[35]

> the antiquity, however, of the aforementioned fumigations may be perceived by him who considers that many now also sacrifice certain portions of odoriferous wood.[36]

> III 6.2: ὅθεν ἔτι καὶ νῦν πρὸς τῷ τέλει τῶν θυηλῶν τοῖς ψαισθεῖσι θυλήμασι χρώμεθα, μαρτυροῦντες μὲν τῷ πραττομένῳ τὴν ἐξ ἀρχῆς τῶν θυμάτων αὔξησιν

hence also now, at the end of the sacrifices, we use fruits that are bruised and ground; testifying by this how much fumigations have parted from their ancient simplicity;

F 7.1 οἷς μαρτυρεῖν ἔοικε καὶ ἡ Ἀθήνησιν ἔτι καὶ νῦν δρωμένη πομπὴ Ἡλίου τε καὶ Ὡρῶν.

and these things appear to be testified by the splendid procession in honor of the Sun and the Hours, which is even now performed at Athens.[37]

One could continue along this line and pile up more instances of this kind of language,[38] but it is perhaps more interesting to point out one process in which Aristotle takes a somewhat different tack from that of his predecessors and contemporaries. When evidence exists to argue from a modern survival to a distant origin, accceptance of that evidence seems to have been automatic, except for Aristotle. The passages:

A 3.3 [on the origin of the eponymous archonship]:
ἔνιοι δ᾽ ἐπὶ Ἀκάστου φασὶ γενέσθαι ταύτην· τεκμήριον δ᾽ ἐπιφέρουσιν ὅτι οἱ ἐννέα ἄρχοντες ὀμνύουσι . . . . ἐπὶ Ἀκάστου τὰ ὅρκια ποιήσειν, ὡς ἐπὶ τούτου τῆς βασιλείας παραχωρησάντων τῶν Κοδριδῶν ἀντὶ τῶν δοθεισῶν τῷ ἄρχοντι δωρεῶν.

some place it in the time of Acastus: champions of the latter view cite in support the fact that the nine archons swear that they will abide by their oaths as in the time of Acastus, and claim that it was in his time that the descendants of Codrus stepped down from the archonship in exchange for the rights given to the archon.

B 5.3 [on the opportunity for Solon to become a tyrant]:
ὡς ἔκ τε ἄλλων ὁμολογεῖται καὶ αὐτὸς ἐν τοῖσδε τοῖς ποιήμασιν μαρτυρεῖ [cp. 6.4: ἐν τοῖς ποιήμασιν αὐτὸς πολλαχοῦ μέμνηται καὶ οἱ ἄλλοι συνομολογοῦσι πάντες. 12.1: οἵ τ᾽ ἄλλοι συμφωνοῦσι πάντες καὶ αὐτὸς ἐν τῇ ποιήσει μέμνηται.]

the other evidence agrees on this, and in particular he bears witness to it himself in these poems [cp. 6.4: he frequently mentions it in his poetry, and everyone else agrees; 12.1: everyone agrees that that is how he acted, and he has mentioned it himself in his poetry.)

C 6.2–4 [on Solon's alleged peculation in the disburdenment]:
ἐν οἷς πειρῶνταί τινες διαβάλλειν αὐτόν. . . . ὅθεν φασὶ γενέσθαι τοὺς ὕστερον δοκοῦντας εἶναι παλαιοπλούτους. οὐ μὴν ἀλλὰ πιθανώτερος ὁ τῶν δημοτικῶν λόγος· οὐ γὰρ εἰκός. . . . ὅτι δὲ ταύτην ἔσχε τὴν ἐξουσίαν, τά τε πράγματα νοσοῦντα μαρτυρεῖ, καὶ ἐν τοῖς ποιήμασιν πολλαχοῦ μέμνηται καὶ οἱ ἄλλοι συνομολογοῦσι πάντες.

some people try to slander Solon in this matter . . . this is said to be how men who were later reputed to be of ancient wealth had come by their riches. However, the democratic version of the story is more credible . . . that he had the opportunity (to become tyrant) is evident from the diseased state of affairs: he frequently mentions it in his poetry, and everyone else agrees.

D 7.4 [on the definition of the second census class];
ἱππάδα δὲ τοὺς τριακόσια ποιοῦντας, ὡς δ᾽ ἔνιοι φασι τοὺς ἱπποτροφ-
εῖν δυναμένους. σημεῖον δὲ φέρουσι τό τε ὄνομα τοῦ τέλους, ὡς ἂν ἀπὸ
τοῦ πράγματος κείμενον, καὶ τὰ ἀναθήματα τῶν ἀρχαίων· ἀνάκειται γὰρ
ἐν ἀκροπόλει εἰκὼν Διφίλου, ἐφ᾽ ᾗ ἐπιγέγραπται τάδε·

Διφίλου ᾽Ανθεμίων τήνδ᾽ ἀνέθηκε θεοῖς,
θητικοῦ ἀντὶ τέλους ἱππάδ᾽ ἀμειψάμενος.

καὶ παρέστηκεν ἵππος ἐκμαρτυρῶν, ὡς τὴν ἱππάδα τοῦτο σημαίνουσαν·
οὐ μὴν ἀλλ᾽ εὐλογώτερον τοῖς μέτροις διῃρῆσθαι καθάπερ τοὺς
πεντακοσιομεδίμνους.

some people say that the cavalry were defined as those capable of maintaining a horse. They cite both the name of the class, as reflecting that criterion, and also ancient dedications; for there stands on the Acropolis a statue of Diphilus bearing this inscription:

Anthemion son of Diphilus made this dedication to the gods,
Having exchanged the laborers' for the cavalry class.

There is a horse standing beside him, as an indication that this is what the cavalry class signifies. Even so it is more reasonable that the cavalry should have been defined by measures of produce like the five-hundred-bushel class.

E 9.2 [on the intended effect of Solon's legislation]:
οἴονται μὲν οὖν τινες ἐπίτηδες ἀσαφεῖς αὐτὸν ποιῆσαι τοὺς νόμους, ὅπως
ᾖ τῆς κρίσεως ὁ δῆμος κύριος. ἀλλὰ τὸ μὴ δύνασθαι καθόλου περιλαβεῖν
τὸ βέλτιστον·οὐ γὰρ δίκαιον ἐκ τῶν νῦν γιγνομένων ἀλλ᾽ ἐκ τῆς ἄλλης
πολιτείας θεωρεῖν τὴν ἐκείνου βούλησιν.

some people think that he made his laws unclear deliberately, in order that the power of decision should rest with the people. However, it is not likely that he was unclear for that reason, but rather because it is impossible to define what is best in general terms. It is not right to estimate his intentions from present-day practice: one should judge from the rest of his political programme.

Three more passages do not, strictly speaking, belong with this set, but I include them for purposes of comparison.

F 14.4 [on the first restoration of Peisistratus]:
προδιασπείρας γὰρ λόγον ὡς τῆς ᾽Αθηνᾶς καταγούσης Πεισίστρατον, καὶ
γυναῖκα μεγάλην καὶ καλὴν ἐξευρών, ὡς μὲν ῾Ηρόδοτός φησιν, ἐκ τοῦ
δήμου τῶν Παιανιέων, ὡς δ᾽ ἔνιοι λέγουσιν ἐκ τοῦ Κολλυτοῦ στεφαν-
όπωλιν Θρᾷτταν, ᾗ ὄνομα ἦν Φύη . . .

he circulated a rumor that Athena was reinstating Peisistratus; and he found a tall and impressive woman called Phyē (from the deme of Paeania according to Herodotus, but a Thracian garland seller from Collytus according to some writers . . .

G 18.4N (whether participants of the procession were armed) ἀλλ' ὁ λεγόμενος λόγος . . . οὐκ ἀληθής ἐστιν. the story . . . is untrue.

H 18.5 [the aftermath of assassination]: κατηγόρει δὲ τῶν τοῦ τυράννου φίλων, ὡς μὲν οἱ δημοτικοὶ φασιν, ἐπίτηδες, ἵνα ἀσεβήσαιεν ἅμα καὶ γένοιντο ἀσθενεῖς ἀνελόντες τοὺς ἀναιτίους καὶ φίλους ἑαυτῶν, ὡς δ' ἔνιοι λέγουσιν, οὐχὶ πλαττόμενος ἀλλὰ τοὺς συνειδότας ἐμήνυεν.

democratic writers say that [Aristogeiton] denounced friends of the tyrants deliberately, so that the tyranny should simultaneously be polluted and weakened by the killing of men who were both innocent and friendly; but others say that he was not inventing it but that the men whom he named actually were involved in the plot.

It seems that from these passages a number of principles arise which embody a certain attitude toward the recovery of (distant) historical truth.

1. Where information is only from secondary sources and these sources are in conflict, it may be impossible to choose one over the other (F).
2. This is so even when one source can use a sign (τεκμήριον)[39] in support of the claim.
3. This is so because signs do not also guarantee the validity of the inference (D).
4. While great authority (Thucydides) is not infallible (G),
5. Truth is guaranteed by unanimity among the sources (B), especially when that is supported by a primary source (ποιήματα).
6. Precise chronological accuracy is not important so long as both dates coexist with the thesis which is based on the chronology (A).
7. It seems especially dangerous to make inferences about intentions (ἐπίτηδες: E, H).

These are particular principles. A more general attitude can be gleaned from his use of terms like εἰκός (C, E), πιθανός (C), and εὔλογος (D). When explanations are chosen in C and D, it is ultimately because of consistency: (C) if Solon turned down the opportunity to become a tyrant, he would not have besmirched himself in small matters;[40] (D) if the criterion for one census class is produce, it is reasonable that the same kind of criterion should obtain for another.[41]

The attitude exemplified in both examples, it will come as no surprise, is that of the famous passage in the *Poetics* 1451A36–B10:

ὅτι οὐ τὸ τὰ γενόμενα λέγειν, τοῦτο ποιητοῦ ἔργον ἐστίν, ἀλλ' οἷα ἂν γένοιτο καὶ τὰ δυνατὰ κατὰ τὸ εἰκὸς ἢ τὸ ἀναγκαῖον . . . διὸ καὶ φιλοσοφώτερον καὶ σπουδαιότερον ποίησις ἱστορίας ἐστίν· ἡ μὲν γὰρ ποίησις μᾶλλον τὰ καθόλου, ἡ δ' ἱστορία τὰ καθ' ἕκαστον λέγει. ἔστιν δὲ καθόλου μὲν τῷ ποίῳ τὰ ποῖα ἄττα συμβαίνει λέγειν ἢ πράττειν κατὰ τὸ εἰκὸς ἢ τὸ ἀναγκαῖον . . . τὸ δὲ καθ' ἕκαστον, τί 'Αλκιβιάδης ἔπραξεν ἢ ἔπαθεν.

that the poet's job is not to tell what has happened but the kind of things that *can* happen, i.e., the kind of events that are possible according to probability or necessity . . . and in fact that is why the writing of poetry is a more philosophical activity, and one to be taken more seriously than the writing of history; for poetry tells us rather the universals, history the particulars. "Universal" means what kind of thing a certain kind of person will say or do in accordance with probability or necessity . . . while "particular" is what Alcibiades did or had done to him [tr. Else]

I am not of course claiming that the 'Αθπολ is an example of ποίησις but only that Aristotle saw that there were areas of human action (like the life of Solon) in which "universal" laws of explanation took precedence over "particular" biographical suggestions. I also suggest that this factor explains why he has chosen Alcibiades as an example of particulars.

In discussing history, the single ἱστορικός he mentions here is Herodotus, who is also the only historian mentioned by name in the 'Αθπολ. Why Herodotus? Or, to put it another way, why not also Thucydides? I suggest that there is an allusion to Thucydides in that his is the work in which Alcibiades is most prominent, at least up to Aristotle's time. The suggestion is consonant with another allusion to Thucydides in our passage G above. The word ἀληθής occurs only here in the 'Αθπολ, and a look at the Thucydidean context reveals why. The story of the assassination of Hipparchus is told in the first instance as an illustration of the conclusion (1.20.3): οὕτως ἀταλαίπωρος τοῖς πολλοῖς ἡ ζήτησις τῆς ἀληθείας (so careless are most people in the search for truth). The mention that the judgment of Thucydides is not always correct looks forward to a heavier criticism in Aristotle's treatment of Theramenes.

NOTES

1. G. Else, *Aristotle's Poetics: The Argument* (Cambridge, Mass. 1957) 152 ff.
2. Cp. *Pol.* 1305A12: νῦν δὲ τῆς ῥητορικῆς ηὐξημένης.
3. In chapter 6, "Methods and Purposes," I will argue that in chapters 27 and 28, there is a kind of parody of this pattern in which Aristotle talks about regression in political leadership. Initially, one may compare ἐκ διαδοχῆς of this passage with 28.4: διεδέχοντο συνεχῶς τὴν δημαγωγίαν.
4. Cf. Keaney 1963.1.
5. It is clear that ἐξ ἀρχῆς is used here in a process of political development: compare F 3 (= Plut. *vitThes* 25.3: ὅτι δὲ πρῶτος ἀπέκλινε πρὸς τὸν ὄχλον, ὡς 'Αριστοτέλης φησί, καὶ ἀφῆκε τὸ μοναρχεῖν [that he was the first to lean toward the mob, as Aristotle says, and gave up single rule) and 41.2: ἡ ἐπὶ Θησέως γενομένη, μικρὸν παρεγκλίνουσα τῆς βασιλικῆς (the change under Theseus, which deviated slightly from monarchy). The phrase is used at the head of other excerpts from Heraclides, but never again in a political context: cf. *Exc.* 22, 30, 46, 49 and 68.
6. A subtext of this passage may be Isoc. *Antid.* 316: αὐξηθείσης τῆς πόλεως καὶ λαβούσης τὴν ἀρχήν κτλ (when the city grew and took over rule).

7. ὑποφέρεσθαι is the opposite of αὐξάνεσθαι: Kaibel (48) supposes a medical metaphor in these verbs.

8. My reasons for adding these last four texts to Else's pattern will become clear in the discussion of analogous passages from Theophrastus and Dicaearchus.

9. Cp. 47.1: ἔτι γὰρ ὁ νόμος κύριός ἐστιν (this law is still in force).

10. Compare, from the Λακεδαιμονίων πολιτεία, Her. *Exc.* 10: τὴν κρυπτὴν . . . καθ' ἣν ἔτι καὶ νῦν ἐξιόντες ἡμέρας κρύπτονται (the *krypteia* . . . . In accordance with this institution even now they go out by day and conceal themselves). This pattern of development would have been applicable to many Greek societies, and Aristotle used it for more widespread analysis (*Pol.* 5.1297B15 ff.): ἡ πρώτη πολιτεία μετὰ τὰς βασιλείας (the first constitution after kingships). Cp. 41.2 of Theseus: δευτέρα δὲ καὶ πρώτη μετὰ ταύτην ἔχουσα πολιτειας τάξιν (second, and first after this, involving a form of constitution) ἡ μὲν ἐξ ἀρχῆς ἐκ τῶν ἱππέων (was composed of warriors). At a later stage of development αὐξανομένων δὲ τῶν πόλεων (when states became larger), it was the hoplite class. For the establishment of tyrannies ἤδη τῶν πόλεων ηὐξημένων, cf. 1310B16–18.

11. By implication from the fact that the first of them is called μέγιστον.

12. All confined to the descriptive section: 43.5; 52.2; 53.1,7; 56.3; 63.4; 64.1; and 67.2.

13. Not to be ignored in this connection is the praise Aristotle gives the Athenian regime at this time (23.2): ἐπολιτεύθησαν καλῶς καὶ κατὰ τούτους τοὺς καιρούς. Similarly high praise is found elsewhere only of the government of the 5000 (33.2).

14. It is also through a repetitive pattern that Aristotle suggests another (counterfactual) development, Theramenes' leadership of the δῆμος: cf. chapter 14 below, "Aristotle and Theramenes."

15. E.g., Herod. 1.167.2; 173.3 al.; Thuc. 2.15.2; 15.5.

16. Thuc. 1.5.2; 6.5.

17. Rhodes 8.

18. *AA* 1.187. Compare Jacoby, *Atthis* 212: "that philosopher, in accordance with the general nature of his thinking, recognized that the description of the existing form of a State does not teach us anything unless it is shown at the same time how the form of the State concerned arrived at its φύσις, as one might say."

19. Aristotle never referred explicitly to fourth-century Athenian democracy as an example of an ἐσχάτη δημοκρατία (nor in fact does he give historical examples of any of his four forms of democracy).

20. For the use of "nature" and "natural" in this work, cf. 1448B20, 1449A4, 24, 1450B18, 29 and 1460A4.

21. There are two differences in the vocabulary: the phrase ἀπὸ συμπτώματος is not used in the Ἀθπολ, and προαίρεσις is replaced by βούλησις. I am tempted to suggest that the reason for the first is generic, that the phrase is too "philosophical" for the genre. Such an exclusion would be consistent with other non-uses (e.g, the verb μεταβάλλειν [cp. of Athenian history, *Pol.* 1304B11] is avoided but not the noun; σπουδαῖος and φαῦλος are frequent in the *Politics* but avoided in the Ἀθπολ); but precisely to define the criteria of exclusion seems impossible. βούλησις is less intellectually grounded than προαίρεσις (itself avoided; the verb once, at 27.2).

22. This was, in fact, the purpose and effect of his liberation of the δῆμος, καὶ ἐν τῷ παρόντι καὶ εἰς τὸ μέλλον (both immediately and for the future) at 6.1.

23. On the structure of this chapter, cf. chapter 9, "Horizontal Structure: Chiasmus."

24. For the Cleisthenic origin of this institution, cf. Keaney 1970¹; 1976¹.

25. Also in the *Politics*: cp. again 1319B21: βουλόμενος αὐξῆσαι τὴν δημοκρα-τίαν.

26. This is presumably Aristotle's response to those who overstated the "demo-cratic" character of the Solonian reforms: cf. E. Ruschenbusch, "Πάτριος πολιτεία. Theseus, Drakon, Solon und Kleisthenes in Publizistik und Geschichtschreibung des 5. und 4. Jahrhunderts v. Chr.," *Historia* 7 (1958) 398–424.

27. τούτων δε γενομένων refers to the reforms described in chapter 21, ἐγένετο to what follows in 22.2–7.

28. As I once wrongly assumed: Keaney 1984.161 n. 2.

29. The precise parallel is the account of Solon's constitution at *Pol.* 2.1273B39–41 in which the three most important elements therein are described as ὀλιγαρχικόν, ἀριστοκρατικόν, and δημοτικόν.

30. References at Rhodes 260.

31. E.g., the scientific ἱστορίαι (ἀριθμητική, γεωμετρική, ἀστρολογική) of Eudemus, the physical and medical doxographies of Theophrastus and Menon, the *Laws* of Theophrastus.

32. The transitional stages are marked by Porphyry as ὕστερον ὁ νομαδικὸς εἰσῆλθεν βίος and *προιόντος δὲ κατὰ μικρὸν οὕτω τοῦ χρονου . . . εἰς τὸ τρίτον τε καὶ γεωργικὸν ἐνέπεσον εἶδος* (afterwards the nomadic way of life came in . . . as time gradually went on in this way, they came upon the third form, the agricultural).

33. I use the text in W. W. Fortenbaugh, *Quellen zur Ethik Theophrasts = Studien zur antiken Philosophie* 12 (Amsterdam 1984) L 91.

34. Within this stage, when sacrifices from nuts were abandoned, arose the proverb ἅλις δρυός, "enough of the oak." According to Dicaearchus (F 49 W), the same adage was probably (οἷα εἰκός) introduced by ὁ πρῶτος μεταβάλλων the ancient way of life. Aristotle, Theophrastus, and probably Dicaearchus (F 100–03) wrote works on proverbs, the use and explanation of which were important tools of analysis in the πολιτεῖαι. Cf. F 505 (Ithaca), 513 (Corcyra), 523 (Kythnos), 528 (Cyrene), 545 (Lakedaemon), 557 (Miletus), 558 (Naxos), 571, and 574 (Samos), 586, (Syracuse), and 593 (Tenedos).

35. πολλοί entails a comparative overview. To what extent κατίδοι ἐπιβλέψας implies personal observation on Theophrastus' part is impossible to tell: for autopsy of things Cyrenaic and Egyptian, cf. W. Capelle, "Theophrast in Kyrene?" *RhM* 97 (1954) 169–89 and "Theophrast in Aegypten," *WS* 49 (1956) 173–86.

36. Translations of Porphyry are taken from the Platonist Thomas Taylor's *Porphyry, On Abstinence from Animal Food* (London 1823; repr. Barnes & Noble 1965).

37. Cp. ᾿Αθπολ 7.4: καὶ παρέστηκεν ἵππος ἐκμαρτυρῶν κτλ.

38. For ἀπ᾿/ἐξ ἀρχῆς: 26.1, 27.1, for νῦν, νῦν ἔτι, ἔτι καὶ νῦν: 8.3, 21.4, 26.1, for documentary evidence: 21.1 (tablets in Crete), 28.1 (altar in Delos), 30.4–5 (festival at Athens).

39. It is possible that a τεκμήριον is a stronger sign than a σημεῖον (as it is at *Rhet.* 2.1402B18–20, for reasons which do not apply to the *AP*), for here Aristotle seems to agree with the "Akastos group": (a) he gives the reason for their claim and is silent about the other claim; (b) he supplies a genitive absolute in support of their claim. Elsewhere (5.3; 13.5), he agrees with the contents of genitives absolute, while he dis-agrees with that of accusatives absolute (7.4, in support of a σημεῖον; 29.3): the dis-tinction just drawn does not hold for 36.1 (ὡς . . . τῆς ἀρετῆς ὡρισμένης), though there Aristotle may be reproducing his source, as he does elsewhere in the same passage

(cp. Xen., *Hell*.3.19). Secondly, inferences made from σημεῖα are elsewhere treated as valid (3.3; 3.5; 8.1; 13.5).

40. This is an example of the τόπος ἐκ τοῦ μᾶλλον καὶ ἧττον (from the more to the less): cf. *Rhet*. 2.1397B12ff. and *Top*. 114B37ff.

41. This seems to be an example of the τόπος ἐκ τοῦ ὁμοίως ὑπάρχειν (in a like degree): cf. *Top*. 2.115A15ff.

3

The πολιτεία Genre
and Its Origin

I

As in general, Aristotle's early steps in political theory continue the work of
Plato,[1] so in particular we might expect to find the seeds of the collections of
nomoi and *politeiai* in Plato's work. In formal terms, that expectation is only
half-fulfilled for, while it is clear enough that the inspiration of Theophrastus'
Νόμοι is to be found in Plato's work of the same title, no such connection
exists between that work and the *politeiai*.

The first half of the connection is clear, even if we do not accept, in part or
in whole, Jacoby's[2] claim that Plato's work is inconceivable without the kind
of research which went into the collections of Aristotle and his pupil. It is
clear, in the first instance, because the works of Plato and Theophrastus show
the requisite minimum of similar features, interest in historical law[3] and interest in comparative law.[4] The latter feature is explicitly incorporated in Plato's
ongoing system. Although he restricts foreign travel by the citizens of his state,
in certain instances it will be allowed:

> οὔτε γὰρ ἄπειρος οὖσα πόλις ἀνθρώπων κακῶν καὶ ἀγαθῶν δύναιτ' ἄν
> ποτε, ἀνόμιλητος οὖσα, ἥμερος ἱκανῶς εἶναι καὶ τέλεος, οὐδ' αὖ τοὺς
> νόμους διαφυλάττειν ἄνευ τοῦ γνώμῃ λαβεῖν αὐτοὺς ἀλλὰ μὴ μόνον ἔθεσιν.
> εἰσὶ γὰρ ἐν τοῖς πολλοῖς ἄνθρωποι ἀεὶ θεῖοί τινες—οὐ πολλοί—παντὸς
> ἄξιοι συγγίγνεσθαι, φυόμενοι οὐδὲν μᾶλλον ἐν εὐνομουμέναις πόλεσιν
> ἢ καὶ μή, ὧν κατ' ἴχνος ἀεὶ τὸν ἐν ταῖς εὐνομουμέναις πόλεσιν οἰκοῦντα
> ἐξιόντα κατὰ θάλατταν καὶ γῆν, ζητεῖν ὃς ἂν ἀδιάφθαρτος ᾖ, τὰ μὲν βε-
> βαιούμενον τῶν νομίμων, ὅσα καλῶς αὐτοῖς κεῖται, τὰ δ' ἐπανορθούμε-
> νον, εἴ τι παραλείπεται. ἄνευ γὰρ ταύτης τῆς θεωρίας καὶ ζητήσεως οὐ
> μένει ποτὲ τελέως πόλις, οὐδ' ἂν κακῶς αὐτὴν θεωρῶσιν. (*Laws* 12.951A5–
> C4)

> no state will ever be able to live at a properly advanced level of civilization if it
> keeps to itself and never comes into contact with all the vices and virtues of man-
> kind; nor will it be able to preserve its laws intact if it just gets used to them
> without grasping their *raison d'etre*. In the mass of mankind you'll invariably find
> a number—though only a small number—of geniuses with whom it is worth any-

thing to associate, and they crop up just as often in badly ruled states as in the well-ruled. So the citizen of a well-run state, provided he's incorruptible, should go out and range over land and sea to track them down, so that he can see to the strengthening of the customs of his country that are soundly based, and the refurbishing of any that are defective. Without this observation and research a state will never stay at the peak of perfection; nor will it if the observers are incompetent.

Theophrastus' *Nomoi* were generated, partially at least, by the kind of process of travel and investigation which Plato recommended.

An equally close connection between Plato's *Laws* and the *politeiai* could not exist, for various reasons. One is the difference in content between the *Laws* and Aristotle's collection. At least partially because of that difference, Plato was aware of the distinction between πολιτεία and νόμοι[5] but it could become blurred.[6] For Aristotle,[7] on the other hand, δεῖ πρὸς τὴν πολιτείαν κεῖσθαι τοὺς νόμους (the constitution must set the pattern for the laws, 1282B10–11), although he never expatiated on this principle or gave examples of how it worked. We will look again at the relation between law and constitution.

II

There is another set of terms, somewhat different and broader, in which to see one relationship between Plato and Aristotle. For Plato, I refer to a major difference between the *Republic* and the *Laws,* namely, his willingness to come to grips with the facts and constraints of historical circumstances over against the more theoretical analyses of political evolutions in *Republic* 8 and 9.[8] For Aristotle, I refer not so much to the large development from the discussion of the best state in *Pol.* 7–8 to the study of deviant forms (παρεκβάσεις) and actual states in *Pol.* 4–6 as to a development of briefer compass within book 2. This approach involves Aristotle's increasing use of historical data, most relevantly here in two ways: he includes among states reputedly well-governed some beyond the traditional canon of Sparta and Crete, e.g., Carthage;[9] secondly, he contrasts the intention of the legislator with what has happened in history to point to defects in the legislation itself, particularly with Sparta.

The Structure of Politics 2

This book is descriptive and critical rather than prescriptive and normative. The process starts from the utopian[10] and ends with the historical; Plato's *Republic* (1261A5), his *Laws* (1264B26), the "constitutional schemes"[11] of Phaleas of Chalcedon (1266A39) and Hippodamus of Miletus (1267B22), the actual constitutions of Sparta (1269A29), Crete (1271B20), and Carthage (1272B24). Finally, in what some have claimed[12] to be an addition or a set of additions[13] to the original plan of the book as outlined at 1260B27–36, there is an account of Solon (1273B35), a capsule history of Athenan democracy (1274A35), and a catalog of other lawgivers (1274A22).

There is nothing in book 2 to suggest that, at this stage, Aristotle was deliberately thinking of a collection of *politeiai,* but the historical direction of the
structure and contents of the book would seem to make such a collection logi-
cally a next or near step. Two elements were involved in this step: one was a
move out of the constraints of "best-state" theorization, when Aristotle began
to deal with the issues we find at the beginning of book 4.[14] The second element is a new set of questions which Aristotle posed and which took Greek
political theory in new directions. As noted, some think that the end of book 2
is a later addition to the original plan of that book. That, I think, is correct,
but two further observations need to be made. There is a conscious attempt on
Aristotle's part to link this segment to the rest of the book in structure and
in content. The first is achieved by the use of a common stylistic device,
summarizing/transitional μὲν οὖν: περὶ μὲν οὖν τῆς Λακεδαιμονίων
εἴρηται, Σόλωνα δ᾽ ἔνιοι μὲν οἴονται κτλ. (1273B35–6: of the Spartan
constitution I have spoken already. Some think that Solon etc.); the second, by
linking Solon and Lycurgus in the same context: οἷον καὶ Λυκοῦργος καὶ
Σόλων· οὗτοι γὰρ καὶ νόμους καὶ πολιτείας κατέστησαν (B33–4: like
Lycurgus and Solon: for they established both constitutions and laws). The one
significant difference between the descriptions of the Spartan and Athenian *politeiai* is that the former is static,[15] once the imprint had been laid on it by
Lycurgus, the latter shows development from the time of Solon and development toward a political τέλος. It is this feature which is especially characteristic of the scientific *politeia,* as we know it from the *AP* and which especially
justifies calling this segment a ur-*AP.*

The segment may be divided into six parts:

1. A "relatively uninformed"[16] and extreme view of Solon as a "radical"
   who effected broad changes in existing institutions toward the goal of a
   mixed constitution (1273B35–39).
2. These changes affected the council of the Areopagus, the election of magistrates, and the popular law courts (1273B39–41).
3. A cautious[17] reply to this, based on we-know-not-what evidence, to the
   effect that Solon made no changes in the first two of these institutions[18]
   but had established the *demos* by setting up popular law courts.
4. A criticism of some[19] that, by this last act, Solon destroyed the power of
   council and magistrates (1274A2–5).
5. A capsule history of the distribution of political power in Athens (1274A5–
   11).
6. A defence of Solon's intentions and an alternative explanation for the
   changes since his time.[20]

Table 3-1 will show what a short distance there is between this segment and
the historical section of the *AP.*

Some general differences between *Pol.* 2.12 and the *AP* will be clear: (a)
the account in *Pol.* 2 is not fleshed out in detail; (b) the account is based
entirely on a limited number of secondary sources, including Academic discus-

Table 3-1

Politics 2	*AP*
(A) Areopagus (no changes)	8.4 largely unchanged (ὥσπερ ὑπῆρχεν καὶ πρότερον)
elections (no changes)	8.1 change from election to sortition
popular court	9.1–2 popular court
strength (ἴσχυσεν) of courts leads to democracy	9.1 establishment of court causes strength of people (ἰσχυκέναι τὸ πλῆθος)
(B) Ephialtes and Pericles diminished the Areopagus	25.1 Ephialtes diminished the Areopagus; Pericles diminished it further
Pericles made the courts μισθοφόρα	27.3–4 Pericles made the courts μισθοφόρα
(C) activity of the demagogues	28.3–5; 41.2 activity of the demagogues
(D) contemporary democracy not Solon's προαίρεσις:	9.3 power of the people through courts not Solon's βούλησις
the *demos,* responsible for naval supremacy in the Persian Wars, ἐφρονηματίσθη	22.3 after Marathon, θαρροῦντος ἤδη τοῦ δήμου, the Athenians first used ostracism
	24.1 θαρρούσης ἤδη τῆς πόλεως, Aristeides advised hegemony
	27.1 Pericles especially turned the city into a naval power, as a result of which τοὺς πολλοὺς θαρρήσαντας took total political power for themselves
and got bad δημαγωγοί ἀντιπολιτευομένων τῶν ἐπιεικῶν	28.1 after Pericles' death, for the first time the *demos* got a προστάτην οὐκ εὐδοκιμοῦντα παρὰ τοῖς ἐπιεικέσιν
(E) Solon gave the people basic privileges, τὰς ἀρχὰς αἱρεῖσθαι καὶ εὐθύνειν	9.1 a two-stage process, initial election followed by sortition
magistrates chosen from the upper three census classes; τὸ δὲ τέταρτον θητικόν, οἷς οὐδεμιᾶς ἀρχῆς μετῆν	7.3–4 magistrates chosen from the upper three census classes; τοὺς δ' ἄλλους θητικόν, οὐδεμιας μετέχοντας ἀρχῆς

sion, some works of Isocrates, Theopompus,[21] and others less identifiable [22] (c) it shows no knowledge of Androtion's *Atthis.*

It is in these areas and others that the specific differences are to be found. When Aristotle in the *AP* describes the functions of the council of the Areopagus before and after Solon, his second description significantly differs only in that he is specific about two details (8.4):

καὶ τὰς ἐκτίσεις ἀνέφερεν εἰς πόλιν, οὐκ ἐπιγράφουσα τὴν πρόφασιν διὰ τὸ εὐθύνεσθαι, καὶ τοὺς ἐπὶ καταλύσει τοῦ δήμου συνισταμένους ἔκρινεν, Σόλωνος θέντος νόμον εἰσαγγελίας περὶ αὐτῶν

the council brought the fines up to the Acropolis, not writing the reason for the punishment and judged those who formed a group to break up the *demos,* Solon having established a law about bringing them to trial.

The phrase οὐκ ἐπιγράφουσα τὴν πρόφασιν implies that Aristotle had seen old inscriptions or other records in which no reasons for the penalty were set down, and his reference to a law of Solon implies documentary research. The same implication is present in the revision of his earlier view that Solon had made no change in the manner of electing magistrates. The revision is based upon knowledge of a Solonian law (*AP* 8.1; 47.1).

The ways in which the narrative of the *AP* was fleshed out in comparison with *Pol.* 2 showed that his research included secondary sources, like Herodotus on Solon and Cleisthenes, Thucydides on the Peisistratids, Plato and Theopompus on Athenian politicians, and Androtion on ostracism.

III

The first two parts of this chapter have been devoted, respectively, to νόμος and πολιτεία, and the division may be thought to be encapsulated in the last section of book 2, with 1273B35—A21 dealing with the πολιτεία of Athens, and 1274A22–B28 concerned with laws and lawgivers. Although we can analyze the two separately, the split is artificial and the split is, historically, unreal. A large portion of law codes, especially that part which dealt with magistrates, is imbedded in the πολιτεία: research into law entailed research into constitutions

That research into both was carried on *pari passu* seems to be indicated by several phenomena: (when Aristotle, at the end of the *Nichomachean Ethics*, outlines the programme of political philosophy which he never completed, he says that, partly on the basis of the collected constitutions (συνηγμέναι πολιτεῖαι), we might more readily see what constitution is best (ποία πολιτεία ἀρίστη) and how each constitution is arranged (πῶς ἑκάστη ταχθεῖσα), using which laws and customs (τίσι νόμοις καὶ ἔθεσι χρωμένη).[23] There is here an obvious link between πολιτεία and νόμοι/ἔθη, and I suggest that one of the ways in which this link is forged is the conception of τάξις.

(1) It is a Platonic notion that νόμοι may be viewed as a τάξις, a notion expressed through the verb (*Leg.* 772B6: νόμων οὓς ἔταξε) or through the noun, whether it be the quasi-synonymous pairing of μετὰ νόμων καὶ τάξεως (673E4: cf. 780D5) or the phrase τάξις τῶν νόμων (688A1: cf. 707D2). The notion as phrased is taken over by Aristotle (*Pol.* 1271B29 and 32) but the field of τάξις is broadened by him in two parallel ways. The first is to apply the notion to the πολιτεία: τάξις τῆς πολιτείας (1264B31; 1272A4, B 10 and 31; 1281B39: cp. *AP* 3.1: ἡ τάξις τῆς ἀρχαίας πολιτείας). The second is to define νόμος as τάξις: ἡ γὰρ τάξις νόμος (1287A18: cp. 1326A30): the parallel step here is to define πολιτεία as τάξις:

1274B38: ἡ δὲ πολιτεία τῶν τὴν πόλιν οἰκούντων ἐστὶ τάξις τις

the constitution is a kind of organization of the state's inhabitants

1278B8–10: ἔστι δὲ πολιτεία πόλεως τάξις τῶν τε ἄλλων ἀρχῶν καὶ μάλιστα τῆς κυρίας πάντων

the constitution of a state is the organization of the offices, and in particular of the one that is sovereign over all the others

1289A15–20: πολιτεία μὲν γάρ ἐστι τάξις ταῖς πόλεσιν ἡ περὶ τὰς ἀρχάς, τίνα τρόπον νενέμηνται, καὶ τί τὸ κύριον τῆς πολιτείας καὶ τί τὸ τέλος ἑκάστης κοινωνίας ἐστίν· νόμοι δ' οἱ κεχωρισμένοι τῶν δηλούντων τὴν πολιτείαν, καθ' οὓς δεῖ τοὺς ἄρχοντας ἄρχειν καὶ φυλάττειν τοὺς παραβαίνοντας αὐτούς

a constitution is the arrangement which a state adopts for the distribution of offices, and for the determination of sovereignty in the constitution and of the end which the particular association aims at realizing: laws distinguishable from descriptions of constitutions are those according to which the rulers shall rule and shall watch out for those who transgress them

1290A7–8: πολιτεία μὲν γὰρ ἡ τῶν ἀρχῶν τάξις ἐστί

for a constitution is the arrangement of the offices

(2) The process which resulted in these new conceptions is reflected in the Epicurean comment about the collecting activities of Aristotle and Theophrastus.[24]

(3) Some aspects of the process can be traced. The *Vita Menagiana* contains a list of Aristotle's works with one interesting item (no. 140 Rose): περὶ τῶν Σόλωνος ἀξόνων ε' (Five books on Solon's *axones*).[25] No fragment of the work has survived, and some have tried to explain the title away.[26] Recourse to that would deprive us of an almost unique[27] chance to observe the workings of a specific effect of research. We saw above that, in his sketch of Athenian constitutional history in *Pol* 2.12, Aristotle thought that Solon made no change in the appointment of officials and that they continued to be elected. He apparently held the same view in book 3: the masses should be involved in election of officials (ἀρχαιρεσίαι: 1281A33). In the 'Αθπολ (8.1), we learn that Solon τὰς δ'ἀρχὰς ἐποίησε κληρωτάς (had the officials appointed by allotment). As if recognizing the novelty of this assertion, Aristotle buttresses it with an argument:

σημεῖον δ' ὅτι κληρωτὰς ἐποίησεν ἐκ τῶν τιημάτων ὁ περὶ τῶν ταμιῶν νόμος, ᾧ χρώμενοι διατελοῦσιν ἔτι καὶ νῦν· κελεύει γὰρ κληροῦν τοὺς ταμίας ἐκ πεντακοσιομεδίμνων.

that Solon stipulated appointment by lot from the property classes is confirmed by the law on the treasurers, which remains in use even today: it orders the appointment of the treasurers by lot from the five-hundred-bushel class.

Uniquely, this law and this law alone is repeated in the description (47.1): on the ταμίαι, . . . κληροῦται δ' εἷς ἐκ τῆς φυλῆς ἐκ πεντακοσιομεδίμνων κατὰ τὸν Σόλωνος νόμον· ἔτι γὰρ ὁ νόμος κύριός ἐστιν (one appointed by lot from each tribe, from the five-hundred-bushel class in accordance with Solon's law—this law is still in force). The reason the treasurers are mentioned first in the list of Solonian magistrates in the narrative is because their manner of appointment is itself an argument, but the fact that they are also mentioned first in the list of allotted officials in the description points up the importance of that argument.

In sum, although there is not enough evidence to show the kind of relationship between the *politeiai* and Plato's Νόμοι as is visible between the latter and Theophrastus, I think that the evidence suffices to show that research into comparative law was indispensable to the origin of Aristotle's series.

NOTES

1. Cf. Jaeger 267 ff.

2. *Atthis* 386 n. 51. Evidence does not permit the claim to be adequately tested.

3. Cf. especially A. H. Chase, "The Influence of Athenian Institutions Upon the *Laws* of Plato," *HSCP* 44 (1933) 131–92, Morrow 6 ff. et passim.

4. The evidence for this is limited, but specific Spartan influence on Plato's homicide law is shown by the Vatican A fragment of Theophrastus: Keaney 1976.189–91. Plato also occasionally praises the political institutions of Greek and non-Greek peoples. See list in Morrow 6.

5. 4.714B3–4: ἐννοεῖς οὖν ὅτι νόμων εἴδη τινές φασιν εἶναι τοσαῦτα ὅσαπερ πολιτειῶν. Cf. also 751A5–7.

6. As at 5.735A5–6. Compare Aristotle's critical remark (*Pol.* 2. 1265A1–2): τῶν δὲ Νόμων τὸ μὲν πλεῖστον μέρος νόμοι τιγχάνουσιν ὄντες, ὀλίγα δὲ περὶ τῆς πολιτείας εἴρηκεν.

7. *Pol.* 3.1282B10: cf. Newman ad loc. and 1289A13–25.

8. Note that Aristotle criticizes these analyses on historical grounds: *Pol.* 5.1316A29 ff.

9. He was preceded in this by Isocrates, 2.24.

10. 1260B27–32: ἐπεὶ δὲ προαιρούμεθα θεωρῆσαι περὶ τῆς κοινωνίας τῆς πολιτικῆς, τίς κρατίστη πασῶν τοῖς δυναμένοις ζῆν ὅτι μάλιστα κατ' εὐχήν, δεῖ καὶ τὰς ἄλλας ἐπισκέψασθαι πολιτείας, αἷς τε χρῶνταί τινες τῶν πόλεων τῶν εὐνομεῖσθαι λεγομένων, κἂν εἴ τινες ἕτεραι τυγχάνουσιν ὑπό τινων εἰρημέναι καὶ δοκοῦσαι καλῶς ἔχειν κτλ (we have undertaken to discuss that form of association which is the state, and to ask which of all such associations would be best if we were in a position to live exactly as we would like. So we must look at the other constitutions too, for example those that are in use by states that have the reputation of being governed by good laws, or any others that have been sketched by writers and appear to be good).

11. Newman *ad* 1266A31.

12. I have discussed the accuracy of this claim with reference to 1272A22–end in Keaney 1981.97–99.

13. Cf. Newman *ad* 1273B27, 1274A22 and 1274B9.

14. 1288B21–1289A1: ὥστε δῆλον, ὅτι καὶ πολιτείαν τῆς αὐτῆς ἐστιν ἐπιστήμης τὴν ἀρίστην θεωρῆσαι τίς ἐστι καὶ ποία τις ἂν οὖσα μάλιστ' εἴη κατ' εὐχὴν μηδενὸς ἐμποδίζοντος τῶν ἐκτὸς καὶ τίς τίσιν ἁρμόττουσα· πολλάκις γὰρ τῆς ἀρίστης τυχεῖν ἴσως ἀδύνατον, ὥστε τὴν κρατίστην τε ἁπλῶς καὶ τὴν ἐκ τῶν ὑποκειμένων ἀρίστην οὐ δεῖ λεληθέναι τὸν ἀγαθὸν νομοθέτην καὶ τὸν ὡς ἀληθῶς πολιτικόν, ἔτι δὲ τρίτην τὴν ἐξ ὑποθέσεως· δεῖ γὰρ καὶ τὴν

δοθεῖσαν δύνασθαι θεωρεῖν ἐξ ἀρχῆς τε πῶς ἂν γένοιτο καὶ γενομένη τίνα τρόπον ἂν σῴζοιτο πλεῖστον χρόνον· λέγω δὲ οἷον εἴ τινι πόλει συμβέβηκε μήτε τὴν ἀρίστην πολιτεύεσθαι πολιτείαν ἀχορήγητόν τε εἶναι καὶ τῶν ἀναγκαίων μήτε τὴν ἐνδεχομένην ἐκ τῶν ὑπαρχόντων, ἀλλά τινα φαυλοτέραν· παρὰ πάντα δὲ ταῦτα τὴν μάλιστα πάσαις ταῖς πόλεσιν ἁρμόττουσαν δεῖ γνωρίζειν. ὥσθ᾽ οἱ πλεῖστοι τῶν ἀποφαινομένων περὶ πολιτείας, καὶ εἰ τἄλλα λέγουσι καλῶς, τῶν γε χρησίμων διαμαρτάνουσιν. οὐ γὰρ μόνον την ἀρίστην δεῖ θεωρεῖν, ἀλλὰ καὶ τὴν δυνατήν, ὁμοίως δὲ καὶ τὴν ῥᾴω καὶ κοινοτέραν ἁπάσαις· νῦν δ᾽ οἱ μὲν τὴν ἀκροτάτην καὶ δεομένην πολλῆς χορηγίας ζητοῦσι μόνον, οἱ δὲ μᾶλλον κοινήν τινα λέγοντες τὰς ὑπαρχούσας ἀναιροῦντες πολιτείας τὴν Λακωνικὴν ἤ τινα ἄλλην ἐπαινοῦσι (so it is clearly true also that it is the task of one and the same science to consider the best constitution, what it is and what it would be like if it were constructed exactly as one would wish, without any hindrance from outside. Another of its tasks is to consider what constitution is suited to what persons, because for many the best is perhaps impossible to attain; so the good lawgiver and the genuine statesman will have to bear in mind both the "absolutely best" constitution and the "best in the circumstances." There is also a third, which starts from an assumption—I mean he must be able to consider a constitution which is given, both how it could come into being and how once in being it may last longest. I am speaking particularly of a state which happens to operate neither the best constitution—being without provision even for its basic needs—nor the one possible in the actual circumstances, but a worse. Besides these there is a fourth he must recognize: the constitution which will suit pretty well all states. This is why the majority of those who give their views on constitutions, however well they may do it in other respects, fall down on questions of utility. For we must consider not only the best constitution but also the possible, and likewise also that which is easier and more within the reach of all states).

15. Aristotle discussed developments of the Spartan constitution in the Λακεδαιμονίων πολιτεία: Keaney 1980.

16. H. T. Wade-Gery, *Essays in Greek History* (Oxford 1958) 195 n. 4.

17. ἔοικε δὲ Σόλων ἐκεῖνα μὲν ὑπάρχοντα πρότερον οὐ καταλῦσαι.

18. In the *AP* (8.1), Aristotle corrects this view about election of officials: see below.

19. Again, we do not know who: Morrow (82) thinks of Academic discussion, probably correctly.

20. Note that no similar attempt is made to defend Lycurgus for things which went bad in his *politeia*.

21. If the use of the word ἀντιπολιτεύεσθαι betrays his influence: cf. chapter 13, "Aristotle and Theopompus."

22. The importance of the law courts and the Solonian establishment thereof predates Aristotle, but we do not know who first asserted it: cf. E. Ruschenbusch, "ΔΙΚΑΣΤΗΡΙΟΝ ΠΑΝΤΩΝ ΚΥΡΙΟΝ," *Historia* 6 (1957) 257–74.

23. Cp. *Pol*, 1263A23: ἔθεσι καὶ τάξει νόμων.

24. See above, "Origin and Authorship."

25. The ἄξονες were archaic inscriptions containing Solon's laws: Rhodes 131–34.

26. Weil 125. E. Heitz, writing in 1865, supposed that the work formed part of the Ἀθπολ: he was not totally wrong.

27. For some examples of changes of mind based on newer evidence or knowledge between the *Politics* and the *politeiai*, cf. Keaney 1980.

4

The Unity of the Ἀθπολ

It is a traditional[1] conception that there is a basic division of the Ἀθπολ into two parts, chapters 1–41 containing the narrative[2] history of the Athenian constitution, and chapters 42–69 describing the constitution as it existed when Aristotle wrote the work ca. 334–331.[3] The simplicity of this conception has an abstract satisfaction, and the conception has some slight support in the text. Both the language and the structure of the work, however, suggest a more complex interpretation, namely, that this division of the work is almost entirely a chronological one, and that the more important relation between the parts of the work is one of connection rather than division.

I

The traditional conception centers on chapter 41. In that chapter, Aristotle notes the (restoration and final re-)establishment of the democracy which continues into the fourth century: this happened in 404/3, ἐπὶ Πυθοδώρου ἄρχοντος (41.1). The account of the last events leading up to that establishment would seem to have provided a good opportunity to mark this division, i.e., to have the thematic split between the end of the development and the description of that result (D) coincide with the chronological split. It is precisely this opportunity which Aristotle did not take.

By the usual standards of structure and content, chapter 41 serves as the transition between N and D, and the chapter could hardly serve better the double function of looking forward and backward. Chapter 41 contains a (selective)[4] summary of the constitutional changes which led up to the final restoration of democracy. Nevertheless, Aristotle has deliberately obscured this function and blurred any sharp division in two ways. First, the statement of the establishment of the democracy and its date are found in 41.1. This does not represent the chronological final point of the narrative, for chapter 39 begins with a process dated ἐπ᾽ Εὐκλείδου ἄρχοντος (403/2) and chapter 40 ends with the final point in the same process dated ἐπὶ Ξεναινέτου ἄρχοντος (401/0). Second, one phrase at the beginning of 41 is used oddly: ταῦτα μὲν οὖν ἐν τοῖς ὕστερον συνέβη γενέσθαι καιροῖς, τότε δὲ κύριος ὁ δῆμος γενόμενος κτλ. Most frequently, μὲν οὖν signals the end of a segment.[5] Here, it has that function but only partially, for the sequel, ὕστερον, at once takes

43

us back to the period before the beginning of that segment and, thematically, looks forward to the contents of 41, the μεταβολὴ πολιτειῶν.[6]

Similarly, this list of πολιτεῖαι ends at 404/3, but the contents of the chapter take us beyond that date with the measures of Heraclides and Agyrrhius.[7]

This interpretation of part of chapter 41 is intended to support the suggestion that the major structural segments of the ᾿Αθπολ are to be looked upon as mutually integrated rather than as sharply demarcated from each other. This structural consideration reflects Aristotle's conception—inferrable from the way he has shaped his material—that, while the history of the Athenian constitution can be broken up into discrete segments for purposes of analysis, that history is at the same time a record of process and continuity. In this chapter I propose to argue that the most accurate division of the work is quadripartite, I (lost beginning to chapter 1), II (2–41), III (42–62), and IV (63–69).

In the passages just discussed, the transition from N to D is effected by the repetition of νῦν: (41.1) τὴν νῦν[8] οὖσαν πολιτείαν; (41.3) μέχρι τῆς νῦν; (42.1) ἡ νῦν κατάστασις. The process of constitutional development in Athens involved both continuity and change. Both aspects are encapsulated in Aristotle's use of the adverb νῦν. Wherever used in N, it invariably looks forward to D and is at once descriptive of circumstances of the fourth century.

The list:[9]

1ab. 3.5: ὁ μὲν βασιλεὺς εἶχε τὸ *νῦν* καλούμενον Βουκόλιον . . . σημεῖον δε· ἔτι καὶ *νῦν* occurs the *hieros gamos* of the king's wife.

2. 3.5 (οἱ ἄρχοντες): κύριοι δ᾿ ἦσαν καὶ τὰς δίκας αὐτοτελεῖς κρίνειν καὶ οὐκ ὥσπερ *νῦν* προανακρίνειν.

3. 3.6 (Areopagus): διὸ καὶ μόνη τῶν ἀρχῶν αὕτη μεμένηκε διὰ βίου καὶ *νῦν*.

4. 7.1 (archons' oath): ὅθεν ἔτι καὶ *νῦν* οὕτως ὀμνύουσι.

5. 7.4 (census classes): διὸ καὶ *νῦν* whenever a candidate is asked his class, he would never reply "thetic."

6. 8.1 (allotment of officials): σημεῖον . . . ὁ περὶ τῶν ταμιῶν νόμος, ᾧ χρώμεμοι διατελοῦσιν ἔτι καὶ *νῦν*.

7. 9.2 (criteria for judging Solon): οὐ γὰρ δίκαιον ἐκ τῶν *νῦν* γιγνομένων ἀλλ᾿ ἐκ τῆς ἄλλης πολιτείας θεωρεῖν τὴν ἐκείνου βούλησιν.

8. 22.2 (institution of the bouleutic oath): ὃν ἔτι καὶ *νῦν* ὀμνύουσιν.

Of these eight instances, six are formulaic (4x: ἔτι καὶ νῦν; 2x: διὸ καί), and it is immediately clear why. In all six instances, there has been continuity of institution without change. On the other hand, in case 2, Aristotle is contrasting the current practice with that of the past,[10] and in case 7 there has been an unforeseeable development of an earlier institution.[11]

The other side of the coin is the use of νῦν in D. Apart from the introductory words of chapter 42, νῦν is used 11 times, always and only in a πρότερον–νῦν formula or a variation thereof.[12] The instances: 45.3; 49.3; 51.3; 53.4; 54.3; 55.1; 55.2; 55.4; 56.4; and 61.1. All these refer to changes in institutions, some of which had been mentioned in N. It is sufficient here to refer to two.[13] At 55.1, Aristotle says οἱ δὲ καλούμενοι ἐννέα ἄρχοντες τὸ μὲν ἐξ ἀρχῆς ὃν τρόπον καθίσταντο εἴρηται. This is the single back-reference to N in D, and the imperfect tense of the verb shows that he is talking about a process rather than a single act. The previous texts concerned are 3.2, the establishment and development of the pre-Solonian archons; 8.1, the Solonian innovations; 22.5, the reestablishment of sortition after the tyranny; and 26.2, the expansion of the numbers eligible for the office. At 53.1, Aristotle says that the number of deme judges, formerly thirty, was increased to forty after the oligarchy of the Thirty. This institution was first mentioned at 16.5 and its reestablishment at 26.2.

Besides the kind of explicit reference we have at 55.1, there is a kind of implicit reference which involves more than repetition of fact. This occurs when Aristotle uses aspects of a contemporary institution to make an inference about the earlier history of that institution. At 57.1, Aristotle says of the king-archon that ὡς δ᾽ ἔπος εἰπεῖν καὶ τὰς πατρίους θυσίας διοκεῖ οὗτος πάσας. At 58.1 he says ὁ δὲ πολέμαρχος θύει μὲν θυσίας τήν τε τῇ Ἀρτέμιδι τῇ Ἀγροτέρᾳ καὶ τῷ Ἐνυαλίῳ. Both texts, the first in a general, the second in a specific, way supply the basis for an inference made in N about the relative antiquity of the three major archonships; 3.3: ὅτι δὲ τελευταία [sc. ὁ ἄρχων] τούτων ἐγένετο τῶν ἀρχῶν, σημεῖον καὶ τὸ μηδὲν τῶν πατρίων τὸν ἄρχοντα διοικεῖν, ὥσπερ ὁ βασιλεὺς καὶ ὁ πολέμαρχος, ἀλλ᾽ ἁπλῶς τὰ ἐπίθετα. This inference is reinforced by another at 13.3. The period after Solon was especially characterized by στάσις, and different kinds of difficulties were experienced in filling the archonship. Aristotle inferred from these that this was the most powerful magistracy: καὶ δῆλον ὅτι μεγίστην εἶχεν δύναμιν ὁ ἄρχων.

II

Aristotle pursued the histories of three institutions, the Council of the Areopagus, the Council of the Five Hundred, and the popular law courts, the δικαστήρια. Although he did not trace the history of the archonship in the same way, that institution, like the other three, is characterized by its relationship to the courts; and, apart from the references we have noted to the manner of election thereto, there is only one statement in N about the competence of the archons. At 3.4, Aristotle says κύριοι δ᾽ ἦσαν καὶ τὰς δίκας αὐτοτελεῖς κρίνειν καὶ οὐχ, ὥσπερ νῦν, προανακρίνειν. Three aspects of this sentence may be remarked: its language, its content, and its context. For the first, the word κύριος links the office thematically with the Areopagus and βουλή, as we will shortly see. The content of the statement is taken up in D at 56–59, in which Aristotle fleshes out this statement by detailing what are the kinds of cases each of the archons ἀνακρίνει. Finally, there appears in the same context a statement about the judicial functions of the pre-Solonian Areopagus:

ἡ δὲ τῶν Ἀρεοπαγιτῶν βουλὴ τὴν μὲν τάξιν εἶχε τοῦ διατηρεῖν τοὺς νόμους, διῴκει δὲ τὰ πλεῖστα καὶ τὰ μέγιστα τῶν ἐν τῇ πόλει, καὶ κολάζουσα καὶ ζημιοῦσα πάντας τοὺς ἀκοσμοῦντας κυρίως

(the Council of the Areopagus had the function of watching over the laws, and it administered most and the greatest of the city's affairs, having full power to chastise and punish all the disorderly.)

The language is very general and probably inspired by Isocrates:[14] the only function mentioned which is at all specific is a judicial one. The same is true of the next passage, which summarizes the role of the Areopagus under Solon (8.4):

τὴν δὲ τῶν Ἀρεοπαγιτῶν ἔταξεν ἐπὶ τὸ νομοφυλακεῖν, ὥσπερ ὑπῆρχεν καὶ πρότερον ἐπίσκοπος οὖσα τῆς πολιτείας, καὶ τά τε ἄλλα τὰ πλεῖστα καὶ τὰ μέγιστα τῶν πολιτικῶν διετήρει καὶ τοὺς ἁμαρτάνοντας ηὔθυνεν κυρία οὖσα καὶ ζημιοῦν καὶ κολάζειν

(he appointed the council of the Areopagus to guard the laws, just as previously it had been overseer of the constitution. In general it watched over most and the greatest of the city's affairs; it corrected wrongdoers, having full power to punish and chastise).

Access to more information allowed him to add two details,[15] both judicial in nature.

The next stage in this process is marked by another verbal link, τῆς πολιτείας φυλακή, in the note on the year 462/1 (25.2): ἅπαντα περιεῖλε [sc. Ephialtes] τὰ ἐπίθετα δι' ὧν ἦνή τῆς πολιτείας φυλακή, καὶ τὰ μὲν τοῖς πεντακοσίοις τὰ δὲ τῷ δήμῳ καὶ τοῖς δικαστηρίοις ἀπέδωκεν (he took away from the council all the accretions which gave it its guardianship of the constitution, giving some to the Council of Five Hundred and some to the people and the jury courts). The fact that we are told nothing of the content[16] of the ἐπίθετα but only that they were handed over partly to the βουλή, partly to the assembly and law courts, has two effects: one is to set up a distinction or an opposition between the βουλή on the one hand and the δῆμος/δικαστήρια on the other; the second is that this note is included specifically for thematic reasons, and its import is not clear until it can be supplemented by another text or texts.

The first of these is in the summary/transitional chapter 41(.2),[17] at which Aristotle points up the salient characteristic of the final democracy: ἁπάντων γὰρ αὐτὸς αὑτὸν πεποίηκεν ὁ δῆμος κύριον, καὶ πάντα διοικεῖται ψηφίσμασιν καὶ δικαστηρίοις, ἐν οἷς ὁ δῆμός ἐστιν ὁ κρατῶν (the people have made themselves masters of everything, and control all things by means of jury courts, in which the sovereign power resides with the people). Here, we have the same opposition as above between δῆμος/δικαστήρια and βουλή. The salience of the opposition comes in the next sentence: καὶ γὰρ αἱ τῆς βουλῆς κρίσεις εἰς τὸν δῆμον ἐληλύθασιν (even the jurisdiction of the council has been transferred to the people). There is an ambiguity in this sentence, and I suggest that the ambiguity is deliberate. It centers on the meaning of κρίσεις. Does this mean only judicial decisions or does it include nonjudicial decisions as well? I think it means both, but in different ways. At 25.2, we had βουλή distinguished from δῆμος and δικαστήρια. Here we initially have δῆμος characterized by assembly and courts, and next distinguished from βουλή. The matchup is not precise, but the texts can be made perfectly to coincide if we assume—an assumption justified by the central position of chapter 41—that the statement looks both backward and forward. In 25, we know only that some functions of the Areopagus were transferred to three organs: assembly, courts, and council. We cannot say that specific kinds of functions were exclusively assigned to one, nor can we say that judicial functions were exclusive to the courts.[18] This is consistent with the statements on the Areopagus at 3.6 and 8.4. Although I have suggested that the specific functions there noted are judicial, the broader functions include, but are not restricted to, these.

It is, however, precisely these which carry the thematic burden, and to emphasize judicial κρίσεις in 41 looks forward to chapter 45, which continues the theme and the language of 41. In 45,[19] Aristotle begins by contrasting present and past—ἡ δὲ βουλὴ πρότερον μὲν ἦν κυρία—and ends τούτων μὲν οὖν ἄκυρός ἐστιν ἡ βουλή. This both continues and reverses the notion of a magistracy which is κύριον, a point made of the archons in chapter 3 and of the Areopagus in chapters 3 and 8. In terms of content, the focus is on judicial decisions and the transfer thereof to a δικαστήριον: linguistically, this is effected by picking up the theme of κρίσεις in 41. The turning point of the anecdote of 45.1 comes κρίσεως ἐν δικαστηρίῳ γενομένης. The next phase of the council's activity is when it κρίνει[20] τὰς ἀρχὰς τὰς πλείστας . . . οὐ κυρία δ' ἡ κρίσις, ἀλλ' ἐφέσιμος εἰς τὸ δικαστήριον (the council has jurisdiction over most officials . . . its judgment is not final but referrable to the jury court). The emphasis on ἔφεσις εἰς τὸ δικαστήριον is repeated in the next two of the areas of the council's former competence.

Overarching and controlling all these texts is a thesis, namely that the history of Athenian politics is the development of the constitution toward the democracy of the fourth century, and that this development is the history of the Athenian δῆμος coming to power by appropriating functions which originally belonged to other organs of the society. Aristotle never articulates this thesis either in general terms or at specific points,[21] but he develops it piecemeal. Important aspects of his method are verbal allusion, as we have seen, and structure. The organs whose functions the δῆμος appropriates are, in order, archons, Areopagus, and Council of the Five Hundred. The archons are treated in I, the Areopagus in II, and the Five Hundred in III. The context in which the archons are treated is the discussion of the buildings in which they carry on their (judicial and other) business. I will suggest[22] that this section is especially linked to IV in that it is here that we find the description of the δῆμος exercising its power.

The theme of the courts also provides another structuring link, now between II and IV. At 27.4 Aristotle says that one effect of Pericles' creating pay for jurymen (δικαστήρια μισθοφόρα) was that inferior men would get on the lists of jurors which were chosen by allotment (κληρουμένων). Near the beginning of his discussion of the courts, Aristotle describes the allotment machines (κληρωτήρια: 63.2) and the allotment process (ἐπικληρώσῃ: 63.5; κληροῖ: 64.3). The end of the description of the court process coincides with the end of the work: ἀπολαμβάνουσιν τὸν μισθὸν ἐν τῷ μέρει οὗ ἔλαχον ἕκαστοι (they receive their stipend, each in the division to which they are assigned by lot).

NOTES

1. Cf. e.g., (early) Sandys lxxi: "The work is divided into two parts;" (later) V. Ehrenberg, *The Greek State* (Oxford, 1960) 243: the *AthPol* "is divided into two parts, unconnected but set side by side, a history of the constitution and a systematic survey of the various elements in the state at the time of Aristotle;" and (most recently) Rhodes 5: "the contents of *A.P.* fall into two parts."

2. In what follows I shall refer to these chapters as N(arrative), and to 42–69 as D(escription).

3. For the date, Keaney 1970.2; Rhodes 51–58.

4. For the criteria of selection, cf. Keaney 1963.125–28.

5. Cf. chapter 8,"Vertical Structure: Ring Composition."

6. There is a parallel to this structure in 21. This begins διὰ μὲν οὖν ταύτας τὰς αἰτίας ἐπίστευεν ὁ δῆμος τῷ Κλεισθένει, τότε δὲ τοῦ πλήθους προεστήκως. The latter clause refers to the events of 20.1 and leads into the theme of ch. 21: cf. Keaney 1969². 419–21. There are further parallels: each τότε-clause is marked by a participle (γενόμενος, προεστηκώς), and each main clause contains an archon date.

7. Cf. Rhodes ad loc.

8. νῦν is Kaibel's certain supplement for the gap in the papyrus: cf. Chambers' apparatus and Rhodes ad loc. The only other suggestion, Papabasileios' πρίν, is ruled out by the fact that Aristotle does not use πρίν adverbially.

9. The approach I use here was initiated by R. W. Macan, "᾿Αθηναίων πολιτεία," *JHS* 12 (1891) 17–40 at 18–19. This analysis treats twice as many passages as did Macan.

10. This passage is also of thematic interest: see below.

11. It is interesting to note that two of the verses of Solon quoted by Aristotle contrast pre-Solonian conditions with those of his time: (12.3) χαῦνα μὲν τότ᾿ ἐφράσαντο, νῦν δέ μοι χολούμενοι and (12.4) πρόσθεν γε δουλεύουσα, νῦν δ᾿ ἐλευθέρα.

12. πρότερον (like νῦν) implies a static condition. Thus, at 55.1, it is avoided because Aristotle refers to a process of change in the selection of archons. It may be avoided at 51.3 because Aristotle realized that the larger number of grain commissioners could be temporary (and by the third century, the number had been reduced). ποτε at 49.3 is, I suppose, *uariationis causa*.

13. For a differently focused discussion, see Keaney 1970².

14. Cf. Rhodes 108: the Atthidographers' view of the wide dicastic powers of the early Areopagos is best represented by Androtion, 324 F 3 Jacoby.

15. Deposit of fines on the Acropolis and trial of conspirators against the democracy.

16. Cf. Rhodes ad loc. and G. Cawkwell, "*Nomophulakia* and the Areopagus," *JHS* 108 (1988) 1–12.

17. I use this term to refer to chapters which not only contain references to events of conditions outside their chronological boundaries (e.g., chs. 9, 23, 27) but also and especially summarize phenomena which Aristotle thought should be placed at decisive points in his narrative (e.g., chs. 3, 28, 41).

18. The clearest example of this is the various kinds of εἰσαγγελίαι: these were handled by all three bodies: cf. Rhodes 524–25.

19. For fuller discussion of this, cf. chapter 18, "Chapter 45: ἡ βουλή."

20. I think the word is used here as it is used by Aristotle at *Pol.* 3.1286A26: δικάζουσι καὶ βουλεύονται καὶ κρίνουσιν, of judicial decisions made by a body primarily nonjudicial in function. Newman ad loc. and Rhodes *ad* 41.2 believe that the word covers both judicial and nonjudicial decisions. This is the only passage in which Aristotle uses the three verbs together. Elsewhere in the *Politics,* βουλεύεσθαι is distinguished from κρίνειν (6x, e.g., 1281B31, 1329A4) and δικάζεσθαι (5x, e.g., 1275B17, 1328B27).

21. The closest he comes to it are his statements at 9 and 41 about δῆμος κύριος, statements connected also by the figure of initial anaphora.

22. Cf. chapter 7, "Structure and Meaning."

5

Observation and Explanation

This part of my title perhaps itself deserves explanation. I think of a double process. Its first part consists of drawing attention to smaller or larger portions of the text about which it is desirable to ask further questions. Although few of these passages have in the past been singled out for special treatment, it will, I hope, become clear that one basic principle of interpretation can be applied to them, namely that to look at them only in their initial and immediate context is a limited, and limiting, approach, and one which does not adequately respond to Aristotle's intentions. It is the matter of these intentions and their identification which constitutes the second part of the process. However successful or not this part of the process turns out to be, the context of intentionality must be the correct one, for two related reasons. The first is that Aristotle had, for practical purposes, no preexisting genre[1] within which to work but had to define in practice and as he went along a new subgenre. In that process, he had to make choices—at the most basic level—of what to include and what to exclude.

The second reason has to do with sources. Since the πολιτεῖαι were not works of fiction or of the free imagination, Aristotle was heavily dependent on secondary sources. To use or not to use a source, to accept or to deny what a source said, to adjust or adapt a source for individual purposes: all of these operations Aristotle engaged in and all of them entailed choices of one kind or another. The question of sources I address more explicitly in the next chapter. Here, I will illustrate the first part of the process—observation—by listing ten short portions of the text and asking of each the question, why?

1. 2.1: Aristotle describes the opposed political/economic groups before Solon as οἱ γνώριμοι [the notables] and τὸ πλῆθος. At 5.1 the same opposition is in terms of οἱ γνώριμοι and ὁ δῆμος. Why the change from πλῆθος to δῆμος?
2. 2.2: in the first reference to Solon, he is termed προστάτης τοῦ δήμου. [champion of the people] Why?
3. 3.1–5: In discussing the early development of the archontic system at Athens, Aristotle uses the order βασιλεύς, πολέμαρχος, ἄρχων, three times in a row. The fourth time the order is βασιλεύς, ἄρχων, πολέμαρχος. Why the change?
4. 6.3: Aristotle says that Solon had the opportunity τυραννεῖν τῆς πόλεως.

At 11.2 he says that Solon had the opportunity τυραννεῖν. Why the repetition?

5. At 7.1: Solon κατέστησε τὴν πολιτείαν. At 11.1 there is another repetition: Solon διαταξας δὲ τὴν πολιτείαν ὅνπερ εἴρηται τρόπον. Why?

6. 8.5: Solon saw τὴν μὲν πόλιν πολλάκις στασιάζουσαν. He made a law to take effect στασιαζούσης τῆς πόλεως. Why the change in word order?

7. 9.1: κύριος γὰρ ὢν ὁ δῆμος τῆς ψήφου κύριος γίγνεται τῆς πολιτείας. This is the first instance of initial anaphora in the ᾿Αθπολ. There is one other (41.2): ἁπάντων γὰρ αὐτὸς αὑτὸν πεποίηκεν κυριον, καὶ πάντα διοικεῖται ψηφίσμασιν καὶ δικαστηρίοις. Why should there be only two instances of this figure?

8. 13.4: when Peisistratus is introduced, he is described as δημοτικώτατος εἶναι δοκῶν. When the account of his activities begins, at 14.1, he is again δημοτικώτατος δ᾿ εἶναι δοκῶν. Why this form of introduction? Why the repetition?

9. 23.1: Aristotle recounts the ascendancy of the Council of the Areopagus after the Persian Wars, οὐδενὶ δόγματι λαβοῦσα τὴν ἡγεμονίαν. δόγμα is universally translated by "decree" *vel sim.*, but the term is never so used by Aristotle, nor is it the usage of official epigraphic language. Why is it used? What does it mean?

10. 27.5: πρώτου καταδείξαντος ᾿Ανύτου μετὰ τὴν ἐν Πύλῳ στρατηγίαν. Aristotle points to the introduction of bribery in the law courts. The language he uses, however, is decidedly odd, for καταδεικνύναι is almost a technical term to describe the introduction of a cultural benefit. What is the point of its use here?

The passages have not been selected at random, and others could have been used; but these provide an adequate sample of questions which the text of the ᾿Αθπολ provokes. It will be clear almost immediately that the general principle articulated at the beginning of this chapter applies to each of these, namely that each is connected in one way or another with other parts of the text. That is to say that Aristotle frequently expresses his meaning through repetition, whether this be formal, through structure, or a matter of content, through pattern or theme.

1. δῆμος and πλῆθος, although believed by some to be synonymous, are in fact not. Aristotle's use of them is consistent: when the two terms are found in the same context, there is always involved an implicit process whereby a large segment of the population becomes a unified group, acting cohesively.[2]

2. The initial purpose of this characterization is to show to which side Solon attached himself, in terms of a moral stance. An ultimate purpose is to introduce and establish the theme of leadership of the δῆμος: we have allusions to this at 20.4 and 23.3, and it becomes one of the central themes of chapter 28, at which the language here used of Solon is repeated.[3]

3. As we will see,[4] there are structural reasons why Aristotle changed the

order of listing of the three archons, but another process also influenced that change. For Aristotle, the archons were principals in two theses. The first was that the δῆμος came to power by appropriating to itself functions which had belonged to three other organs—archons, Areopagus, βουλή. We are told how the process of appropriation took place in the cases of the latter two,[5] but of the archons we are told only that it took place, not when or how. The second is the chronology of the development within the archontic college whereby the archon came to be the most important official. Again, we are told that this change took place, but not when or how.

4. In the first passage in which the expression is used, the phrase shows the reaction of Solon to one state of affairs: that reaction is to be implicitly recalled in the new context in which τυραννεῖν is repeated.[6]

5. The passages are structured by means of a device used frequently in the Ἀθπολ, framing ring composition.[7]

6. The phrases are illustrations of the related phenomenon of chiasmus, an A/B/B¹/A¹ order.[8]

7. Why there should be only two instances of initial anaphora cannot be totally clear, but the fact that the figure is restricted in this way highlights as strongly as possible the thematic link between the two passages. 9.1 sets up a result (κύριος–πολιτείας) which is dependent upon a condition (κύριος–ψήφου): by 41.2, both condition and result have been achieved.

8. Two comments are relevant. From a purely formal point of view, the repeated language frames material which one may call a digression in so far as it concerns an event, the διαψηφισμός, which occurred much later than the chronological context in which it is found. The repetitions, however, serve other functions. First, the use of repetition is a stylistic marker for the narrative of the tyranny.[9] Second, the use of δοκῶν is one instance of a pattern according to which major figures come upon the political scene already accompanied by a certain reputation.[10]

9. This will turn out to be another instance of the same pattern.

10. The occurrence of πρώτου *cum* verb will show that we are dealing with an idiom with which Aristotle signals the degeneration of political leadership in Athens. Overtly, this begins in chapter 28 with Cleon, but the idiom is first applied to Pericles, in chapter 27.[11]

NOTES

1. Cf. chapter 2, "The 'Cultural' Origin of the πολιτεία." The cultural genre within which Aristotle worked was not rigorous enough to determine what went into the contents of the πολιτεῖαι.

2. Cf. chapter 16, "δῆμος, πλῆθος, and πόλις."

3. Cf. chapter 14, "Aristotle and Theramenes."

4. Ch. chapter 6, "Methods and Purposes."

5. Cf. chapter 8, "Vertical Structure: Ring Composition."

6. Cf. chapter 9, "Horizontal Structure: Chiasmus."

7. Cf. chapter 10, "The Politics of Institutions versus the Politics of Personality."

8. Cf. chapter 11, "The δοχειγ Formula."

9. Cf. my remarks on the deconstruction of Pericles in chapter 6, "Methods and Purposes."

10. Cf. chapter 6.

11. Areopagus, ch. 26; βουλή, chs. 41 and 45.

6

Methods and Purposes

By Jacoby's definition, the ᾿Αθπολ is the single extant example of a genre invented by Aristotle. The other πολιτεῖαι exist only in titles and/or fragments: the MS of the end of the ᾿Αθπολ is defective, and the beginning is missing. Thus, any attempt to create criteria for the genre *qua* genre must fail; the ᾿Αθπολ has no specific generic antecedents and no specific synchronic comparanda.

If then Aristotle had no generic criteria to guide him, what criteria did he use? Initially, these flow from his intentions. Once the choice was made to split the work into a narrative part and a systematic part, that choice was both a restraining factor and a liberating factor. It restrained because a relation between the first and second parts had to be determined and, once determined, had to be fleshed out in detail. Once, however, this kind of need was filled, it seems that Aristotle was totally free to include in the narrative whatever he wished to. This is not to say that the contents of the narrative are randomly chosen. They are not, but they are not all, nor most of them, determined by the demands of the second part.

I will try to be more specific here under two rubrics: choice of sources and use of sources. The historical part of the ᾿Αθπολ obviously needs a chronological backbone. For this, Aristotle chose the system of dating by archon year, a system rejected by Thucydides (5.20) but used by the local historians of Attica, the Atthidographers. Once that choice was made, it entailed using or considering the *Atthides'* versions of the events they described. It also meant not using much of the material they contained, for it would not have been relevant to the kind of political history which Aristotle was writing. In the context of historiography, it was natural for Aristotle to use sources closer to the events they were describing. Thus, normal historical sources (Herodotus, Thucydides, Androtion [perhaps Cleidemus], Ephorus); and primary sources where available (the poems of Solon, laws, inscriptions). This much is predictable for a work grounded in historical events. Other sources are less predictable (Isocrates, Plato's *Apology* and *Gorgias,* Theopompus). From the point of view of pure historical information or historical objectivity, these latter three would not be expected to provide the same kind of material as the writers of the first group, and the choice of these as sources, if they are correctly identified as such, already bespeaks a different way of treating sources other than as historical quarries. Let us look briefly at four passages which show four different ways of source use, or, more precisely, source adaptation.

The first is the account of the assassination of Hipparchus. The main source of this is Thucydides, but in one detail Aristotle corrects him, namely, that weapons were not carried in processions at that time (18.4). This is a simple and basic use of sources with no further implication.

The second text is 14.1: Peisistratus persuades the assembly to give him a group of bodyguards, with Aristion making the motion, Ἀριστίωνος γράψαντος τὴν γνώμην. The detail is found in Plutarch, *vitSol* 30.2, and was presumably drawn from Androtion's *Atthis*. There, it was a historical event to be recorded in a specific context. For Aristotle it served two other functions, the first as one element of a pattern of deceitful actions on the part of Peisistratus,[1] the second as one element in a pattern of introducing nondemocratic governments.[2] There is no reason to think that either pattern was in Androtion's Ἀτθίς *as a pattern*.

The third text describes the establishment of the oligarchy of the Thirty (34.3): καταπλαγεὶς ὁ δῆμος ἠναγκάσθη χειροτονεῖν τὴν ὀλιγαρχίαν (terrified, the δῆμος was compelled to vote in the oligarchy). Some of the language is borrowed directly from the source (Ephorus?) of Diodorus 14.3.7: ὁ δῆμος καταπλαγεὶς ἠναγκάζετο χειροτονίᾳ καταλῦσαι τὴν δημοκρατίαν. The borrowing seems straightforward, but the choice of χειροτον- is complicated. This is the only time the word is used in the narrative, but it is used in the systematic part eighteen times as a constituent element of the normal democratic process. Aristotle's substitution of χειροτονεῖν τὴν ὀλιγαρχίαν for χειροτονίᾳ καταλῦσαι τὴν δημοκρατίαν heightens the ironic contrast between the democratic process and the oligarchic result. The oxymoron becomes the more striking given the close-knit structure of Aristotle's work: such an effect would not have been possible in the discursiveness of Ephorus' general history.[3]

The last text is more complex. In the same chapter in which Aristotle reports that Pericles instituted pay for the jury courts, he says (27.5): ἤρξατο δὲ μετὰ ταῦτα καὶ τὸ δεκάζειν, πρώτου καταδείξαντος Ἀνύτου μετὰ τὴν ἐν Πύλῳ στρατηγίαν (after this judicial corruption began. The way was first shown by Anytus after he had served as general at Pylos). With this may be compared two parallel texts, Diodorus 13.64.6: πρῶτος Ἀθηναίων δοκεῖ δικαστήριον δωροδοκῆσαι and Σ Aeschines 1.87: ἐδέκαζεν οὖν διέφθειρεν ἀργυρίῳ τοὺς δικαστάς. ἤρξατο δὲ τοῦ τοιούτου πρῶτος Ἄνυτος. The event referred to took place in 409 and is in Diodorus' narrative under that year. It will have been in that year in all the *Atthides* as well. Therefore, the fact that in general Aristotle used *Atthis* chronology did not entail that he use all elements of *Atthis* form. He took this event out of normal chronology because he wanted to make a thematic point.[4]

So far we have seen that, while Aristotle can use his sources in a very matter-of-fact way (example 1), he also used them to create elements of patterns (example 2), to produce rhetorical effects (example 3), and, by ignoring restraints placed upon authors writing in traditional genres, to put an historical datum in an entirely new context (example 4).

My use of terms like "pattern," "theme/thematic," and, shortly, "subtext" and "paratext" arises from a different way of looking at the text from what has been followed in nearly all previous treatments of the work. This interpretation is intended to suggest that an important method of communication in the work is through what may be called extrareferentiality. I use this ugly term to express a comparatively simple notion, namely that many statements in the Ἀθπολ are not to be read in and for themselves in their immediate context but are related to and more fully understood in the light of other passages, both within and without the work. This notion involves three compositional devices: I. structure, which I discuss in the next chapter; II. formula, pattern, and theme, which I discuss throughout; and III. subtext and paratext.

Since we have begun with a brief view of Aristotle's manipulation of his sources, I propose to refer to such sources as "subtexts" and will be using further instances of them in future chapters. I will also use the term "paratext" to refer to passages in one part of the *AP* which, by greater or lesser repetition of language and/or theme, are linked to other passages and may serve to clarify them. I begin by discussing passages concerning two of the major figures in Athenian history, Solon and Pericles, illustrating how Aristotle used subtexts and paratexts.

THE THREE LIVES OF SOLON

One of the σοφισταί who came to Croesus' court, according to Herodotus 1.29, was Solon,

> ὃς Ἀθηναίοισι νόμους κελεύσασι ποιήσας ἀπεδήμησε δέκα ἔτεα, κατὰ θεωρίης πρόφασιν ἐκπλώσας, ἵνα δὴ μή τινα τῶν νόμων ἀναγκασθῇ λῦσαι τῶν ἔθετο.

> who, having made laws at the bidding of the Athenians, left the country for ten years, so that he wouldn't be compelled to abrogate any of his legislation.

The source (whom I take to be Androtion) of Plutarch, *vitSol* 25.6 says:

> πρόσχημα τῆς πλάνης τὴν ναυκληρίαν ποιησάμενος ἐξέπλευσε, δεκαετῆ παρ' Ἀθηναίων ἀποδημίαν αἰτησάμενος. τοῖς νόμοις αὐτοὺς ἔσεσθαι συνήθεις.

> using trade as a cover for his journey, he sailed off, having requested and obtained leave to be away for ten years from the Athenians. For he expected that they would become accustomed to his laws in this period.

Aristotle's version (11.1) runs:

> ἀποδημίαν ἐποιήσατο κατ' ἐμπορίαν ἅμα καὶ θεωρίαν εἰς Αἴγυπτον, εἰπὼν ὡς οὐχ ἥξει δέκα ἐτῶν· οὐ γὰρ οἴεσθαι δίκαιον εἶναι τοὺς νόμους ἐξηγεῖσθαι παρών, ἀλλ' ἕκαστον τὰ γεγραμμένα ποιεῖν.

he went on his travels, going to Egypt to trade and to see the sights, saying that he would not return for ten years; he did not think it right that he should stay and expound his laws, but everyone should simply do what he had written.

There are two major differences in these accounts: (1) both Herodotus and *vitSol* impute an alleged motive for travel to Solon (πρόφασις, πρόσχημα): the aspect of allegation is absent from *AP;* (2) Herodotus and *vitSol* each provides one motive, while Aristotle has both.

The differences between Aristotle's narrative here and those of his two sources have apparently not been felt to be serious enough to attract the attention of the commentators, all of whom maintain silence, but the discrepancies in the sources can and should be explained. Solon's motive for his journey was the dissatisfaction—economic and political—felt by γνώριμοι and δῆμος at his reforms. The sources of dissatisfaction are detailed in the rest of chapter 11, and this ends:

> ὁ δὲ Σόλων ἀμφοτέροις ἠναντιώθη, καὶ ἐξὸν αὐτῷ μεθ᾽ ὁποτέρων ἐβούλετο συστάντα τυραννεῖν εἵλετο πρὸς ἀμφοτέρους ἀπεχθέσθαι, σώσας τὴν πατρίδα καὶ τὰ βέλτιστα νομοθετήσας.

Solon was opposed to both; and, while he could have combined with whichever party he chose and become tyrant, he preferred to incur the hatred of both, by saving his country and legislating for the best.

There is a paratext in 6.3. In rejecting the accusation that Solon had personally profited from his cancellation of debts, Aristotle had to resort to an argument from probability (κατὰ τὸ εἰκός):

> οὐ γὰρ εἰκὸς ἐν μὲν τοῖς ἄλλοις οὕτω μέτριον γενέσθαι καὶ κοινόν, ὥστ᾽ ἔξον αὐτῷ τοὺς ἑτέρους ὑποποιησάμενον τυραννεῖν τῆς πόλεως ἀμφοτέροις ἀπεχθέσθαι καὶ περὶ πλείονος ποιήσασθαι τὸ καλὸν καὶ τὴν τῆς πόλεως σωτηρίαν ἢ τὴν αὐτοῦ πλεονεξίαν, ἐν οὕτω δὲ μικροῖς καὶ φανεροῖς καταρρυπαίνειν ἑαυτόν.

Solon was so moderate and impartial in other respects that, when he could have gotten the rest of the people into his power and made himself tyrant over the city, he instead accepted the hatred of both sides and set a higher value on honor and on the safety of the city than on his own advantage; so it is not plausible that he should have defiled himself in so petty and easily detected a matter.

Why the repetition? Its purpose is to remind the reader of the context in which the statement of 6.3 was made and what that statement was intended to establish, the moral quality of Solon. The repetition is not a further proof of that, but it reinforces what was established, and the reinforcement signals that the πρόφασις of Herodotus and the πρόσχημα of Plutarch's source are inconsistent with Solon's morality. The paratext gave Solon a certain moral stance, its repetition—the text—shows that the same stance applies in another context.

In using his subtexts in this way, Aristotle was making two choices. The first was to use their information rather than to suppress it. The second was to correct what they had to say. The correction may be thought to be negative in character: he is silent as to πρόφασις and πρόσχημα. But this choice had a positive aspect as well. In the *AthPol,* Solon's political activity is described at length. After his work is done, he departs, partly for the sake of commerce, partly for the sake of inquiry.[5] It is not difficult to see here a version of the motif of the "three lives," of which Solon is the only representative in the *AthPol.* This motif was exploited differently by different ancient authors, but the basic division, as here, is into economic, political, and intellectual activity.[6] It is part of the philosophical tradition, especially the strain represented by Plato, that one of these lives is to be preferred to the others. While it is doubtless true that Aristotle's Solon was especially to be remembered for his political activity, no pride of place is given to one of these lives over the other. Each is relevant to the different circumstances of Solon's career. In a sense, moreover, Solon is like the segments of the Athenian population in Pericles' *epitaphios*: as each individual does not embody all the lives but all are represented harmoniously by the total, so Solon's activities do not rival but chronologically complement each other.

THE DECONSTRUCTION OF PERICLES

Chapter 28 begins: ἕως μὲν οὖν Περικλῆς προειστήκει τοῦ δήμου, βελτίω τὰ κατὰ τὴν πολιτείαν ἦν, τελευτήσαντος δὲ Περικλέους πολὺ χείρω (while Pericles was champion of the people, the constitution was in a rather good condition, but after his death it became much worse). The beginning of chapter 29 is: ἕως μὲν οὖν ἰσόρροπα τὰ [πράγματα] κατὰ τὸν πόλεμον ἦν, διεφύλαττον τὴν δημοκρατίαν (as long as the war was evenly balanced, the Athenians preserved the democracy). The phenomenon of formulaic and identical chapter beginnings is not unparalleled[7] even in contiguous chapters,[8] but the repetitions here are of a different order. Only here does ἕως begin a chapter, and only here do we have two further repetitions: τὰ κατά–τὰ κατά; ἦν–ἦν. The repetitions suggest that the two chapters form a kind of unity and are to be read together, and the general theses they sustain are similar: in 28 the decline of political leadership after Pericles, in 29 the inability to preserve the democracy after the expedition to Syracuse.

Further, the beginning of 28 suggests that Aristotle is upholding a thesis first put forward by Thucydides,[9] that the quality of leadership worsened after Pericles. But a closer reading of 28 and some paratexts suggest that the position of Pericles in the 'Αθπολ is consistently undermined. In fact, Aristotle denigrates[10] Pericles in four ways.

I. Pericles is introduced with the usual formula (27.1):[11]

πρὸς τὸ δημαγωγεῖν ἐλθόντος Περικλέους καὶ πρῶτον εὐδοκιμήσαντος ὅτε κατηγόρησε τὰς εὐθύνας Κίμωνος στρατηγοῦντος νέος ὤν·

coming to *demos* leadership and first winning fame as a young man by prosecuting at the examination of Cimon the general.

The verb εὐδοκιμ- is used twice in the δοκ formula and there is doubtless an intended cut at Pericles here. The first instance is of Peisistratus (14.1), σφόδρ᾽ εὐδοκιμηκὼς ἐν τῷ πρὸς Μεγαρέας πολέμῳ.[12] Nothing is said in the ᾽Αθπολ about Pericles' military abilities, and the contrast between the successful generalship of Peisistratus and Pericles' prosecution of a general is striking.

II. Three political figures are reported in the ᾽Αθπολ to have been subject to personal attack: Solon (6.2–4: ψευδῆ τὴν αἰτίαν), Pericles (27.4: ἀφ᾽ ὧν αἰτιῶνται), and Theramenes (28.5). Solon and Theramenes are defended by Aristotle, Pericles is not.

III. The first part of the introduction of Pericles is πρὸς τὸ δημαγωγεῖν ἐλθόντος . Rhodes (335) remarks that "this use of δημαγωγεῖν is not necessarily hostile." I suggest that it is, when read in a wider context, and that this context is supplied by a series of paratexts. The first of these is at 26.1, at which Cimon is introduced συνέπεσε μηδ᾽ ἡγεμόνα ἔχειν τοὺς ἐπιεικεστέρους, ἀλλ᾽ αὐτῶν προεστάναι Κίμωνα τὸν Μιλτιάδου, νεώτερον ὄντα καὶ πρὸς τὴν πόλιν ὀψὲ προσελθόντα (at this time, it happened that the better sort had no leader, but their champion was Cimon, son of Miltiades, a youngish man who had only recently turned to public affairs). A main part of chapter 27 is devoted to the rivalry of Cimon and Pericles, but this is already anticipated by the linguistic parallels, νεώτερον[13] ὄντα with νέος ὤν, and προσελθόντα with ἐλθόντος, both used metaphorically only here.

One result of the rivalry was the institution of pay for dicasts, a measure suggested to Pericles by an intellectual adviser (27.4): συμβουλεύσαντος αὐτῷ Δαμωνίδου τοῦ Οἴηθεν, ὃς ἐδόκει τῶν πολλῶν εἰσηγητὴς εἶναι τῷ Περικλεῖ, διὸ καὶ ὠστράκισαν αὐτὸν ὕστερον (on the advice by Damonides of Oe—who seems to have been the originator of most of Pericles' measures, and for that reason was subsequently ostracized).[14] The fate of Damonides is linked with that of Cleophon and Callicrates, each of whom also proposed state pay (28.3): τούτων μὲν οὖν ἀμφοτέρων θάνατον κατέγνωσαν ὕστερον· εἴωθεν γάρ, κἂν ἐξαπατηθῇ, τὸ πλῆθος ὕστερον μισεῖν τούς τι προαγαγόντας ποιεῖν αὐτοὺς τῶν μὴ καλῶς ἐχόντων (both . . . were subsequently condemned to death by the Athenians: the masses generally come to hate those who have led them on to do anything wrong, particularly if they have been deceived).

The next sentence in 28 begins: ἀπὸ δὲ Κλεοφῶντος ἤδη διεδέχοντο συνεχῶς τὴν δημαγωγίαν (since Kleophon there has been an unending succession of popular leaders . . .). Allusion to the demagogues takes us backward to a context we have just seen. Immediately before the sentence introducing Cimon in 26.1, we have: μετὰ δὲ ταῦτα συνέβαινεν ἀνίεσθαι μᾶλλον τὴν πολιτείαν διὰ τοὺς προθύμως δημαγωγοῦντας (afterwards the constitution was further slackened through the men who devoted themselves eagerly to demagogy). The same allusion takes us forward (41.2), to Aristotle's summary of this period of constitutional history: ἐν ᾗ πλεῖστα συνέβη τὴν πόλιν διὰ τοὺς δημαγωγοὺς ἁμαρτάνειν διὰ τὴν τῆς θαλάττης ἀρχήν (in which it happened that the state because of the demagogues made many mistakes through its rule of the sea).

I am suggesting, then, that the wider context in which the remark about Pericles' δημαγωγία is to be placed extends from chapter 26 to the period covered by the reference in 41. This is not to say that Pericles is to be grouped with the demagogues of 28.3–4: it was not directly because of him that Athens ἁμαρτάνει, but those errors were due to ἡ τῆς θαλάττης ἀρχή, they were committed by ἡ πόλις, and it was Pericles who μάλιστα προύτρεψεν τὴν πόλιν ἐπὶ τὴν ναυτικὴν δύναμιν (27.1). It is rather in the earlier period that his activity is to be placed and judged, as will become clear from the next set of passages.

IV. The thesis that the political leadership of Athens degenerated is exemplified by actions of individual demagogues: these are linked by a pattern involving the repetition of the word πρῶτος (28.3): Κλέων . . . *πρῶτος ἐπὶ* τοῦ βήματος. . . . Κλεοφῶν. . . . ὃς καὶ τὴν διωβελίαν ἐπόρισε *πρῶτος*. . . . Καλλικράτης Παιανιεὺς *πρῶτος ὑποσχόμενος*. . . .[15] Thus, the phenomenon which links the "bad" politicians is that they were the first to perform certain actions. The same phenomenon also occurs shortly before in a passage we have seen earlier in this chapter: at 27.5 Aristotle observes:

> ἤρξατο δὲ μετὰ ταῦτα καὶ τὸ δεκάζειν *πρώτου* καταδείξαντος Ἀνύτου μετὰ τὴν ἐν Πύλῳ στρατηγίαν· κρινόμενος γὰρ ὑπό τινων διὰ τὸ ἀποβαλεῖν Πύλον, δεκάσας τὸ δικαστήριον ἀπέφυγεν·

. . . . he was brought to trial for losing Pylos, and escaped by bribing the jury.

Pericles introduced jury pay ca. 460, and the battle of Pylos was in 409. Thus, from the historian's point of view, the comment of Rhodes (343) is representative: "the interval of about fifty years makes nonsense of *A.P.*'s implication (ἤρξατο δὲ μετὰ ταῦτα) that it was the introduction of jury pay which was responsible for corruption in the courts."

It does not seem, however, that anyone has recognized what Aristotle is doing here, in terms of structure, theme and language. Let us begin with structure and chronology. What follows is the order of events as Aristotle has them in chapters 25.2 to 28.1:

1. 25.2: Ephialtes	462/1 archon date
2. 26.2: revision of archonship	457/6 archon date
3. 26.3: reestablishment of 30 dicasts	453/2 archon date
4. 26.3: citizenship law	451/0 archon date
5. 27.1: Pericles attacks Cimon	?462
6. 27.3: payment for court services	ca. 460
7. 27.5: Pylos	409
8. 28.1: death of Pericles	429

It is not only, then, the item about Anytus and Pylos which is odd, but the chronological relationship of 25/6 and 27 is skewed. I suggest that there are two indications that the skewing is deliberate. The first is the appearance of Pericles in 26.3 before he is introduced with the δοχ-formula.[16] The second is the absence of archon dates in 27, when contrasted with 25/6. This suggests that the focus of that chapter is not chronological, and the content shows that the the focus is thematic.

There are several themes taken up in this chapter, but the central one is Pericles' introduction of pay for jury duty. This justifies the account of the rivalry between Pericles and Cimon, which itself justifies the remark about Pericles' initial attack on Cimon. The gap between Pericles' measure and Anytus' bribery is thematically bridged by the phrase (27.4): κληρουμένων ἐπιμελῶς ἀεὶ μᾶλλον τῶν τυχόντων ἢ τῶν ἐπιεικῶν ἀνθρώπων (since ordinary people rather than the better sort were careful to get themselves on the allotment lists at any given time).

I want to suggest that this passage belongs to the congery of texts which made up the context discussed under III. The first such text held that as a result of the activity of the demagogues ἀνίεσθαι μᾶλλον τὴν πολιτείαν (the constitution became more relaxed). The metaphor from tightening and relaxing strings of instruments was used elsewhere by Plato and Aristotle,[17] but it is not at all clear how precisely the metaphor is to be applied to Athenian political life of this period. There are two passages which may throw light on the question. Aristotle says that the generals in charge of military expeditions were inexperienced in warfare and chosen because of family reputations (26.1: ἀπείρων μὲν τοῦ πολεμεῖν τιμωμένων δὲ διὰ τὰς πατρικὰς δόξας). The result was that ἀναλίσκεσθαι τοὺς ἐπιεικεῖς καὶ τοῦ δήμου καὶ τῶν εὐπόρων (26.1: the better people both from the wealthy and from the common people were expended). That Aristotle wants to put the failure of the selection process into a context of ''loosening'' is suggested by his next sentence which is both summary and transitional: τὰ μὲν οὖν ἄλλα πάντα διῴκουν οὐχ ὁμοίως καὶ πρότερον τοῖς νόμοις προσέχοντες (in other respects the Athenians in their administration did not abide by the laws as they had done before). If this is correct, the paratext for the ''loosening'' which resulted in the loss of ἐπιεικεῖς is our text of 27 in which the statement that ordinary people rather than ἐπιεικεῖς will fill the jury panels is directly followed by the first instance of bribery in the courts.[18]

Finally, the language: καταδεικνύναι is for both Plato and Aristotle an extremely rare word. In the latter, the other occurrence is also in conjunction with πρῶτος, in the versus in laudem Platonis preserved by Olympiodorus in Gorg. pr. 41 (= F 673 R):

ὃς μόνος ἢ πρῶτος θνητῶν κατέδειξεν ἐναργῶς
οἰκείῳ τε βίῳ καὶ μεθόδοισι λόγων
ὡς ἀγαθός τε καὶ εὐδαίμων ἀνήρ

who alone or first among mortals established clearly by his personal life and philosophical argument how a man comes to be good and fortunate.

As Jaeger[19] has pointed out, καταδεικνύναι ''is used, often in conjunction with πρῶτος, of inventors of a τέχνη.''

It seems that we can be certain of two things. Used of Anytus, Aristotle found πρῶτος in his source, whether that source was Ephorus[20] or an *Atthis*, for all ancient references to the affair note the fact that this was the first such instance.[21] The second thing is that καταδεικνύναι is Aristotle's insertion, by which he creates a parody of the language of *kulturgeschichtlich* progress. Thus, Anytus belongs with the series of what may be called the πρῶτοι εὑρέται of political degeneration in Athens.[22] But, of course, this list does not begin with Anytus, but fifty years earlier: ἐποίησε δὲ καὶ μισθοφόρα τὰ δικαστήρια Περικλῆς πρῶτος, and Pericles' action is the first such action mentioned in the text.

I have previously argued that Aristotle made important points about his conception of the development of Athenian democracy by selection of matter to include and choice of where to put it.[23] One of these points concerned the unique aspects of chapter 45,[24] its structure and its contents, and how these related to the theme of the importance of the law courts. One critic[25] has suspended belief: "I am not persuaded that this purpose governed arrangement of his [sc., Aristotle's] material, and think that if he had wanted to point this moral he would have done so more obviously." I trust that the freedom implicit in his new genre allowed Aristotle to point his moral in any legitimate way, and surely one of these ways was that set out by Theophrastus,[26] as preserved by [Demetrius] *de Elocutione*, par. 222:

ἐν τούτοις τε οὖν τὸ πιθανόν, καὶ ἐν ᾧ Θεόφραστός φησιν, ὅτι οὐ πάντα ἐπ᾽ ἀκριβείας δεῖ μακρηγορεῖν, ἀλλ᾽ ἔνια καταλιπεῖν καὶ τῷ ἀκροατῇ συνιέναι, καὶ λογίζεσθαι ἐξ αὑτοῦ· συνιεὶς γὰρ τὸ ἐλλειφθὲν ὑπὸ σοῦ οὐκ ἀκροατὴς μόνον, ἀλλὰ καὶ μάρτυς σου γίνεται, καὶ ἅμα εὐμενέστερος. συνετὸς γὰρ ἑαυτῷ δοκεῖ διά σε τὸν ἀφορμὴν παρεσχηκότα αὐτῷ τοῦ συνιέναι, τὸ δὲ πάντα ὡς ἀνοήτῳ λέγειν καταγινώσκοντι ἔοικεν τοῦ ἀκροατοῦ.

these, then, are the main essentials of persuasiveness; to which may be added that indicated by Theophrastus when he says that all possible points should not be punctiliously and tediously elaborated, but some should be left to the comprehension and inference of the hearer, who when he perceives what you have omitted becomes not only your hearer but your witness, and a very friendly witness too. For he thinks himself intelligent because you have afforded him the means of showing his intelligence. It seems like a slur on your hearer to tell him everything as though he were a simpleton. (tr. Roberts)

NOTES

1. Cf. chapter 10, "The Politics of Institutions versus the Politics of Personality."
2. Cf. chapter 12, "The Constitutional Formula."
3. Cf. also Isocrates, *Areop.* 67, of the Thirty: οἱ μὲν γὰρ ψηφίσματι παραλαβόντες τὴν πόλιν πεντακοσίους καὶ χιλίους τῶν πολιτῶν ἀκρίτους ἀπέκτειναν. Aristotle may have known this text, for he gives the same figure for the number of victims of the Thirty (35.4).

4. I discuss this later in the chapter.

5. More precisely, philosophical inquiry. Cf. the words of Croesus to Solon (Herod. 1.29.2): ὡς φιλοσοφέων γῆν πολλὴν θεωρίης εἵνεκεν ἐπελήλουθας.

6. A representative sample may be found in J. S. Rusten, "Two Lives or Three? Pericles on the Athenian Character (Thucydides 2.40.1–2)," *CQ* 35 (1985) 14–19.

7. μετὰ δὲ ταῦτα: 2, 19, 24, 27, 38; ἡ μὲν οὖν: 15, 16, 25, 26; οἱ μὲν οὖν: 30, 32, 35.

8. 15, 16, 25, 26.

9. 2.65.10; 8.89.3–4.

10. Wider aspects of this question are treated in chapter 14, "Aristotle and Theramenes."

11. Cf. chapter 11, "The δοκεῖν Formula."

12. Cf. Herodotus 1.59.4: πρότερον εὐδοκιμήσας ἐν τῇ πρὸς Μεγαρέας γενομένη στρατηγίῃ.

13. A great deal of effort has been expended on emendation: I agree with Rhodes (326) that the text should be retained in spite of the chronological problems thereby created.

14. This is another cut at Pericles. Not only did he lack the financial resoures with which to compete with Cimon, he could not even think of the device on his own.

15. πρῶτος was emended to πρῶτον by Leeuwen (accepted by e.g., Rhodes, Chambers) but the reading is guaranteed by the pattern.

16. The function of Pericles in the ᾿Αθπολ is thematic, but his law on citizenship was irrelevant to this function; that is, on my reading, there was nothing "demagogic" about it.

17. Discussion in Rhodes 322–23.

18. Note that the application of ἐπιεικεῖς in 26.1 to both δῆμος and εὔποροι shows that Aristotle intended it to be understood in a moral, not a social, sense.

19. W. W. Jaeger, "Aristotle's Verses in Praise of Plato," *CQ* 21 (1927) 13–17.

20. Diod. 13.64: καὶ πρῶτος ᾿Αθηναίων δοκεῖ δικαστήριον δωροδοκῆσαι.

21. They are listed by Rhodes 343.

22. For πρῶτος/τὸ πρῶτον used with ἄρχειν/ἄρχεσθαι in cultural contexts, cf. *Met.* 982B13; *Poet.* 1449B7, 1456A39; *Rhet.* 1404A20 and F 677 R. For δεικνύναι τὰ ἱερά *vel. sim.*, cf. already C. Lobeck, *Aglaophamus* (Königsberg 1829) 48–49; for καταδεικνύναι, 205–6; more recently, cf. Richardson on *HDem* 474–76. πρῶτος is found in combination with καταδεικνύναι at Comica Adespota, F 106–7.2 Kock, Antiphanes F 123.1 K, Machon F 1 K, Aristophanes, *Aves* 500, Ephorus 70 F 149 J, Athenaios 8.360D, Diodorus Sic. 1.6.1 and Josephus, *AJ* 11.8. Although the vocabulary may be used to comic effect (Machon on the Macedonians and ματτύη) , the only pejorative connotation I have found in this context is Diodorus 1.45.2 (πολυτελεία).

23. Keaney 1963 [1].

24. On which cf. chapter 18, "Chapter 45: ἡ βουλή."

25. Rhodes 37.

26. The passage is ascribed to the Περὶ λέξεως *(On Diction)* = F VIII Schmidt on grounds of probability, not necessity.

7

Structure and Meaning

I

If, as I have argued, Aristotle's basic cultural pattern in the Ἀθπολ did not furnish him with generic guidelines of sufficient clarity and rigidity to aid him overly much in the composition of the work, we must ask how he expected his reader to know what was going on once he got below a superficial level, i.e., statements of unambiguous content. I am going to suggest that he did this in two ways: the second, which I discuss later, is through structure; the first is of relatively rare occurrence and involves manipulation of language.

This can be illustrated by single words and by phrases, and I choose three. Eight times in the Ἀθπολ and forty-three times in the *Politics,* Aristotle uses the word γνώριμοι in the sense of "political elite," "notables." For practical purposes, this nuance is a coinage, but with what precise intention Aristotle coined it is unclear, nor is it clear whether recognition of the nuance depends upon the repetition of the word.[1]

One phrase has a nuance peculiar to the Ἀθπολ: this is the restriction of κυρι- τῆς πόλεως to tyrants, actual or potential.[2] The important point of the idiosyncratic use of this phrase is that its meaning can be fully comprehended only through repetition: the nuance could not be extracted if the phrase occurred only once.[3]

A third example is like the first in that it is found in the *Politics.* It is analogous to the second example, not in the fact that its full semantic value depends upon repetition, for it is not repeated, but in that recognition of its full functional value is not possible until it is realized that it is one of a set of thematically connected paratexts. The word is προανακρίνειν,[4] coined and used only by Aristotle in the classical period. At *Pol.* 4.1298A30–1, he says that it is characteristic of final democracy (ἡ τελευταία δημοκρατία) that magistrates make judicial decisions about nothing but only conduct preliminary hearings: τὰς δ᾽ ἀρχὰς περὶ μηθενὸς κρίνειν ἀλλὰ μόνον προανακρι-'νειν. Here, the προ- element is necessary because, unlike the noun ἀνάκρισις, the verb ἀνακρίνειν is not restricted only to legal proceedings, but the function of the verb is purely semantic.

At 3.5, Aristotle says κύριοι [sc., οἱ ἄρχοντες] δ᾽ ἦσαν καὶ τὰς δίκας αὐτοτελεῖς κρίνειν καὶ οὐχ ὥσπερ νῦν προανακρίνειν (they had full authority to judge suits and not as now to hold preliminary hearings). The context in which this sentence is found opens the way to several lines of development, two of which I discuss later in the chapter. For the third, we may focus on the προ- element. On one level, as in the *Politics,* it is used for the sake of clarity. On another level, however, its value is more than semantic. The combination of προ- and νῦν brings to mind a theme which is developed especially in the description of the contemporary constitution, a theme which is usually signaled by the contrast of πρότερον (formerly) and νῦν.[5] Some of the changes so signaled refer to processes whereby an organ of the government loses prerogatives which are taken over by the δῆμος. Thus, the προ- of προανακρίνειν initiates a theme which finds its full expression many chapters later.

More frequently, communication of meaning on a subsurface level is achieved by structure. This can be illustrated in various ways, and I begin with one structural feature which is almost pervasive in the non-Peisistratean chapters of the narrative:[6]

B (2.2): ἦν γὰρ αὐτῶν ἡ πολιτεία τοῖς τε ἄλλοις ὀλιγαρχικὴ πᾶσι καὶ δὴ καὶ (the constitution was oligarchic in all other respects and in particular)

C (2.2): ἐδούλευον οἱ πένητες τοῖς πλουσίοις. (the poor were enslaved to the rich)

x 2.2 The basis of the economic δουλεία is explained.

C¹ (2.3): χαλεπώτατον μὲν οὖν καὶ πικρότατον ἦν τοῖς πολλοῖς τῶν κατὰ τὴν πολιτείαν τὸ δουλεύειν· (the harshest and bitterest aspect of the constitution for the masses was the fact of their enslavement,)

B¹ (2.3): οὐ μὴν ἀλλὰ καὶ ἐπὶ τοῖς ἄλλοις ἐδυσχέραινον· οὐδενὸς γὰρ ὡς ἔπος εἰπεῖν ἐτύγχανον μετέχοντες. (though they were discontented on other grounds too: it could be said that there was nothing in which they had a share).

This is the first instance of complex ring structure[7] in the extant part of the work. We cannot tell if the structure was used earlier, but even if this were its first instance, we could not expect it to be fully normative for future uses. The analog is the phrase κυρι- τῆς πόλεως, which takes on its full nuance only after repetition. So here, in ways larger and smaller, the meaning of the device becomes clear only after comparison with repeated uses. I attempt now to show how a basic structure is manipulated—uniquely in the Ἀθπολ—by the intrusion of another repeated idiom.

The idiom ἀλλ- plus καὶ δὴ καί.

The idiom is used when the the author intends to draw attention to a particular subject: this subject is immediately preceded and introduced by καὶ δὴ καί; this itself is preceded by a generalizing ἀλλ- (in other respects), the purpose of which is to delay mention of the subject and thus to focus attention on it by creating a miniclimax. In terms of meaning, ἀλλ- is a throwaway. The idiom is not used by every prose author (not e.g., by Thucydides or Demosthenes), but it is favored by Herodotus,[8] by Plato, especially in the *Laws*,[9] and by Aristotle in the Ἀθπολ.

The ordinary usage of the idiom can be illustrated by three passages:

Poetics 1460A5–6: Ὅμηρος δὲ ἄλλα τε πολλὰ ἄξιος ἐπαινεῖσθαι καὶ δὴ καὶ ὅτι μόνος τῶν ποιητῶν οὐκ ἀγνοεῖ ὃ δεῖ ποιεῖν αὐτόν.

Homer deserves praise in many other respects and specifically because he alone of the poets is not unaware of what he should be doing.

Diog. Laert. 2.45 = F 32 R: φησὶ δ' Ἀριστοτέλης μάγον τινὰ ἐλθόντα ἐκ Συρίας εἰς Ἀθήνας τά τε ἄλλα καταγνῶναι καὶ δὴ καὶ βίαιον ἔσεσθαι τὴν τελευτὴν αὐτῷ.

Aristotle says that a magician came to Athens from Syria and made other detrimental predictions about Socrates, in particular that he would have a violent death.

16.10: οἱ περὶ τῶν τυράννων νόμοι πρᾷοι κατ' ἐκείνους τοὺς καιροὺς οἵ τ' ἄλλοι καὶ δὴ καὶ ὁ μάλιστα καθήκων πρὸς τὴν τῆς τυραννίδος ⟨κατάστασιν⟩.

at that time the Athenians' laws about tyrants were mild, in particular the one relating to the setting up of a tyranny.

These, like the instances in Herodotus and Plato, illustrate what may be called the traditional, uncomplicated usage of the idiom. A general rubric (reasons for praise of Homer, troubles to come, laws on tyrants) is applied first loosely, and then, with one example, specifically. A slightly complicated usage is found at 16.2:

ἔν τε γὰρ τοῖς ἄλλοις φιλάνθρωπος ἦν καὶ πρᾷος καὶ τοῖς ἁμαρτάνουσι συγγνωμονικός καὶ δὴ καὶ τοῖς ἀπόροις προεδάνειζε χρήματα πρὸς τὰς ἐργασίας, ὥστε διατρέφεσθαι γεωργοῦντας.

in general he was humane, mild, and forgiving to wrongdoers, and in particular he lent money to those who were in difficulties, to support their work, so that they could continue to maintain themselves by farming.

This is different in several respects. The rubric is not focused but diffuse (although all the adjectives belong in the same moral field). The relationship of the specific example to the rubric(s) is not, as it usually is, uncluttered, for while Peisistratus' loans to those in difficulty may have been motivated by φιλανθρωπία, that was not their only motivation, and Aristotle goes on to make explicit to what degree Peisistratus' self-interest was involved.

The usage in chapter 2 is still more complicated. The repetition of τοῖς ἄλλοις (A/A[1]) is paralleled, in a way,[10] but the usual transition from general to specific is not quite what Aristotle is doing here, at least overtly. The normal procedure in ring composition is to distinguish outer (here, B/B[1]) from inner (C/C[1]) elements: both sets are part of a larger picture, but they are discrete parts. Here, he exploits the τὰ ἄλλα idiom and melds the terms of B and C so that the general rubric is that of politics but the specific example is one of economics. The priority of importance normal to the structure is preserved, since the economic sphere (C/C¹) is subordinate to the political sphere (B/B¹).

A final touch in this structure: if we were to ask in which sphere it is that οἱ πολλοὶ οὐδενὸς ἐτύγχανον μετέχοντες, the structure should tell us that it was the political. That this is so is confirmed by the technical uses of μετέχειν in the work: it is applied to civic magistracy (ἀρχή: 7.4) and to enfranchisement (πόλις: 8.5 and 26.3; πολιτεία: 42.1).

II. CHAPTER 3

As chapter 2 described the economic conditions existing before Solon, so chapter 3 describes the political conditions of the same period. Apart from differences in content, however, the chapters diverge sharply in structure and approach. For the first, there is simple ring frame in 3 but nothing corresponding to the rather complex form of 2. This is partly because Aristotle chose to make the economic conditions part of, and described within, the political system, broadly outlined (τοῖς τε ἄλλοις ὀλιγραχικὴ πᾶσι); and an A/B/B¹/A¹ structure suited that complexity. Another reason why the complex structure is not used in chapter 3 is Aristotle's approach: as opposed to the static description of 2, separate sections in 3 are dynamic and linear. They go in A¹¹ from earliest times to Medon and/or Acastus; in B from that cutoff to some time after Solon; in C, by a double process, from early times to Solon, and from Solon to the fourth century; and in D from the origin of the Areopagus to the fourth century.

I want initially to suggest that we have in chapter 3 (as we did not have in 2) a programme in practice and base the suggestion on both the structure and the content of the chapter. The latter may be summarized as follows: the topic of the work will be the πολιτεία; the early πολιτεία functioned especially through the institution of the archonship; that institution was not static throughout its history but developed and changed. Although the activity of Solon represented a kind of watershed in Athenian history, the period before him as well as the period after him were marked by change reaching down to the fourth century (νῦν).

Unlike the elaborate ring structure of chapter 2, chapter 3 is set out in a series of panels, headed by a rubric: ἦν δ᾽ ἡ τάξις τῆς ἀρχαίας πολιτείας τῆς πρὸ Δράκοντος τοιάδε.¹² (the organization of the ancient constitution before the time of Draco was as follows.)

A. τὰς μὲν ἀρχὰς καθίστασαν ἀριστίνδην καὶ πλουτίνδην· ἦρχον δὲ τὰ μὲν πρῶτον διὰ βίου—τοῦτο μὲν οὖν ὁποτέρως ποτ᾽ ἔχει, μικρὸν ἂν παραλλάττοι τοῖς χρόνοις· (officials were appointed on the basis of good birth and wealth; at first men held office for life—whichever view is right, it would make little difference to the chronology.)

B. ὅτι δὲ τελευταῖα—διὸ καὶ μόνη τῶν ἀρχῶν οὐκ ἐγένετο πλείων ἐνιαυσίας· τοῖς μὲν οὖν χρόνοις τοσοῦτον προέχουσιν ἀλλήλων. (that the office of archon was last—for that reason this alone of the chief offices has never been held for more than a year. That is the chronological sequel of the offices.)

C. (a) ἦσαν δ' οὐχ ἅμα πάντες οἱ ἐννέα ἄρχοντες (the nine archons used not to work together)

   (b) ὁ μὲν βασιλεὺς εἶχε τὸ νῦν καλούμενον Βουκολεῖον (the *basileus* occupied what is now called the *Boukoleion*,)
   [explanatory comment]

   (c) ὁ δὲ ἄρχων τὸ πρυτανεῖον (the archon the town hall,)

   (d) ὁ δὲ πολέμαρχος τὸ Ἐπιλύκειον (and the polemarch the *Epilukeion*)
   [explanatory comment]

   (e) θεσμοθέται δ' εἶχον τὸ θεσμοθετεῖον. ἐπὶ δε Σόλωνος ἅπαντες εἰς τὸ θεσμοθετεῖον συνῆλθον. (the *thesmothetae* occupied the *thermotheteion*. In the time of Solon they all came together in the *thesmotheteion*.)

   (f) κύριοι δ' ἦσαν καὶ τὰς δίκας αὐτοτελεῖς κρίνειν καὶ οὐχ ὥσπερ νῦν προανακρίνειν. (They had full power to give a final judgment in lawsuits not simply to hold a preliminary inquiry as they do now.)

   (g) τὰ μὲν οὖν περὶ τὰς ἀρχὰς τοῦτον εἶχε τὸν τρόπον. (This is how offices were arranged.)

D. ἡ δὲ τῶν Ἀρεοπαγιτῶν—ἀκοσμοῦντας κυρίως. ἡ γὰρ αἵρεσις τῶν ἀρχόντων ἀριστίνδην καὶ πλουτίνδην ἦν ἐξ ὧν οἱ Ἀρεοπαγῖται καθίσταντο· διο καὶ μόνη τῶν ἀρχῶν αὕτη μεμένηκε διὰ βίου καὶ νῦν. (The council of the Areopagus—full power [to punish] the disorderly. The appointment of the archons was based on good birth and wealth, and it was the archons who became members of the Areopagus: for that reason membership of the Areopagus alone has remained to this day an office held for life.)

The structure, as I have articulated it, raises questions, among them:

1. Why is the first sentence of chapter 3 styled a rubric?
2. Why is the history of the archonship broken up into two segments?
3. Why are magistrates' office buildings mentioned, and why here?
4. Why are only judicial functions of the archons mentioned?
5. What is the relationship of this chapter to others?
6. Why does Aristotle twice use inferential διὸ καί when no inference is involved?

Although the πολιτεία is important for structural purposes in and for the argument of chapter 2, and although it resumes its structural importance at the beginning of chapter 5 (τοιαύτης δὲ τῆς τάξεως οὔσης ἐν τῇ πολιτείᾳ), it does not recur in chapter 3, nor is it implicated in the structure there. I suggest that the reason it is not so implicated is to be found in three structural decisions: the first was to enclose the economic sphere within the political sphere in 2;

the second was to enclose the structure of 2 within a larger structure which is not completed until 5; the third was to carry over the implications of the structure of 2, and 2 *cum* 5, into the contents of chapters 6 (Solon's economic response) and 7 (his political response). It was especially the second of these decisions which precluded the use of ἦν δ' ἡ τάξις κτλ. as part of a ring frame. If it had been so used, Aristotle would either have had to drop the larger structure connecting 2 with 5 or to have created a new structure by inserting a framing remark about the πολιτεία at the end of 3: this would have been stylistically intolerable in contiguity with the beginning of 5.

Regarding our question 2, the repetitions of μὲν οὖν and τοῖς χρόνοις show two things: the fact of repetition that there are two separate segments here, the kind of repetition that the two segments are related. Since the transition between panels A and B comes in the treatment of the eponymous archon, the main purpose of this part of the structure is to emphasize the importance of that official over against the king and the polemarch. One effect of this is to focus attention on the point made and the argumemt for it, namely, that the archon has become powerful only comparatively recently, τοῖς ἐπιθέτοις αὐξηθεῖσα (being augmented by newly created functions), as is signaled (σημεῖον) by the fact that the archon, unlike the king and polemarch, has no ancestral functions. The point and the argument take us into the future; the point into the period immediately after Solon when Aristotle says that it was the kind of election of Damasias as archon ᾧ καὶ δῆλον ὅτι μεγίστην εἶχεν δύναμιν ὁ ἄρχων· φαίνονται γὰρ ἀεὶ στασιάζοντες περὶ ταύτης τῆς ἀρχῆς (13.2: this makes it clear that it was the archon who wielded the greatest power: we see that that was the office over which strife always arose). The argument takes us into panel D, the description of the contemporary constitution, in which the king and the polemarch—but not the archon—are described as performing certain kinds of sacrifices: polemarch (58.1), king (57.1): ὡς δ' ἔπος εἰπεῖν καὶ τὰς πατρίους θυσίας διοικεῖ οὗτος πάσας (one might say that he administers all the ancestral sacrifices).

The summary formula closing off panel C (τὰ μὲν οὖν–τὸν τρόπον) takes us in the same directions, for it is the formula used to round off the Solonian disposition (9.1) and that of the fourth century (60.1).

Referring to question 3, we may defer, for a moment, consideration of our original question about the buildings, to look at an anomaly. The anomaly is the change in the order in which the magistrates are mentioned in panels A and B. They are introduced in the order: king, polemarch, archon; in their relative chronology there is the same order. The same is true of the first part of B (βασιλεύς, πολέμαρχος, ἡ ἀρχὴ μεγάλη). After the institution of the *thesmothetai* is noted, there is the section on the buildings: here the order is changed to king, archon, polemarch, *thesmothetai*. The reason for the change is solely the symmetry Aristotle[13] has imposed on this section, as articulated above: (bcde) have the essential elements (magistrate, building), (b) is linked to (e) by the presence of the verb ἔχειν, (b) to (d) by the presence of a comment, and (c) to (e) by the absence of comment. The whole is enclosed within a chiastic structure (verb, πάντες, ἅπαντες, verb).

In this segment, however, (f) is isolated from the structure, and it is necessary to ask why: this smaller question is a convenient route to the larger one which we had previously deferred, as well as to questions 4 and 5. It is to be noted that the motivation for the institution of the *thesmothetai* is judicial, that the single specific function ascribed to the archons is judicial, and it will be seen [14] that some of the judicial language used of the Areopagus will be used again of that body for the period after Solon and of the Council of the Five Hundred in the fourth century. In the second place, if we work with the quadripartite structure of the ᾿Αθπολ, some of the contents of chapter 3 have a clear parallel with chapter 41. There, one has an (almost) complete record of constitutional development before the description of fourth-century democracy: in 3, there is a record of the development of the most important single board and official before the description of the πολιτεία of Solon, ἀφ᾿ ἧς ἀρχὴ δημοκρατίας ἐγένετο (41.2: the change which brought about the origin of the democracy). In the third place, the contrast of the judicial authority wielded by the archons before Solon and in the fourth century is just one of a series of instances in which elements of chapter 3 are brought forward in time: it is unique within these for it alone shows a discontinuity and not a continuity of practice. Given the building context in which the contrast is found, I suggest that the parallel to panel C is to be found in that later section of the work in which the people who have taken over the judicial decisions of the archons and their operation in public buildings is described, namely, the citizens in the popular law courts (63–69).

Finally, we have the double use of an inferential particle, διό, where no inference is intended. I suggest, again, that this repetition is one of three by which the chapter is organized. The connection of panels A and B is signalled by the repetition of μὲν οὖν: the organization of C(a-e) is internal; C(f) is connected to D by the repetition of κύριοι and κυρίως: A is connected to D by the repetitions ἀριστίνδην καὶ πλουτίνδην and διὰ βίου, and B to D by that of διὸ καὶ μόνη τῶν ἀρχῶν.

NOTES

1. A reader for the Press points out that the first usage of the word of a political group is in the *Hellenica Oxyrhynchia* VI.2: καὶ τ[ῶν] ᾿Αθηναίων ἀγανακτούντω[ν ὅσοι γνώ]ριμ[οι (the supplement is all but certain)]. I do not know if Aristotle was aware that he had been preceded in this nuance.

2. 20.3, 34.2, 35.1. Cf. chapter 16, "δῆμος, πλῆθος, and πόλις.

3. A hint of the nuance—no more than that—could have been gotten from the first use of the phrase τῆς πόλεως at 6.3: τυραννεῖν τῆς πόλεως.

4. For my use of this term, cf. chapter 6, "Methods and Purposes."

5. 45.3; 53.4; 54.3; 55.2; 56.3, 4: cf. Keaney 1970.[2] 329–31.

6. On the structure of these chapters, cf. chapter 10, "The Politics of Institutions versus the Politics of Personality."

7. For full discussion, see chapter 8, "Vertical Structure: Ring Composition."

8. Pervasive, e.g., 1.1.7; 1.82.2; 2.1.8 al.

9. Approximately a dozen times in the earlier works, thirteen times in *Laws*, e.g., 659A3; 666B4; 698D7 al.

10. In simple ring frame at 19.3.

11. For this sectioning, see immediately below.

12. I assume that the text read πρὸ Σόλωνος before the activity of the interpolator of chapter 4. Some (e.g., Rhodes 97) assume that the whole phrase, τῆς πρὸ Δράκοντος, was inserted at that time.

13. After the archon has achieved preeminence, a new order is used: archon, king, polemarch, *thesmothetai* (56–59).

14. Cf. chapter 18, "Chapter 45: ἡ βουλή."

8

Vertical Structure:
Ring Composition

Ring composition, the technique of repeating at the end of a structural unit, a word, phrase, or theme with which the unit began, has a long history in Greek literature.[1] The standard discussion is that of W. A. A. van Otterlo,[2] and I begin with his definitions, qualifying them where necessary. The first type (which I will refer to as the simple form) is defined (p. 3):

> das an den Anfang gestellte Thema eines bestimmten Abschnitts wird nach einer längeren oder kürzeren sich darauf beziehenden Ausfuhrung am Schluss wiederholt, so dass der ganze Abschnitt durch Sätze gleichen Inhalts und mehr oder weniger ahnlichen Wortlauts umrahmt und so zu einem einheitlichen, sich klar vom Kontext abhebenden Gebilde geschlossen wird.

> a theme placed at the beginning of a defined section is repeated after a longer or shorter exposition related thereto, so that the whole section, through clauses of similar content and more-or-less similar wording is framed and thus concludes in a structure clearly set off from the context.

Within this type, van Otterlo (7) distinguishes two functions; the first, as above, he calls *inclusorisch,* the second *anaphorisch.* The functions differ in that the second encloses a digression within a narrative: thus, narrative, beginning of digression (A), digression, end of digression (A[1]), narrative resumed.[3] This distinction is not particularly helpful for the ’Aθπολ, since Aristotle does not use the device to frame digressions.[4] Instead, I will make a distinction between simple and complex types. The complex type would be schematized:

A
B
(C)
x, where x is the content, whether this material is announced by B (as in ch. 2) or is something else (as in ch. 20);
(C[1])
B[1]
A[1]

Ring composition as a stylistic device is potentially flexible, and Aristotle uses it in various ways and for different purposes. Its basic purpose is to focus on one segment of the narrative by isolating it from the rest of the narrative, and this function is achieved by both the simple and complex types. Within the complex type, a variety of purposes is evident. One may make a distinction between an analytic use and a narrative use.[5] In the first Aristotle is describing a set of circumstances set forth as A/A[1] and B/B[1]: here the tendency is for B to be described more fully and also to be less important than A. Two instances are in chapters 3 and 27: in the first, B is a statement of the economic, A of the political conditions before Solon. Since economic conditions are less important than the political situation, B is subordinate to A and is described in chapter 2, while discussion of A is delayed until chapter 3. In 27, Aristotle used Theopompus' account of the private generosity of Cimon as the basis for a more complex picture of a rivalry between Cimon and Pericles on the private *and* public levels. In that chapter, B/B[1] are the public, C/C[1] the private acts of Cimon and Pericles, with the public being more important.

In the narrative use, Aristotle marks off different parts of his account. Here it is possible for one segment of the narrative to be more important than another, but this does not seem always to be the case. For instance, in chapter 19 it is clear that the inner elements of the ring which represent the failed attempts of the Alcmeonids to restore themselves are less productive than the outer elements, the ploy which was successful for them. On the other hand, it is not clear that Cleisthenes' pro-*demos* stance in chapter 20 is less important than the antityrant stance of him and his family (A/A[1]).

What follows is a list of all instances of ring composition in the Ἀθπολ.[6] Discussion of some of the texts will be found in separate chapters.

I. COMPLEX

A (2.1): συνέβη στασιάσαι τούς τε γνωρίμους καὶ τὸ πλῆθος. . . .[7] (there was strife for a long time between the notables and the masses.)

B (2.2): ἦν γὰρ αὐτῶν ἡ πολιτεία τοῖς τε ἄλλοις ὀλιγαρχικὴ πᾶι καὶ δὴ καὶ (for the Athenians' constitution was oligarchic in all other respects, and in particular)

C (2.2): ἐδούλευον οἱ πένητες τοῖς πλουσίοις. (the poor were enslaved to the rich)

[x 2.2: The basis of the economic δουλεία is explained.]

C[1] (2.3): χαλεπώτατον μὲν οὖν καὶ πικρότατον ἦν τοῖς πολλοῖς τῶν κατὰ τὴν πολιτείαν τὸ δουλεύειν· (the harshest and bitterest aspect of the constitution was the fact of their enslavement)

B[1] (2.3): οὐ μὴν ἀλλὰ καὶ ἐπὶ τοῖς ἄλλοις ἐδυσχέραινον· οὐδενὸς γὰρ ὡς ἔπος εἰπεῖν ἐτύγχανον μετέχοντες. (though they were discontented on other grounds too: it could be said that there was nothing in which they had a share).

Linguistic parallels with Plutarch, *vitSol* 13[8] show that the common source of Aristotle and Plutarch discussed pre-Solonian economic conditions,[9] but the same parallels show that this source did not integrate economic and political conditions. The integration in the 'Αθπολ is effected through structure[10] and through language. Economic conditions (C/C^1) form the inner elements of the ring structure and are thus subordinate to the outer elements. Secondly, the verb Aristotle uses to describe the economic condition, ἐδούλευον (C), serves to make that condition one element of the wider political condition: τῶν κατὰ τὴν πολιτείαν τὸ δουλεύειν (C^1).

II. COMPLEX

A (3.1): τὰς μὲν ἀρχὰς καθίστασαν ἀριστίδην καὶ πλουτίνδην (officials were appointed on the basis of good birth and wealth;)

B (3.1): ἦρχον δὲ τὸ μὲν πρῶτον διὰ βίου (at first, men held office for life)

[x 3.2–5: history and function of the archons]

A^1 (3.5): τὰ μὲν οὖν περὶ τὰς ἀρχὰς τοῦτον εἶχε τὸν τρόπον (this was the way ofices were arranged)

[x 3.6: functions of the Areopagus]

A^2 (3.6): ἡ γὰρ αἵρεσις τῶν ἀρχόντων ἀριστίνδην καὶ πλουτίνδην ἦν, ἐξ ὧν οἱ Ἀρεοπαγῖται καθίσταντο. (the appointment of the offices was based on good birth and wealth, and it was the archons who became members of the Areopagus:)

B^2 (3.6): διὸ καὶ μόνη τῶν ἀρχῶν αὕτη μεμένηκε διὰ βίου καὶ νῦν. (for that reason membership of the Areopagus alone has remained to this day an office held for life).

The variations introduced into the normal structure by A^2 and B^2 are unique to this chapter.

III. COMPLEX

These two structures are themselves enclosed within a wider frame:

A (2.1): στασιάσαι τούς τε γνωρίμους καὶ τὸ πλῆθος

B (2.2): ἐδούλευον

C (3.1): ἦν δ' ἡ τάξις τῆς ἀρχαίας πολιτείας (the organization of the ancient constitution)

C^1 (5.1): τοιαύτης δὲ τῆς τάξεως οὔσης ἐν τῇ πολιτείᾳ (while the state was organized in this way,)

B^1 (5.1): καὶ τῶν πολλῶν δουλευόντων τοῖς ὀλίγοις

A^1 (5.1): ἀντέστη τοῖς γνωρίμοις ὁ δῆμος. ἰσχυρᾶς δὲ τῆς στάσεως οὔσης καὶ πολὺν χρόνον ἀντικαθημένων . . . (the people rose against the notables. The strife was fierce, and they held out against one another for a long time).

IV. VARIANT

A small variant of purely horizontal chiasmus is in chapter 5.

A (5.2): τὴν ἐλέγειαν (the elegy)

B (5.2): ἧς ἐστὶν ἀρχή (which begins)

C (5.2): [poem]

D (5.3): κοινῇ παραινεῖ [καταπαύειν] (he urges them to join together [in putting an end to])

E (5.3): τὴν ἐνεστῶσαν φιλονικίαν (the contention dwelling in them)

D¹ (5.3): παραινῶν τοῖς πλουσίοις (urging the rich)

C¹ (5.3): [poem]

D² (5.3): ἀνάπτει τοῖς πλουσίοις (lays the blame [for the strife] on the rich)

B¹ (5.3): ἐν ἀρχῇ (at the beginning)

A¹ (5.3): τῆς ἐλεγείας (of the poem)

E¹ (5.3): τῆς ἔχθρας ἐνεστώσης (of the ill-feeling).

It is difficult to say whether this structure is more properly described as framing ring or as vertical chiasmus, but formally there is little difference between the two.

The position of E¹ disturbs a tightly knit structure, and it may be interesting to see if we can discover Aristotle's intention here. There are two instances of chiasmus: D/D¹ κοινῇ παραινεῖ/ παραινῶν τοῖς πλουσίοις, and E/E¹ τὴν ἐνεστῶσαν φιλονικίαν/τῆς ἐχθρᾶς ἐνεστώσης; and I suggest that the fact of chiastic structure and the repetition of language set up two different parallels, the first between D and E, the second, which breaks and corrects the first, between D¹/D² and E¹. In the first, Aristotle seems to be adapting a subtext which had Solon as absolutely neutral between the two sides. Such a view is found in Plutarch, *vitSol* 14, and we there find the poem, quoted differently by Aristotle, in the version:

τῶν μὲν τὴν φιλοχρηματίαν τῶν δὲ τὴν ὑπερηφανίαν.
(the greed of one group, the arrogance of the other).

The source of Plutarch thought that faults attached to each side.

Aristotle (5.2) begins his account as if Solon were neutral: πρὸς ἑκατέρους ὑπὲρ ἑκατέρων μάχεται (fights against each side on behalf of the other), but uses three steps to correct that beginning. The first step comes at D¹ in which, by replacing κοινῇ with τοῖς πλουσίοις, he attaches the blame to the rich. This is reinforced by the repetition of τοῖς πλουσίοις at D². The third step is the same position illustrated by his version of the verse: [11]

τήν τε φιλ[οπλο]υτίαν τήν θ᾽ ὑπερηφανίαν.

There is no inconsistency here. For Aristotle, Solon was politically, not morally, neutral.

V. SIMPLE

A (6.2): ἐν οἷς πειρῶνταί τινες διαβάλλειν αὐτόν (some people try to slander Solon in this matter)

x 6.2–4

A¹ (6.4): ταύτην μὲν οὖν χρὴ νομίζειν ψευδῆ τὴν αἰτίαν εἶναι. (the accusation must therefore be judged false).

VI. COMPLEX

A (7.1): πολιτείαν δὲ κατέστησε καὶ (Solon established a constitution and)

B (7.1): νόμους ἔθηκεν ἄλλους (enacted other laws)

x 7.1

B¹ (7.2): κατέκλεισεν δὲ τοὺς νόμους (he secured the laws against alteration)

A¹ (7.2): καὶ διέταξε τὴν πολιτείαν τόνδε τὸν τρόπον (and he organized the constitution as follows).

If we compare the structure of this section to a similar structure in chapter 2 for example, we might expect a discussion of Solon's νόμοι with the treatment of the πολιτεία deferred. The latter we have but not the former, for x consists of three brief statements,[12] none of which has anything to do with the content of Solonian law. It seems to me that Aristotle is suggesting a programme here, namely that the πολιτεία genre he is writing does not include the study of laws for their own sake. Historically, this resulted in a division of labor: Theophrastus covered comparative Greek legislation in his work of twenty-four books, Νόμοι.[13]

VII. COMPLEX

A (7.2): διέταξε τὴν πολιτείαν τόνδε τὸν τρόπον

B (7.3): τὰς μεγάλας ἀρχάς[14] (the major offices)

x 7.3–8.1

B¹ (8.2): Σόλων μὲν οὖν οὕτως ἐνομοθέτησεν περὶ τῶν ἐννέα ἀρχόντων. (that is the law which Solon enacted concerning the nine archons.)

B² (9.1): τὰ μὲν οὖν περὶ τὰς ἀρχὰς τοῦτον εἶχε τὸν τρόπον. (that is how the officials were dealt with.)

A¹ (11.1): διατάξας δὲ την πολιτείαν ὅνπερ εἴρηται τρόπον . . . (Solon organized the constitution in the manner stated).

The structure of these chapters is slightly unwieldy. B¹ rounds off discussion of the nine archons, but, just as the discussion of the history of the archonship led to the inclusion of the Council of the Areopagus (composed of ex-archons) in chapter 3, so here B¹ is followed by statements on the Areopagus, and this is rounded off by B². A¹ is necessary to get back to the theme of πολιτεία (within which are included the σεισαχθεία and other laws).[15]

VIII. SIMPLE

A (9.1): δοκεῖ δὲ τῆς Σόλωνος πολιτείας τρία ταῦτ' εἶναι τὰ δημο-τικώτατα (the following seem to be the most democratic features of So-lon's constitution)

x 9.1–2

A¹ (10.1): ἐν μὲν οὖν τοῖς νόμοις ταῦτα δοκεῖ θεῖναι δημοτικά. (those appear to be the democratic features in Solon's laws).

IX. SIMPLE

A (11.1): ἀποδημίαν ἐποιήσατο (he went on his travels)

x 11.1–12.5

A¹ (13.1): τὴν μὲν οὖν ἀποδημίαν ἐποιήσατο. . . .

X. COMPLEX

A (13.4): μία [sc., στάσις] μὲν τῶν παραλίων, ὧν προε@ιστήκει Μεγακλῆς ὁ Ἀλκμέωνος, οἵπερ ἐδόκουν μάλιστα διώκειν τὴν μέσην πολιτείαν. (one [faction] of the men of the coast, led by Megacles son of Alcmaeon, whose particular objective seemed to be the middle form of constitution;)

B (13.4): ἄλλη δὲ τῶν πεδιακῶν, οἳ τὴν ὀλιγαρχίαν ἐζήτουν. ἡγεῖτο δ' αὐτῶν Λυκοῦργος. (another the men of the plain, whose aim was oligarchy, and who were led by Lucurgus;)

C (13.4): τρίτη δ' ἡ τῶν διακρίων, ἐφ' ἡ τεταγμένος ἦν Πεισίστρατος, δημοτικώτατος δ' εἶναι δοκῶν. (and the third, the men of the Diakria, whose leader was Peisistratus, a man who seemed most inclined toward democracy.)

x 13.5–34.2

C¹ (34.3): οἱ μὲν δημοτικοὶ διασῴζειν ἐπειρῶντο τὸν δῆμον, (the democrats tried to preserve the democracy;)

B¹ (34.3): τῶν δὲ γνωρίμων οἱ μὲν ἐν ταῖς ἑταιρείαις ὄντες καὶ τῶν φυγάδων οἱ μετὰ τὴν εἰρήνην κατελθόντες ὀλιγαρχίας ἐπεθύμουν, (of the notables those who belonged to the clubs and the exiles who had returned after the peace treaty were eager for oligarchy;)

(A¹ (34.3): οἱ δὲ ἐν ἑταιρείᾳ μὲν οὐδεμιᾷ συγκαθεστῶτες, ἄλλως δὲ δοκοῦντες οὐδενὸς ἐπιλείπεσθαι τῶν πολιτῶν, τὴν πάτριον πολιτείαν ἐζήτουν. (those who did not belong to any club and who in

other respects seemed inferior to no one of the citizens had as their objective the traditional constitution).
[I discuss this in chapter 14, "Aristotle and Theramenes."]

XI. SIMPLE

A ([4.2]: λέγεται δὲ Σόλωνα (it is said that Solon)
[x 14.2 anecdote of Solon's opposition to Peisistratus]
A¹: (14.2): Σόλων μὲν οὖν οὐδὲν ἤνυσεν τότε παρακαλῶν. (the appeal which Solon made at that time achieved nothing).

XII. SIMPLE

A (14.3): Πεισίστρατος δὲ λαβὼν τὴν ἀρχὴν . . . (Peisistratos on obtaining power)
x 14.2–15.5
A¹ (16.1): ἡ μὲν οὖν Πεισιστράτου τυραννὶς ἐξ ἀρχῆς τοῦτον τὸν τρόπον . . . (that is how Peisistratus' tyranny was established from the beginning).

XIII. SIMPLE

A (14.4): κατήγαγεν [sc., Megacles] αὐτὸν [sc., Peisistratus] ἀρχαίως καὶ λίαν ἁπλῶς. (Megacles reinstituted him in a primitive and oversimple manner.)
[x 14.4 the return of Peisistratus]
A¹ (15.1): ἡ μὲν οὖν πρώτη κάθοδος ἐγένετο τοιαύτη. (such was Peisistratus' first return).

XIV. COMPLEX

A (19.2): ἐν τούτοις δ' ὢν ἐξέπεσεν ὑπὸ Κλεομένους (while work there was in progress, he was expelled by Cleomenes.)
B (19.2): χρησμῶν γιγνομένων ἀεὶ τοῖς Λάκωσι καταλύειν τὴν τυραννίδα διὰ τοιάνδ'αἰτίαν. (a whole series of oracles had commanded the Spartans to put an end to the tyranny, for the following reason.)
C (19.3): οἱ φυγάδες, ὧν οἱ Ἀλκμεωνίδαι προειστήκεσαν, αὐτοὶ μὲν δι' αὑτῶν οὐκ ἐδύναντο ποιήσασθαι τὴν κάθοδον, ἀλλ' ἀεὶ προσέπταιον. (the Athenian exiles, chief among whom were the Alcmeonids, were unable to bring about their return on their own, inspite of several attempts)

D (19.3): ἔν τε γὰρ τοῖς ἄλλοις οἷς ἔπραττον διεσφάλλοντο (among their other failures was one when they)

[x 19.3: attack on Leipsydrion; scholia]

D¹ (19.4): ἀποτυγχάνοντες οὖν ἐν ἄπασι τοῖς ἄλλοις (after they had failed in everything else,)

C¹ (19.4): ἐμισθώσαντο τὸν ἐν Δελφοῖς νεὼν οἰκοδομεῖν . . . (the Alcmeonids obtained the contract to build the temple in Delphi)

B¹ (19.4): ἡ δὲ Πυθία προέφερεν ἀεὶ τοῖς Λακεδαιμονίοις χρηστηριαζομένοις ἐλευθεροῦν τὰς Ἀθήνας . . . (whenever the Spartans consulted the oracle, the priestess always commanded them to liberate Athens)

A¹ (19.6): expulsion of Hippias.

Although Aristotle has used another source or sources in this chapter, the basic source is a linear narrative in book five of Herodotus, and our first step will be to compare the two accounts:

A: not in Herodotus (nor is the material about the fortification of Munychia at the beginning of the chapter)

B: not in Herodotus

C: H. 5.62.2

D: not in Herodotus

x H. 5.62.2

D¹: I take this to be functionally equivalent to H. 5.62.2: πᾶν ἐπὶ τοῖσι Πεισιστρατίδῃσι μηχανώμενοι

C¹: probably a different version from that of H. 5.62.2–3

B¹: H. 5.63.1 with strong verbal echoes of προφέρειν σφι τὰς Ἀθήνας ἐλευθεροῦν

A¹: H. 5.63.2–65.2.

It is clear that Aristotle has converted a linear structure in Herodotus into a ring structure, using material provided by Herodotus in the process. What is not so clear is why.

It is conceivable that the ring structure was a way to integrate the account of Herodotus with that of another source, or sources, but this is true only to a limited extent. The material which Aristotle did not take from Herodotus did not affect the structure: the fortification of Munychia is mentioned before the first element of the structure; details about Leipsydrion and the scholia come at the same point as they do in Herodotus' narrative; and the same is true about the arrangement with Delphi, whatever be the source used here.[16]

It is more precise to say that the non-Herodotean material is used to create this structure by supplying the first half of it, and it may be more profitable to examine it from this point of view. The structure here differs in several ways from other uses of the device. First, exact verbal correspondence between the balanced elements is found only at D/D¹: ἔν τε γὰρ τοῖς ἄλλοις/ἐν ἄπασι τοῖς ἄλλοις. A merely announces the result of a longish account in A¹, and the only verbal parallel is the name of Cleomenes. B gives no more information than is found in the content of B¹. The different language of B may point to a new source, and the language of the oracle's command, καταλύειν τὴν τυραννίδα, over against Herodotus' ἐλευθεροῦν τὰς ᾿Αθήνας, may seem to have more of a political ᾳuance, but it is not clear why such a nuance is needed here, and the paraphrases can be treated as functionally equivalent.

It is in C and C¹ that the differences are greatest. Because of the rest of the structure, these elements must be connected, but there is not a single verbal correspondence, and the contents are different: in B the exiles, led by the Alcmeonids, are unable to effect their return; in B¹, they (= the Alcmeonids, but the subject has to be supplied from the general sense) make a contract with Delphi whence they acquire enough money for Spartan aid. This discrepancy can be explained if we look upon A/B as static, and C/D/D¹/C¹/B¹/A¹ as dynamic elements of the structure. In other words, A/B announce the participation of Sparta and Delphi in the expulsion of the tyrants, and the chronologically correct narrative begins with C.

If this is so, one purpose of the ring structure is to bring Sparta and Delphi onto the scene immediately. Their presence affects the narrative in two ways, one dramatic and one political. The inclusion of the two enables Aristotle to make a separate, structural unit. Within that, he achieves some dramatic effects. We have the insistence of the Delphic oracle with C and C¹, an insistence heightened by the repetition of ἀεί. With this can be contrasted the ἀεὶ προσέπταιον (Herodotus has simply προσέπταιον) of the Alcmeonid efforts in C. Another contrast is in the situations before and after Leipsydrion, where the ἅπασι τοῖς ἄλλοις makes the situation more desperate when contrasted with τοῖς ἄλλοις of C. Finally, there is a balance between C/D/x/D¹/C¹ on the one hand, with two references to general failure surrounding a particular failure in contrast with the initial success in getting money from Delphi, and the two Spartan invasions, the first a failure, the second successful. In describing the affair of Leipsydrion, Herodotus says only Λειψύδριον τὸ ὑπὲρ Παιονίης τειχίσαντες (fortifying Leipsydrion beyond Parnes), which Aristotle expands to (1) τειχίσαντες ἐν τῇ χώρᾳ Λειψύδριον τὸ ὑπὸ Πάρνηθος (they fortified Leipsydrion in the country below Parnes, (2) εἰς ὃ συνεξῆλθόν τινες τῶν ἐκ τοῦ ἄστεως (and were joined by some men from the city), (3) ἐξεπολιορκήθησαν ὑπὸ τῶν τυράννων (but the tyrants besieged them and drove them out). Of the second and third clauses, the third is a necessary inference from the fact of the defeat of men in a fort. The second clause cannot be an inference. It is either from another source,¹⁷ or it is Aristotle's invention. In either case, I suggest that the early mention of Sparta in A and the inclusion of οἱ ἐκ τοῦ ἄστεως are intended to flesh out the statement that the exiles were unable αὐτοὶ δι᾿ αὐτῶν ποιήσασθαι τὴν κάθοδον. I further suggest that there is a contrast between this situation and the final democratic restoration, in the context of which Aristotle makes the statement (41.1) that the δῆμος δικαίως [λαβεῖν] τὴν πολιτείαν διὰ τὸ ποιήσασθαι τὴν κάθοδον δι᾿ αὐτοῦ (the people's taking political power seems justifiable, since it was the people themselves who achieved their return).

Stylistically, it may be suggested that the integration of the linear structure of his major source into his own ring structure, coming as it does at the end of the basically linear narrative of the tyrants, signals Aristotle's return to the style normal to N.

XV. COMPLEX

A (20.1): καταλυθείσης δὲ τῆς τυραννίδος ἐστασίαζον πρὸς ἀλλήλους Ἰσαγόρας ὁ Τεισάνδρου φίλος ὢν τῶν τυράννων καὶ Κλεισθένης τοῦ γένους ὢν τῶν Ἀλκμεωνιδῶν. (when the tyranny had been overthrown, strife broke out between Isagoras son of Teisander, a friend of the tyrants, and Cleisthenes of the Alcmeonid family.

B (20.1–2): ἡττώμενος δὲ ταῖς ἑταιρείαις ὁ Κλεισθένης προσηγάγετο τὸν δῆμον, ἀποδιδοὺς τῷ πλήθει τὴν πολιτείαν. as Cleisthenes was getting the worse of the party struggle, he attached the people to his following)

x 20.2–3

B¹ (20.4): κατασχόντος δὲ τοῦ δήμου τὰ πράγματα, Κλεισθένης ἡγεμὼν ἦν καὶ τοῦ δήμου προστάτης. (thus the people obtained control of affairs, and Cleisthenes became leader and champion of the people.)

A¹ (20.4): αἰτιώτατοι γὰρ σχεδὸν ἐγένοντο τῆς ἐκβολῆς τῶν τυράννων οἱ Ἀλκμεωνίδαι, καὶ στασιάζοντες τὰ πολλὰ διετέλεσαν. (the Alcmeonids bore the greatest responsibility for the expulsion of the tyrants, and had persisted in opposition to them for most of the time).

For a discussion of the structure of this chapter, especially of its implications for the contents of chapters 20 and 21, see Keaney 1969³ (418–21). Chapters 19 and 20 attempt to give a balanced account of the end of tyranny and its threat in Athens, 19 from external, 20 from internal points of view. The introductory sentence of 19 refers to τὴν τυραννίδα, that of 20 to τῆς τυραννίδος. Both devices are used again in chapters 28 and 29, each of which begins ἕως μὲν οὖν, and one of which discusses internal politics, the second external military matters.

XVI: A,B,C. SIMPLE

Chapter 24 is composed of three structural units, each of which has a different kind of frame.

A (24.1): συνεβούλευεν ἀντιλαμβάνεσθαι τῆς ἡγεμονίας (Aristeides advised the Athenians to assert their leadership)

x 24.1: καὶ καταβάντας ἐκ τῶν ἀγρῶν οἰκεῖν ἐν τῷ ἄστει· τροφὴν γὰρ ἔσεσθαι πᾶι, τοῖς μὲν στρατευομένοις, τοῖς δὲ φρουροῦσι, τοῖς δὲ τὰ κοινὰ πράττουσι, (and to leave the fields and live in the city; there would be maintenance for all, some on campaigns, some on guard duty, others attending to public affairs;)

A¹ (24.1): εἶθ' οὕτω κατασχήσειν τὴν ἡγεμονίαν. (and by living in this way, they would secure their leadership).

Aristeides makes two suggestions, that the Athenians seize hegemony and dwell in the city. The fulfillment of the first suggestion depends upon the fulfillment of the second. Since that is guaranteed (τροφὴν γὰρ . . .), the first suggestion will be fulfilled (A1).

A (24.2): πεισθέντες δὲ ταῦτα καὶ λαβόντες τὴν ἀρχὴν (the Athenians were persuaded. They took control of the empire,)

x 24.2: τοῖς συμμάχοις δεσποτικωτέρως ἐχρῶντο πλὴν Χίων καὶ Λεσβίων καὶ Σαμίων· τούτους δὲ φύλακας εἶχον τῆς ἀρχῆς, (and became more domineering in their treatment of the allies, apart from Chios, Lesbos and Samos:)

A¹ (24.2): ἐῶντες τάς τε πολιτείας παρ' αὐτοῖς καὶ ἄρχειν ὧν ἔτυχον ἄρχοντες. (these they kept as guardians of the empire, accepting their existing constitutions and allowing them to retain the subjects over whom they ruled).

The link connecting the two units is the transition from ἡγεμονία to ἀρχή,[18] and the structure depends upon the play with the root ἀρχ-.

A (24.3): κατεστησαν δὲ καὶ τοῖς πολλοῖς εὐπορίαν τροφῆς (they provided ample maintenance for the common people)

x 24.3

A¹ (25.1): ἡ μὲν οὖν τροφὴ τῷ δήμῳ διὰ τούτων ἐγίγνετο. (that is how maintenance for the common people came into being).

XVII. SIMPLE

A (25.1): διέμεινεν ἡ πολιτεία προεστώτων τῶν Ἀρεοπαγιτῶν (the constitution in which the Areopagus predominated persisted)

x 25.1–4

A¹ (26.1): ἡ μέν οὖν τῶν Ἀρεοπαγιτῶν βουλὴ ἀπεστερήθη τῆς ἐπιμελείας. (in this way the council of the Areopagus was deprived of its responsibility).

XVIII. COMPLEX

A (27.2): μετὰ δὲ τῇ ἐν Σαλαμῖνι ναυμαχίαν (after the battle of Salamis)

B (27.2): ἑνὸς δεῖ πεντηκοστῷ ἔτει (in the forty-ninth year)

C (27.2): ἐπὶ Πυθοδώρου ἄρχοντος (the archonship of Pythodorus)

D (27.2): ὁ πρὸς Πελοποννησίοις ἐνέστη πόλεμος (the Peloponnesian War broke out)

x 27.2–32.1

D¹ (32.2): ἡ μὲν οὖν ὀλιγαρχία τοῦτον κατέστη τόν τρόπον (that is how the oligarchy was set up,)

C¹ (32.2): ἐπὶ Καλλίου μὲν ἄρχοντος, (in the archonship of Callias,)

B¹ (32.2): ἔτεσιν . . . ἑκατον (a hundred years)

A¹ (32.2): δ' ὕστερον τῆς τῶν τυράννων ἐκβολῆς (after the expulsion of the tyrants).

[I discuss these passages in chapter 14: "Aristotle and Theramenes."]

XIX. COMPLEX

A (27.3): ἐποίησε δὲ καὶ μισθοφόρα τὰ δικαστήρια Περικλῆς πρῶτος . . . (Pericles was the first man to provide payment for jury service)

B (27.3): ὁ γὰρ Κίμων . . . πρῶτον μὲν τὰς κοινὰς λητουργίας ἐλητούργει λαμπρῶς, (first, Cimon . . . performed the public liturgies lavishly;)

C (27.3): ἔπειτα τῶν δημοτῶν ἔτρεφε πολλούς . . . (secondly, he maintained many of his fellow demesmen)

x 27.3–4

C¹ (27.4): ἐπεὶ τοῖς ἰδίοις ἡττᾶτο [sc. Pericles], (Pericles' property was insufficient)

B¹ (27.4): διδόναι τοῖς πολλοῖς τὰ αὐτῶν, (give the people their own property)

A¹ (27.4): κατεσκεύασε μισθοφορὰν τοῖς δικασταῖς . . . (he devised payment for the jurors).

C and C¹ contrast Cimon's private generosity with Pericles' lack of private means, while B and B¹ mention the public acts of each. I discuss this text in chapter 13 on Theopompus.

XX. SIMPLE

A (29.4): οἱ δ' αἱρεθέντες πρῶτον μὲν ἔγραψαν . . . (the men who were elected proposed first)

x 29.4–5

A¹ (30.1): οἱ μὲν οὖν αἱρεθέντες ταῦτα συνέγραψαν. (those are the proposals made by the elected committee).

XXI. COMPLEX

A (30.1): κυρωθέντων δὲ τούτων, (when they had been ratified,)

B (30.1): εἵλοντο σφῶν αὐτῶν οἱ πεντακισχίλιοι τοὺς ἀναγράψοντας τὴν πολιτείαν ἑκατὸν ἄνδρας. (the Five Thousand elected from their own number a hundred men to draw up the details of the constitution,)

C (30.2): οἱ δ' αἱρεθέντες ἀνέγραψαν καὶ ἐξήνεγκαν τάδε· (and the men who were elected drew up and submitted the following)

x 30.2–6

C¹ (31.1): ταύτην μὲν οὖν εἰς τὸν μέλλοντα χρόνον ἀνέγραψαν τὴν πολιτείαν, ἐν δὲ τῷ παρόντι καιρῷ τήνδε· (the committee drew up that constitution for the future, and the following for the immediate crisis)

x 31.2–3

B¹ (32.1): οἱ μὲν οὖν ἑκατὸν οἱ ὑπὸ τῶν πεντακισχιλίων αἱρεθέντες ταύτην ἀνέγραψαν τὴν πολιτείαν. (that is the constitution drawn up by the hundred men who were elected by the Five Thousand.)

A¹ (32.1): ἐπικυρωθέντων δὲ τούτων ὑπὸ τοῦ πλήθους . . . (it was ratified by the masses).

XXII. COMPLEX

A (34.2): ἐξ ἧς συνέβη κύριον γενομένον τῆς πόλεως Λύσανδρον (as a result of that Lysander became master of the city, and)

B (34.2): καταστῆσαι τοὺς τριάκοντα τρόπῳ τοιῷδε. (set up the Thirty in the following manner)

x 34.3

B¹ (35.1): οἱ μὲν οὖν τριάκοντα τοῦτον τὸν τρόπον κατέστησαν ἐπὶ Πυθοδώρου ἄρχοντος. (in this way the Thirty were established, in the archonship of Pythodorus.)

A¹ (35.1): γενομένοι δὲ κύριοι τῆς πόλεως[19] (having become masters of the city).

A and A¹ underscore the importance of Lysander in setting up the Thirty.

XXIII. COMPLEX

A (37.1): ἔγνωσαν [sc., the Thirty] τῶν μὲν ἄλλων τὰ ὅπλα παρελέσθαι, (they decided to disarm the unprivileged and)

B (37.1): Θηραμένην δὲ διαφθεῖραι τόνδε ⟨τὸν⟩ τρόπον· ⟨to destroy Theramenes in the following way⟩

x (37.1): νόμους εἰσήνεγκαν εἰς τὴν βουλὴν δύο κελεύοντες ἐπιχειροτονεῖν, (they introduced two laws and ordered the council to approve them:)

C (37.1): ὧν ὁ μὲν εἰς αὐτοκράτορας ἐποίει τοὺς τριάκοντα τῶν πολιτῶν ἀποκτεῖναι τοὺς μὴ τοῦ καταλόγου μετέχοντας τῶν τρισχιλίων, (one giving the Thirty full authority to put to death those citizens who were not included in the register of the Three Thousand;)

D (37.1): ὁ δ' ἕτερος ἐκώλυε κοινωνεῖν τῆς παρούσης πολιτείας: (the other excluding from participation in the present constitution)

[the conditions are spelled out]

x (37.1): ὥστε συνέβαινεν ἐπικυρωθέντων τῶν νόμων (so when the laws were ratified the result was that)

D¹ (37.1) ἔξω τε γίγνεσθαι τῆς πολιτείας αὐτόν, (he was excluded from the citizen body)

C¹ (37.1): καὶ τοὺς τριάκοντα κυρίους εἶναι θανατοῦντας. (and the Thirty had the power to put him to death.)

B¹ (37.2): ἀναιρεθέντος δὲ Θηραμένους, (after eliminating Theramenes,)

A¹ (37.2): τά τε ὅπλα παρείλοντο πάντων πλὴν τῶν τρισχιλίων κτλ. (they disarmed all except the Three Thousand).

XXIV. SIMPLE

A (39.1): ἐγένοντο δ' αἱ διαλύσεις ἐπ' Εὐκλείδου ἄρχοντος κατὰ τὰς συνθήκας τάσδε. (The reconciliation took place in the archonshop of Eucleides, in accordance with the following agreements)

x 39.1–6

A¹ (40.1): γενομένεν δὲ τοιούτων τῶν διαλύσεων κτλ. (those were the terms on which the reconciliation took place).

XXV. COMPLEX

A (41.1): τότε δὲ κύριος ὁ δῆμος γενόμενος τῶν πραγμάτων, (meanwhile the people gained control of affairs)

B (41.1: ἐνεστήσατο τὴν νῦν οὖσαν πολιτείαν ἐπὶ Πυθοδώρου ἄρχοντος δοκοῦντος δὲ δικαίως τοῦ δήμου λαβεῖν τὴν πολιτείαν διὰ τὸ ποιήσασθαι τὴν κάθοδον δι' αὐτοῦ τὸν δῆμον.[20] (and set up the present constitution, in the archonship of Pythodorus: the people's taking power seems justifiable, since it was the people themselves who achieved their return.)

C (41.2): ἦν δὲ τῶν μεταβολῶν ἑνδεκάτη τὸν ἀριθμὸν αὕτη. (this was the eleventh of the changes in the constitution.)

x 41.2

C¹ (41.2): ἑνδεκάτη δ' ἡ μετὰ τὴν ἀπὸ Φυλῆς καὶ ἐκ Πειραιέως κάθοδον, (eleventh, the regime after the return from Phylē and the Peiraeus,)

B¹ (41.2): ἀφ' ἧς διαγεγένηται μεχρὶ τῆς νῦν, ἀεὶ προσεπιλαμβάνουσα τῷ πλήθει τὴν ἐξουσίαν. (from which the constitution has continued to that in force today, continually increasing the power of the masses.)

A¹ (41.2): ἁπάντων γὰρ αὐτὸς αὑτὸν πεποίηκεν ὁ δῆμος κύριον, καὶ πάντα διοικεῖται ψηφίσμασιν καὶ δικαστηρίοις, ἐν οἷς ὁ δῆμός ἐστιν ὁ κρατῶν.[21] καὶ γὰρ αἱ τῆς βουλῆς κρίσεις εἰς τὸν δῆμον ἐληλύθασιν. (the people have made themselves masters of everything, and control all things by means of decrees and jury courts, in which the power resides with the people; even the jurisdiction of the council has been transferred to the people).

This chapter is the culmination of the historical sections of the *AP*, and it is best to discuss its richness under the rubrics of structure, language and theme, although some overlapping will be necessary. The chapter begins: ταῦτα μὲν οὖν ἐν τοῖς ὕστερον συνέβη γενέσθαι καιροῖς (the final reconciliation took place subsequently). This makes explicit what would otherwise have to be assumed, namely that there is not a simple chronological progression from chapter 40 to 41, and that the event mentioned in B took place as one of the events during the time frame of 40. This means that 41 is a transitional chapter and transitional both from the past and to the future. This latter aspect of the transition is signalled by τὴν νῦν οὖσαν and by μέχρι τῆς νῦν. Both of these are taken up by the first sentence of the description of the contemporary constitution (42.1): ἔχει δ᾽ ἡ νῦν κατάστασις τῆς πολιτείας τόνδε τὸν τρόπον (the present form of the constitution is as follows). Like other transitional chapters, it is also a summary chapter, as is obvious from the core of its content.

From both the transitional and summary points of view, chapter 41 resembles most closely the pre-Solonian chapter 3. Just as the economic conditions in chapter 2 assume the political conditions of chapter 3, so the resolution of στάσις in 40 assumes the political result described in 41; and, as 4l looks forward to the fourth century (νῦν),[22] so 3 looks forward not only to Solon (3.5: ἐπὶ δὲ Σόλωνος) but also to the fourth century (3.5: οὐχ ὥσπερ νῦν).[23]

This parallelism of content is the first device Aristotle uses to draw parallels between Solon and the last form of democracy. Part of the parallelism is the fact that both Solon and the last democracy are described after a dissolution of *stasis,* even if that dissolution, in Solon's time, was short-lived.

The complex ring structure of 41 has its nearest parallel in the text of chapter 34, in which the intervention of Lysander the Spartan is decisive in establishing the regime of the Thirty. The parallelism is reinforced by an echo of language: (34.2) κύριον γενόμενον, (35.1) γενόμενοι δὲ κύριοι with (41.1) κύριος ὁ δῆμος γενόμενος. But the same language in 41 has an earlier echo at 6.1: κύριος δὲ γενόμενος τῶν πραγμάτων Σόλων τόν τε δῆμον ἠλευθέρωσε κτλ. (on gaining control of affairs, Solon liberated the people). This language is a deliberate pointer toward Solon in the sense that last democracy finally accomplished what Solon began.

Finally, the ring structure ends with the thematic remark about the βουλή. This looks forward to 45.1, a passage unique in the second part of the *AP* in two of its features: it is the only example of complex ring composition in the systematic part, and it contains the only historical anecdote. In structure and theme, 45.1 belongs more closely to the narrative than to the second part of the work.

XXV1. SIMPLE

A (42.1): μετέχουσιν μὲν τῆς πολιτείας οἱ ἐξ ἀμφοτέρων γεγονότες ἀστῶν, ἐγγράφονται δ᾽ εἰς τοὺς δημότας, ὀκτωκαίδεκα ἔτη γεγονότες. ὅταν δ᾽ ἐγγράφωνται (men belong to the citizen body if they are of citizen parentage on both sides, and they are registered as members of their demes at the age of eighteen)

x 42.1–4

A¹ (43.1): τὰ μὲν οὖν περὶ τὴν τῶν πολιτῶν ἐγγραφὴν καὶ τοὺς ἐφήβους τοῦτον ἔχει τὸν τρόπον. (this is what happens with the registration of citizens, and with the cadets).

XXVII. SIMPLE

A (43.1): τὰς δ᾽ ἀρχὰς τὰς περὶ τὴν ἐγκύκλιον διοίκησιν ἀπάσας ποιοῦσι κληρωτάς . . . (all the officials concerned with civilian administration are appointed by lot)

x 43.2–54.8

A¹ (55.1): αὗται μὲν οὖν αἱ ἀρχαὶ κληρωταί τε καὶ κύριαι τῶν εἰρημένων πάντων εἰσίν. (those officials are appointed by lot, and are responsible for all the matters mentioned).

Rhodes (613) believes that what I have printed as A "rounds off *A.P.*'s section on sortitive officials, begun in ch. 50." It is possible that he is correct. One argument against is that discussion of sortitive officials begins not at chapter 50 but at 47.1. Perhaps in favor is a structuring like this:

A (43.1): as above

B (45.1): ·ἡ δὲ βουλὴ πρότερον μὲν ἦν κυρία . . . (formerly the council had full power)

x 45.4–46.2

C (47.1): συνδιοικεῖ δὲ καὶ ταῖς ἄλλαις ἀρχαῖς τὰ πλεῖστα. (in general the council cooperates in the administrative work of the other officials)

C¹ (49.5): συνδιοικεῖ δὲ καὶ ταῖς ἄλλαις ἀρχαῖς τὰ πλεῖστα ὡς ἔπος εἰπεῖν. (in general, one might say, the council cooperates. . . .)

B¹ (50.1): τὰ μὲν οὖν ὑπὸ τῆς βουλῆς διοικούμενα ταῦτ᾽ ἐστίν (this is the work handled by the council.)

Aᵇ (50.1): κληροῦνται δὲ καὶ . . . (there are appointed by lot also)

A¹ as above.

The element most queried here has been C¹. Herwerden deleted it as a doublet of C. Kaibel (25) recognized that it could not be that because of the addition of ὡς ἔπος εἰπεῖν, but he could only account for the repetition by suggesting that 49.5 was part of a first draft which Aristotle failed to excise in a later revision.[24] The fact of repetition is no reason for excision, and the problem lies with the contiguity of C¹ and B¹. It is unexampled for two elements to occur back to back. Unless something has fallen out of the text between 49.5 and 50.1, the juxtaposition is clumsy.

XXVIII. COMPLEX

A (45.1): ἡ δὲ βουλὴ πρότερον μὲν ἦν κυρία (formerly the council had full power)

B (45.1): καὶ χρήμασιν ζημιῶσαι (to impose fines,)

C (45.1): καὶ δῆσαι (to imprison)

D (45.1): καὶ ἀποκτειναι. (and to put to death.)

[x (45.1): the story of Lysimachus, the upshot of which is that ὁ δῆμος ἀφείλετο τῆς βουλῆς (the people took away from the council the right)]

D¹ (45.1): τὸ θανατοῦν (to execute,)

C¹ (45.10: καὶ δεῖν (imprison)

B¹ (45.1): καὶ χρήμασι ζημιοῦν. (and fine.)

[x (45.1) it further passed a law that condemnations and fines by the βουλή were to be referred to a δικαστήριον, καὶ ὅ τι ἂν οἱ δικασταὶ ψηφίσωνται τοῦτο κύριον εἶναι. (whatever the jurors voted should be final.) Further limitations on the judicial powers of the βουλή are specified and Aristotle sums up:]

A¹ (45.4): τούτων μὲν οὖν ἄκυρός ἐστιν ἡ βουλή. (in those matters the council does not have final power). [I discuss this segment in chapter 18, "Chapter 45: ἡ βουλή."]

NOTES

1. The basic bibliography is in Keaney 1969².497 n. 3. Some additions: Rhodes 44–49; I. Beck, *Die Ringkomposition bei Herodot und ihre Bedeutung für die Beweistechnik, Spudasmata* 25 (Hildesheim and New York 1971); O. Wenskus, *Ringkomposition, anaphorisch-rekapitulierende Verbindung und anknüpfende Wiederholung im hippokratischen Corpus* (Frankfurt 1982).

2. "Untersuchung uber Begriff, Anwendung und Enstehung der Griechischen Ringkomposition," *Med. d. Nederl. Akad. v. Wetenschappen, Afd. Letterkunde,* Nieuwe Reeks, 7 (1944) 1–46.

3. An example is taken from Herodotus 5.66–69. The historian says that the Athenian Cleisthenes increased the number of tribes:

A 67.1: ταῦτα δὲ, δοκέειν ἐμοί, ἐμιμέετο ὁ Κλεισθένης οὗτος τὸν ἑωυτοῦ μητροπάτορα Κλεισθένη τὸν Σικυῶνος τύραννον. (in this, it seems to me, Cleisthenes was imitating his maternal grandfather, Cleisthenes, tyrant of Sicyon.)
[digression about the Sicyonian Cleisthenes]
A¹ 69.1: ὁ δὲ δὴ Ἀθηναῖος Κλεισθένης . . . τὸν ὁμώνυμον Κλεισθενέα ἐμιμήσατο (the Athenian Cleisthenes imitated his homonym, Cleisthenes).
[discussion of tribal reforms continues.]

4. An apparent exception is chapter 6, in which Aristotle mentions Solon's disburdenment of debts and goes on to defend him from the charge of peculation in that act. This part of the chapter is framed by a simple ring, but it would not be accurate to refer to this part as a digression when it takes up four-fifths of the chapter and was obviously where Aristotle wanted to put his emphasis.

5. The distinction is not meant to be rigid, for, as in chapter 20, both uses may coexist.

6. It is more complete than the discussion in Keaney 1969[2] and in Rhodes 44–49: it also differs in some details in the discussion of certain passages.

7. Cf. chapter 9, "Horizontal Structure: Chiasmus."

8. Keaney 1963.123–24.

9. There is nothing in Plutarch corresponding to the analysis of political conditions in ch. 3. The only fragment of Androtion relevant to the question shows that he discussed the pre-Solonian Areopagus (324 F 4).

10. Cf. Keaney 1963[1] 123–25.

11. On the problems of the text, cf. Rhodes 125.

12. (1) they preserved only Draco's homicide laws; (2) the laws were inscribed and located in the Royal Stoa; (3) the archons swear an oath to use the laws.

13. Cf. H. Bloch, "Studies in Historical Literature of the Fourth Century B.C.," *Athenian Studies Presented to William Scott Ferguson = HSCP,* Suppl., 1 (Cambridge 1941) 303–76, esp. 355 ff.

14. For this reading, see the discussion in Rhodes 138–39. His point that "any adjective is superfluous here, since the thetes' membership of the ecclesia and heliaea ought not to rank as an ἀρχή at all" ignores the fact that Aristotle in *Politics* 3 explicitly includes such membership as an ἀρχή: (3.1275A23–26) τῶν δ᾽ ἀρχῶν αἱ μέν εἰσι διῃρημέναι κατὰ χρόνον . . . ἀόριστος, οἷον ὁ δικαστὴς καὶ ἐκκλησιαστής (some offices are distinguished in respect of length of tenure . . . not so limited, such as membership of a jury or of an assembly).

15. In ch. 11, the reaction of the citizens concerned the νόμοι (laws), the ἀποκοπαὶ τῶν χρεῶν (disburdenment of debts), and the κατάστασις (constitutional setup). Aristotle's avoidance of the term πολιτεία as a separate item in this list shows that these items are included in the generic πολιτεία.

16. On this, see the discussion and bibliography in Rhodes 236–37.

17. If so, this source will have been responsible for the slight deemphasis on the role of the Alcmeonids. In Herodotus, they act ἅμα τοῖσι ἄλλοισι ᾽Αθηναίων φυγάσι (with the other Athenian exiles); in the ᾽Αθπολ, the activity is of οἱ φυγάδες, ὧν οἱ ᾽Αλκμαιωνίδαι προειστήκεσαν.

18. On which cf. von Fritz and Kapp 168; Rhodes 298.

19. For chiastic structure in chapter 34, see chapter 9.

20. τὸν δῆμον was excised by Kaibel and Wilamowitz: they are followed by Chambers.

21. The allusion to δημοκρατία will not have escaped notice.

22. Ch. 41 ends with references to events presumably later than the archonship of Pythodorus.

23. This last, thematic, detail is parallel, in 40, to the reference to the βουλή: cf. chapter 18.

24. Kaibel did not develop the suggestion, and it is not clear what assumptions prompted it. It is possible that, in the process of composition, Aristotle finished and put down this section. When he took up the work again, he carelessly added B[1] before resuming with ch. 50.

9

Horizontal Structure: Chiasmus

At the end of chapter 11, Aristotle says of Solon that he ἀμφοτέροις ἠναν-τιώθη, καὶ ἐξὸν αὐτῷ μεθ᾽ ὁποτέρων ἐβούλετο συστάντα τυραννεῖν, εἵλετο πρὸς ἀμφοτέρους ἀπεχθέσθαι, σώσας [A] τὴν πατρίδα [B] καὶ τὰ βέλτιστα [B¹] νομοθετήσας [A¹] (Solon was opposed to both; and, while he could have combined with whichever party he chose and become tyrant, he preferred to incur the hatred of both by saving his country and legislating for the best). Rhodes (171) comments: "probably to be read as a formulation of what Solon thought he was doing, rather than as an expression of *A.P.*'s enthusiastic approval." I wonder, and ask a question: if an author has expressed himself through the use of a figure like this,[1] is the use of that figure the result of a deliberate choice, or is it accidental? A second question: if it is the result of choice, what does the author intend by it?

If an author is dealing with two sets of terms, he may use a normal order—A/B/A¹/B¹—or a chiastic order—A/B/B¹/A¹. It would be surprising if the choice of the latter were not made sometimes *causa uariationis*. On the other hand, given the clear evidence that there is at least one passage in the ᾽Αθπολ in which the choice of chiasmus must be deliberate, it may with justice be assumed that it frequently, if not always, is such (cf. 32.1 below).

Kaibel (100–101), indeed, was confident that this was so and, on the basis of eight[2] passages, sought to establish two conclusions: (a) of the two pairs, the outer elements have the greater weight; (b) of the four elements, the fourth and last has the most emphatic position in the clause. In general, he thought, the use of the figure is no mere virtuosity *(blosse Künstlerei)* but a rhetorical means of expressing the thought. It is not clear if Kaibel intended his treatment of chiasmus to be exhaustive, and it is, perhaps, not accidental that the examples he chose support his conclusions. But he restricted his analysis to the immediate context of each example; his list is far from complete, and matters are more complicated.

Granted the assumption that the figure can be chosen deliberately, it is usually not difficult to divine the author's purpose. In the passage we are considering, as frequently, it is necessary to consider form, content, and context. Aristotle says that Solon had the choice of becoming a tyrant by throwing his lot in with one side or the other but chose to incur the enmity of both, σώσας

κτλ. The context is one of factional dissatisfaction with Solon, of implicit criticism and defence. A similar content/context is found previously. When the
Solonian strategy of σεισαχθεία became known in advance and some of his
friends profited from it, he was accused of collusion. In a passage (6.3) we
have considered in another context,[3] Aristotle replied:

> οὐ γὰρ εἰκὸς ἐν μὲν τοῖς ἄλλοις οὕτω μέτριον γενέσθαι καὶ κοινόν, ὥστ᾽
> ἐξὸν αὐτῷ τοὺς ἑτέρους ὑποποιησάμενον τυραννεῖν τῆς πόλεως, ἀμφοτέροις
> ἀπεχθέσθαι καὶ περὶ πλείονος ποιήσασθαι τὸ καλὸν καὶ τὴν τῆς πόλεως
> σωτηρίαν ἢ τὴν αὐτοῦ πλεονεξίαν, ἐν οὕτω δὲ μικροῖς καὶ ἀναξίοις
> καταρρυπαίνειν ἑαυτόν

> Solon was so moderate and impartial in other respects that, when he could have
> gotten the rest of the people into his power and made himself tyrant over the city,
> he instead accepted the hatred of both sides and set a higher value on honor and
> the safety of the city than on his own advantage.

If we take away from this passage what is necessary to its specific context
(viz., οὐ γὰρ–κοινόν; ἢ τήν–ἑαυτόν) both passages are almost exactly alike,
but there is one small detail in which they differ: the phrase περὶ πλείονος
τὸ καλὸν καὶ τὴν τῆς πόλεως σωτηρίαν is matched by σώσας τὴν πατρίδα
καὶ τὰ βέλτιστα νομοθέτησας. The word σώσας goes with σωτηρίαν and
τὸ καλόν with τὰ βέλτιστα. Solon's general principle of acting κατὰ τὸ
καλόν is exemplified by νομοθετήσας. One result of reading these passages
as paratexts is that another chiastic structure is observed: περὶ πλείονος τὸ
καλὸν (A), τὴν τῆς πόλεως σωτηρίαν (B) // σώσας τὴν πατρίδα[4] (B¹),
τὰ βέλτιστα νομοθετήσας (A¹).

On the other hand, occasionally Aristotle's purpose is easier to detect. At
24.3–25.1 chiastic order occurs in a ring frame: after Aristeides has advised
Athens to seize hegemony, κατέστησαν δὲ τοῖς πολλοῖς [A] εὐπορίαν
τροφῆς [B] (they provided ample maintenance for the common people): there
follows a list of citizens and officials who were supported, and Aristotle rounds
off ἡ μὲν οὖν τροφὴ [B¹] τῷ δήμῳ [A¹] διὰ τούτων ἐγένετο (that is how
maintenance for the people came into being). Here, the chiastic order helps to
preserve continuity, τὸ συνεχὲς τοῦ λόγου, as it does in Homer.[5] The continuity is that of process, from number (οἱ πολλοί) to a group functioning
politically (ὁ δῆμος).[6]

In what follows I propose to give a complete list of instances of chiastic
structure. In the course of this investigation, two things should be kept in mind:
(1) some instances of this phenomenon will be verbal, some syntactical, some
both. An example of syntactical structure is the first text discussed above, with
two aorist active participles governing two accusatives. A verbal structure is
illustrated by the larger chiasmus, with σώσας and σωτηρίαν having the same
root. It is legitimate to treat τὸ καλόν and τὰ βελτίστα as verbally linked
because they belong to the same semantic field. (2) It was observed of ring
composition that, when the complex type is used, the outer elements (A/A¹)
have a tendency to be more important than the inner elements (B/B¹), and, if

Kaibel is correct, the same tendency will be operative here. By its nature, chiasmus is complex, but it is not clear what are the criteria by which to judge here the operation of this tendency. In the larger structure above, for example, it is arguable that a general moral principle (A), actualized by a historical example (A¹), is more important, more "philosophic," if you will, than the effect of specific historical acts (B/B¹). With reference to the smaller structure, we cannot look for this tendency: although B¹ (the quality of the act) and A¹ (the act) are separable, A and B are not. Thus, we may expect the tendency to exist in verbal, but not in syntactical, chiasmus.[7]

I

3.6: the Council of the Areopagus διῴκει [A] δὲ τὰ πλεῖστα καὶ τὰ μέγιστα [B] τῶν ἐν τῇ πόλει, καὶ κολάζουσα [C] καὶ ζημιοῦσα [D] πάντας τοὺς ἀκοσμοῦντας κυρίως. 8.4: καὶ τά τε ἄλλα τὰ πλεῖστα καὶ τὰ μέγιστα [B¹] τῶν πολιτικῶν διετήρει [A¹] καὶ τοὺς ἁμαρτάνοντας ηὔθυνεν κυρία οὖσα καὶ ζημιοῦν [D¹] καὶ κολάζειν [C¹] (the Council of the Areopagus had the function of watching over the laws, and it administered most and the greatest of the city's affairs, having full power to chastise and punish all the disorderly) [A/B/B¹/A¹: verbal/syntactical, C/D/D¹/C¹ verbal].

The two passages are thematically[8] related, but the relation is created by the repeated language. It may be that the relation is pointed up or reinforced by the chiasmus, and the most complete treatment of the theme, in chapter 45.1, is characterized by the allied structure of ring composition. κολάζειν does not recur in the Ἀθπολ, but ζημιοῦν and κύριος + inf. belong to the language of documentary description.[9]

5.1: τῶν πολλῶν [A] δουλευόντων τοῖς ὀλίγοις [B], ἀντέστη τοῖς γνωρίμοις [B¹] ὁ δῆμος [A¹] (the many were enslaved to the few, the people rose against the notables) [verbal]. The text completes a ring pattern framing the description of the political and economic conditions prior to Solon. The static tendency of that frame is at once preserved and broken by this passage. It is preserved by the genitives absolute τοιαύτης δὲ τῆς τάξεως οὔσης ἐν τῇ πολιτείᾳ (5.1) and τῶν πολλῶν δουλευόντων : it is broken by the main verb ἀντέστη and by a shift from the economic plane to the political[10] plane effected by the change from the "economic" πολλοί/ὀλίγοι to the "political" γνώριμοι/δῆμος. The emphasis is clearly on οἱ πολλοί/ὁ δῆμος, for, from this point on, the history of the Athenian πολιτεία will be the history of this body.

5.2: εἵλοντο [A] . . . Σόλωνα [B] καὶ τὴν πολιτείαν [B¹] ἐπέτρεψαν [A¹] (appoint Solon . . . and entrusted the state to him) [syntactical].

5.2: εἵλοντο [A] κοινῇ [B] . . . κοινῇ [B¹] παραινεῖ [A¹] (urges them to join together) [verbal, syntactical]. The first elements (A/B) describe the action of both sides in electing Solon, the second set (B¹/A¹) is the articulation of his programme affecting both sides. Within this structure he is portrayed as a political neutral.

5.2/3: κοινῇ [A] παραινεῖ [B] . . . παραινῶν [B¹] τοῖς πλουσίοις [A¹] (urging the rich) [verbal, structural]. Aristotle uses the second term of the previous set in loose anaphora to shift Solon's stance from one of political neutrality to one of moral partiality.

A: ἐν ᾗ πρὸς ἑκατέρους ὑπὲρ ἑκατέρων διαμάχεται κτλ. (in this poem he fights against each side on behalf of the other)

B: κοινῇ παραινεῖ

B¹: παραινῶν τοῖς πλουσίοις

A¹: ἀεὶ τὴν αἰτίαν τῆς στάσεως ἀνάπτει τοῖς πλουσίοις. (he everywhere lays the blame for the strife on the rich).

The objective statements (A/A¹) surround the chiasmus (B/B¹), the chiasmus is effected by the anaphora of παραινεῖν, and the shift from the politico-economic to the moral sphere is signalled by αἰτίαν and underlined by the anaphoric repetition of τοῖς πλουσίοις. It is noteworthy that the structure here is closely enmeshed within the content, or, to put it another way, the literary touches combine with objective statements in a manner which itself produces a chiastic structure:

8.5: ὁρῶν [sc., Solon] δὲ τὴν μὲν πόλιν [A] πολλάκις στασιάζουσαν [B] . . . ὃς ἂν στασιαζούσης [B¹] τῆς πολεως [A¹] (seeing that the city was often in a state of strife . . . when the city was torn by strife) [verbal]. The AB order may have been influenced by the syntax. Having begun with a verb governing two objects,[11] each of which is qualified by a different participle, Aristotle may have thought the order V(erb)V, instead of VO(bject), too confining. A more important determinant will have been the content. The emphasis here is on the πόλις and, I suggest, on the πόλις as unified. The reason for the suggestion is that the language recurs: στασιαζούσης [A] τῆς πόλεως [B] . . . τῆς πόλεως [B¹] μὴ μετέχειν [A¹] [verbal].[12]

9.1–2: κύριος [A] γὰρ ὢν ὁ δῆμος [B] τῆς ψήφου [C] . . . ὅπως ᾖ τῆς κρίσεως [C¹] ὁ δῆμος [B¹] κύριος [A¹] (when the people are masters of the vote . . . in order that the power of decision should rest with the people) [verbal, syntactical]. The purpose of the structure is to set off the treatment of an important theme, which element of the state has τὸ κῦρος. A/B/C set up a condition, C¹/B¹/A¹ a result. That this result was Solon's intention is denied. That the condition is valid is shown by 41.2, which is closely connected in theme to this chapter. Kaibel (101) pointed out that there are only two instances of (initial) anaphora in the *AthPol*. The first is at 9.1: κύριος γὰρ ὤ ν ὁ δῆμος τῆς ψήφου, κύριος γίγνεται τῆς πολιτείας (they are masters of the state). The second is at 41.2: ἁπάντων γὰρ αὐτὸς αὑτὸν πεποίηκεν ὁ δῆμος κύριον, καὶ πάντα διοκεῖται ψηφίσμασιν καὶ δικαστηρίοις, ἐν οἷς ὁ δῆμός ἐστιν ὁ κρατῶν (the people have made themselves masters of everything, and control all things by means of decrees and jury courts, in which the sovereign power resides with the people). Here, the order is the same as in the second set of chapter 9 (B¹/A¹), and ἁπάντων (= C¹) is more inclusive than ψῆφος/κρίσις because decisions of the assembly have been added to those of the courts.

13.1: οὐ κατέστησαν [A] ἄρχοντα [B] . . . ἀναρχίαν [B¹] ἐποίησαν [A¹] (prevented the appointment of an archon . . . there was no archon) [verbal, syntactical]. One phase in the development of the archonship is finished.

13.2: ἔτη [A] δύο [B] καὶ δύο [B¹] μῆνας [A¹] (for two years and two months) [verbal, syntactical]. Another phase is completed.

13.4: ὧν [A] προειστήκει [B] . . . ἐδόκουν μάλιστα διώκειν [C] τὴν μέσην πολιτείαν [D] . . . τὴν ὀλιγαρχίαν [D¹] ἐζήτουν [C¹] · ἡγεῖτο [B¹] αὐτῶν [A¹] (led by . . . whose particular objective seemed to be the middle form of constitution . . . whose aim was oligarchy, and who were led by) [verbal, syntactical]. There are two structures in this segment: the first is serial, μία μὲν τῶν παραλίων . . . , ἄλλη δὲ τῶν πεδιακῶν, . . . τρίτη δ᾽ ἡ τῶν διακρίων (one the men of the coast; another the men of the plain . . . and the third, the men of the Diakria]. This is inclusive and treats all three groups as on the same level. The chiastic structure is exclusive, encloses the first two groups, and thus leaves the emphasis to fall on the third group, that led by Peisistratus.[13]

14.2: αὐτὸς [A] μὲν ἔφη [B] βεβοηθηκέναι [C] τῇ πατρίδι [D] . . . ἀξιοῦν [B¹] δὲ καὶ τοὺς ἄλλους [A¹] ταὐτὸ τοῦτο [D¹] ποιεῖν [C¹] (he said that he had helped his country . . . and called on the others to do likewise) [syntactical]. The contrasts here are A/B over against B¹/A¹, Solon's statement over against his claim on others, and the verbal contrast C/D/D¹/C¹, verb/noun, pronoun/verb.

16.3: ἐν τῷ ἄστει [A] διατρίβωσιν [B] ἀλλὰ διεσπαρμένοι [B¹] κατὰ τὴν χώραν [A¹] (they should spend their time not in the city but scattered about the countryside) [verbal, syntactical].

16.3: εὐπορῶντες [A] τῶν μετρίων [B] καὶ πρὸς τοῖς ἰδίοις [B¹] ὄντες [A¹] (they should have reasonable means of subsistence, and should concentrate on their private affairs) [syntactical].

16.3: πρὸς τοῖς ἰδίοις [A] ὄντες [B] μήτ᾽ ἐπιθυμῶσι μήτε σχολάζωσιν ἐπιμελεῖσθαι [B¹] τῶν κοινῶν [A¹] (and have neither the desire nor the leisure to take an interest in public affairs) [syntactical]. These three passages form part of a larger pattern informing the account of Peisistratean policies.[14]

16.8: αὐτὸς μὲν ἀπήντησεν [A] ὡς ἀπολογησάμενος [B], ὁ δὲ προσκαλεσάμενος [B¹] φοβηθεὶς ἔλιπεν [A¹] (he attended to make his defence—but the prosecutor took fright and defaulted) [syntactical].

18.1: Ἵππαρχος [A] καὶ Ἱππίας [B] . . . Ἱππίας [B¹] . . . Ἵππαρχος [A¹] [verbal, syntactical]. The point of this is presumably to put the emphasis on Hipparchus, the future victim of the assassination.

18.2: οὐ κατεῖχε [A] τὴν ὀργήν [B]. . . .18.6: ὑπὸ τῆς ὀργῆς [B¹] οὐ κατέσχεν [A¹] ἑαυτόν (he could not suppress his anger. . . .unable to control his anger) [verbal, syntactical]: the emotional framework of the assassination of Hipparchus.

19.1: διὰ τὸ τιμωρεῖν [A] τἀδελφῷ [B] καὶ διὰ τὸ πολλοὺς [B¹] ἀνῃρηκέναι καὶ ἐκβεβληκέναι [A¹] (took revenge for his brother's death, with many executions and expulsions) [syntactical]. The emphasis is on the actions of the Peisistratids, illustrating the first sentence of the chapter, πολλῷ τραχυτέραν εἶναι τὴν τυραννίδα (the tyranny became much more cruel), which itself fulfills the prediction of 16.7.

19.2: ἔτει δὲ τετάρτῳ [A] μετὰ τὸν Ἱππάρχου θάνατον [B]. . . . 19.6: ἐπὶ Ἁρπακτίδου ἄρχοντος κατασχόντες τὴν τυραννίδα μετὰ τὴν τοῦ πατρὸς τελευτὴν [B¹] ἔτη μάλιστα ἑπτακαίδεκα [A¹] (about the fourth year after the death of Hipparchus . . . in the archonship of Harpactides: the Peisistratids had held the tyranny for about seventeen years after their father's death) [verbal, syntactical]. This is a unique usage of a chronological formula[15] in which one element (ἐπὶ ἄρχοντος) is delayed, and in which the formula and its repetition frame the narrative.

19.5: κατὰ θάλατταν [A] ἔχοντα [B] στρατιάν [C] . . . στόλον [C¹] ἔχοντα [B¹] μείζω κατὰ γῆν [A¹] (who took a force by sea . . . by land with a larger force) [verbal, syntactical]. The emphasis is on sea and land, and is intended to repeat by means of structure a similar contrast in Herodotus' description (5.64) of the conflict: οὐκέτι κατὰ θάλασσαν στείλαντες ἀλλὰ κατ' ἤπειρον (they did not send these troops by sea but by the mainland).

20.1–2: ἡττώμενος [A] δὲ ταῖς ἑταιρείαις [B] ὁ Κλεισθένης [C]. . . . ὁ δὲ Ἰσαγόρας [C¹] ἐπιλειπόμενος [A¹] τῇ δυνάμει [B¹] (as Cleisthenes was getting the worse of the party struggle. . . . Isagoras then fell behind in power). The chiastic order complements the elaborate ring frame of the chapter. δύναμις is the genus of which ἑταιρεῖαι are a species.

20.3: τῆς δὲ βουλῆς [A] ἀντιστάσης [B] καὶ συναθροισθέντος [B¹] τοῦ πλήθους [A¹] (the council resisted and the common people gathered in force) [syntactical].

21.2–4: ὅπως μετάσχωσι [A] πλείους [B]. . . . ὅπως ἑκάστη [B¹] μετέχῃ [A¹] . . . [verbal, syntactical]. There is a nice verbal–syntactical balance in this section:

1a: ὅπως μετάσχωσι . . . πολιτείας (so that more men would have a share)

1b: ὅθεν ἐλέχθη . . . βουλομένους (this is the origin of the saying . . . wishing)

2: ὅπως αὐτῷ μὴ συμβαίνῃ . . . τριττῦς (to avoid allocating them by the existing thirds)

3: ὅπως ἑκάστη μετέχῃ . . . τόπων (that each tribe should have a share in all the regions)

4a: ἵνα μὴ . . . ἀναγορεύωσιν (that they should not use their fathers' names)

4b: ὅθεν καὶ καλοῦσιν . . . δήμων (this is why the Athenians still call themselves after their demes).

Each of the first four actions of Cleisthenes is accompanied by a purpose clause: the first and third clauses are positive (ὅπως), the second and fourth negative (ὅπως μή, ἵνα μη). The first and last measures are closed off by ὅθεν clauses (ὅθεν ἐλέχθη, ὅθεν καὶ καλοῦσιν).

22.1: καινοὺς δ' ἄλλους [A] θεῖναι [B] . . . ἐτέθη [B¹] καὶ ὁ περὶ τοῦ ὀστρακισμοῦ νόμος [A¹] (enacted other new laws, . . . among them the law about ostracism) [verbal]. This is a variation of the familiar formula in which ἄλλα are mentioned but not specified, and attention is focused on the second, specific, term.

23.3: Ἀριστείδης ὁ Λυσιμάχου [A] καὶ Θεμιστοκλῆς ὁ Νεοκλέους [B], ὁ μὲν [Ba] τὰ πολέμια ⟨δοκῶν⟩, ὁ δὲ [Aa] τὰ πολιτικά. . . . ἐχρῶντο τῷ μὲν [B¹] στρατηγῷ, τῷ δὲ [A¹] συμβούλῳ (Aristeides son of Lysimachus and Themistocles son of Neocles: Themistocles practiced the military arts, while Aristeides was skilled in the political arts . . . the Athenians used the first as a general and the second as an adviser) [verbal, syntactical]. In chapter 2 a ring frame was used to subordinate the economic to the political plane: here the same device functions to make the (political) outer element more important than the (military) inner one.[16]

23.4: ἐπὶ δὲ τὴν ἀπόστασιν [A] τὴν τῶν Ἰώνων [B] ἐκ τῆς τῶν Λακεδαιμονίων [B¹] συμμαχίας [A¹] (urged the Ionians to break away from the Spartan alliance) [syntactical]. The jingle effect may have helped to determine the order: the text continues Ἀριστείδης ἦν ὁ προτρέψας, *τηρήσας* κτλ [verbal, syntactical].

24.1: θαρρούσης [A] ἤδη τῆς πόλεως [B] καὶ χρήματων [B¹] ἠθροισμένων [A¹] πολλῶν (now that the city was confident and a large amount of money had been collected) [syntactical].

25.2: πρῶτον μὲν ἀνεῖλεν [A] πολλοὺς [B] τῶν Ἀρεοπαγιτῶν [C]. . . . ἔπειτα τῆς βουλῆς [C¹] ἐπὶ Κόνωνος ἄρχοντος ἅπαντα [B¹] περιεῖλε [A¹] (first he eliminated many of its members, . . . then in the archonship of Conon he took away from the council all) [verbal, syntactical].[17]

This is the first part of an unusually complex display of chiastic structure. As it stands, it is incomplete, because ἅπαντα has no referent. By making use of the figure of hyperbaton, Aristotle effects a transition to another instance of the structure: the text continues: περιεῖλε [A] τὰ ἐπίθετα [B] δι' ὧν ἦν τῆς πολιτείας φυλακή, καὶ τὰ μὲν [B¹] τοῖς πεντακοσίοις τὰ δὲ (B¹) τῷ δήμῳ καὶ τοῖς δικαστηρίοις ἀπέδωκεν [A¹] (all the accretions which gave it its guardianship of the constitution, giving some to the Council of Five Hundred and some to the people and the jury courts). The complexity of this structure is surely intended to underscore the importance of the content. We have seen that the δῆμος increases its power and it does so by appropriating to itself functions antecedently wielded by other organs of the state. The phrase, δι' ὧν ἦν τῆς πολιτείας φυλακή, echoes Aristotle's previous statement on the Council of the Areopagus (8.4): ἐπὶ τὸ νομοφυλακεῖν, ὥσπερ ὑπῆρχεν καί πρότερον ἐπίσκοπος οὖσα τῆς πολιτείας (to guard the laws, just as previously it had been overseer of the constitution). Aristotle here says that some functions were transferred to the assembly and courts, some to the Council of the Five Hundred. The process will be continued until (41.2): αἱ τῆς βουλῆς κρίσεις εἰς τὸν δῆμον ἐληλύθασιν (even the jurisdiction of the council has been transferred to the people).[18]

26.1: ἡγεμόνα [A] ἔχειν (B) τοὺς ἐπιεκεστέρους [C], ἀλλ' αὐτῶν [C¹] προεστάναι [Β¹] Κίμωνα τὸν Μιλτιάδου [Α¹] (the better sort had no leader, but their champion was Cimon son of Miltiades) [syntactical].

27.3, 5: Περικλῆς [Α] πρῶτος [Β] . . . πρώτου [Β¹] καταδείξαντος Ἀνύτου [Α¹] (Pericles was the first. . . . the way was first shown by Anytus) [verbal, syntactical]. The structure locks together Pericles' measure and one result of it.[19]

27.3: Κίμων [Α] ἅτε τυραννικὴν ἔχων [Β] οὐσίαν [C]. . . . 27.4: ἐπιλειπόμενος [Β¹] ὁ Περικλῆς [Α¹] τῇ οὐσίᾳ [C¹] (Cimon was as rich as a tyrant. . . . Pericles' property was insufficient for this kind of service) [verbal, syntactical]. As in chapter 21, this pattern occurs within a highly structured chapter. The next two examples also show slight divergences from the rigid structure.

28.1: Περικλῆς [Α] προεστήκει [Β] τοῦ δήμου, βελτίω [C] τὰ κατὰ τὸ πόλεμον ἦν, τελευτήσαντος [Β¹] δὲ Περικλέους [Α¹] πολὺ χείρω [C¹] (while Pericles was champion of the people the constitution was not in too bad a state, but after his death it became much worse) [verbal, syntactical]. The formula is partly preserved, insofar as we have A/B/B¹/A¹. Aristotle needs to keep this to implement other strategies in the chapter.[20] A by-product of that choice was to sharpen the contrast between C and C¹ because of their unusual (for this structure) position.

27.3–28.3: ἐποίησε [Α]. . . . Περικλῆς πρῶτος [Β] . . . πρώτου [Β¹] καταδείξαντος [Α¹] . . . πρῶτος [Β²] . . . ἀνέκραγε [Α²]. . . . ἐπόρισε [Α³] πρῶτος [Β³]. . . . πρῶτος [Β⁴] ὑποσχόμενος [Α⁴] [verbal, syntactical]. The complex linking is another indication that chapters 27 and 28 belong together: cf. chapter 6, ''Methods and Purposes.''

29.1: εἰπόντος [Α] . . . λόγον [Β] Μηλοβίου [C], τὴν δὲ γνώμην [Β¹] ἀναγράψαντος [Α¹] Πυθοδώρου [C¹] (the speech introducing the decree was made by Melobius, and the motion stood in the name of Pythodorus) [syntactical]. [Cf. chapter 12, ''A Constitutional Formula.''] Here, the position of C/C¹ may be for purposes of balance rather than contrast.

32.1: Θαργηλιῶνος [Α] τετράδι ἐπὶ δέκα [Β], . . . ἐνάτῃ [Β¹] φθίνοντος Θαργηλιῶνος [Α¹] (on 14 Thargelion. . . . on 22 Thargelion) [verbal, syntactical]. This is the clearest sign of the fact that chiastic structure can be the result of deliberate choice. In the Athenian formula for dating, the month precedes the day, and does not follow it, as it does in B¹/A¹.[21]

33.2: ἅπαντα [Α] γὰρ δι᾽ αὐτῶν [Β] ἔπραττον [C], οὐδὲν [Α¹] ἐπαναφέροντες [C¹] τοῖς πεντακισχιλίοις [Β¹] (they did everything on their own and referred nothing to the Five Thousand) [syntactica]. The usual order is broken to create a strong contrast between A and A¹.

34.3: Λυσάνδρου [Α] δὲ προσθεμένου [Β] τοῖς ὀλιγαρχικοῖς [C], καταπλαγεὶς [Β¹] ὁ δῆμος [Α¹] ἠναγκάσθη χειροτονεῖν τὴν ὀλιγαρχίαν [C¹] (Lysander gave his support to the oligarchs, and the people were intimidated and compelled to decide in favor of the oligarchy) [syntactical].

34.2: κύριον [Α] γενόμενον [Β] τῆς πόλεως [C]. . . . 35.1: γενόμενοι [Β¹] κύριοι [Α¹] τῆς πόλεως [C¹] (became master of the city. . . . having become masters of the city). [verbal, syntactical]. Both of these passages exhibit the same structure: A/B/C/B¹/A¹/C¹. The phrase κύριος τῆς πόλεως has overtones of tyranny, and I suggest that the purpose of the arrangement is to emphasize Lysander's support of an oligarchy which turned into a tyranny.

35.1–2: τὰ μὲν ἄλλα [A] τὰ δόξαντα περὶ τῆς πολιτείας παρεώρων [B]. . . . τοῦτ' ἔδρων [B¹] καὶ ἐπὶ τῶν ἄλλων [A¹] (they ignored the other resolutions about the constitution. . . . they did likewise in the other cases) [verbal, syntactical].

35.4: οὐδενὸς [A] ἀπείχοντο [B] τῶν πολιτῶν ἀλλ' ἀπέκτειναν [B¹] τοὺς καὶ ταῖς οὐσίαις καὶ τῷ γένει καὶ τοῖς ἀξιώμασιν προέχοντας [A¹] (they left none of the citizens alone, but put to death those who were outstanding for their wealth, birth, or reputation). There is a contrast between οὐδενός and προέχοντας and word play in ἀπείχοντο and ἀπέκτειναν.

36.1: τῆς μὲν ἀσελγείας [A] αὐτοῖς [B] παρῄνει παύσασθαι [C], μεταδοῦναι [C¹] δὲ τῶν πραγμάτων [A¹] τοῖς βελτίστοις [B¹] (urged the Thirty to abandon their outrageous behavior and give the best men a share in affairs) [syntactical]. The contrast in A/A¹ is between aberrant behavior (ἀσέλγεια) and normality (πράγματα) . There is also an implicit moral contrast between αὐτοῖς and βελτίστοις.

36.1: διεσπάρησαν [A] οἱ λόγοι [B] πρὸς τὸ πλῆθος [C] καὶ πρὸς τὸν Θηραμένην [C¹] οἰκείως εἶχον [A¹] οἱ πολλοί [B¹] (when his arguments gained currency among the masses and the ordinary people became well disposed to him) [syntactical]. Both passages from 36.1 have the same order: ABC/C¹A¹B¹, but a verbal parallelism leaves τὸ πλῆθος and οἱ πολλοί in the same position in the second passage. The positions of C and C¹ may be intended to link Theramenes and τὸ πλῆθος.

36.2: μεταδοῦναι [A] τοῖς ἐπιεικέσι [B] τρισχιλίοις μόνοις [B¹] μεταδιδόασι [A¹] (to give a ahare to the better sort, but were going to give a share only to three thousand) [verbal, syntactical].

36.2: βίαιόν [A] τε τὴν ἀρχὴν [B] καὶ τῶν ἀρχομένων [B¹] ἥττω [A¹] κατασκευάζοντες (set up a regime based on force, and make the rulers weaker than the subjects) [verbal, syntactical]. A memorable phrase, the point of which is sharpened by Aristotle's order: compare Xenophon's (*Hell.* 2.3.19): βιαίαν τε τὴν ἀρχὴν καὶ ἥττονα τῶν ἀρχομένων.

36.2: τὸν δὲ κατάλογον [A] . . . ὑπερεβάλλοντο [B] καὶ παρ' αὑτοῖς ἐφύλαττον [B¹] τοὺς ἐγνωσμένους [A¹] (they postponed publishing the register . . . and kept to themselves the names of those they had decided upon) [syntactical].

38.1: τοὺς μὲν τριάκοντα [A] κατέλυσαν [B], αἱροῦνται [B¹] δὲ δέκα [A¹] (they deposed the Thirty and elected ten) [verbal, syntactical].

38.3: τὰς διαλύσεις [A] γενέσθαι [B] καὶ κατελθεῖν [B¹] τὸν δῆμον [A¹] (the reconciliation took place and the people returned to Athens) [syntactical].

38.4: λαβόντες [A] τὴν ἐπιμέλειαν [B] ἐν ὀλιγαρχίᾳ [C], τὰς εὐθύνας [B¹] ἔδοσαν [A¹] ἐν δημοκρατίᾳ [C¹] (having accepted responsibility under the oligarchy they submitted to examination under the democracy) [verbal, syntactical]. The rigid pattern is broken to put oligarchy and democracy in contrasting positions, again with A/B/B¹/A¹ forming an enclosure.

38.4: the passage just discussed is enclosed within another chiastic structure: οἱ δὲ περὶ τὸν Ῥίνωνα [A] . . . ἐπηνέθησαν [B], . . . ἡρέθη [B¹] Ῥίνων [A¹] (Rhinon and his supporters were praised, . . .Rhinon was elected) [verbal, syntactical].

39.1: αὐτοκράτορας [A] ἑαυτῶν [B] καὶ τὰ αὐτῶν [B¹] καρπουμένους [A¹] (with full power and authority over themselves, and continue to draw the revenues from their own property) [syntactical].

39.2: μὴ ἐξεῖναι [A] δὲ μήτε τοῖς Ἐλευσινόθεν [B] εἰς τὸ ἄστυ [C] μήτε τοῖς ἐκ τοῦ ἄστεως [C¹] Ἐλευσινάδε [B¹] ἰέναι [A¹] (no one from Eleusis was to go to the city, and no one from the city was to go to Eleusis) [verbal, syntactical].

39.6: ἐὰν διδῶσιν [A] εὐθύνας [B]. εὐθύνας [B¹] δὲ δοῦναι [A¹] (if they successfully submitted to an examination. The examination was to take place) [verbal, syntactical]. In all three passages from 39, Aristotle is using documentation, but the form may be his own.

II

The next set of instances is taken from chapters 42–69.

42.2: ἐκ τῶν φυλετῶν [A], . . . σωφρονιστὴν [B] καὶ κοσμητὴν [B¹] ἐκ τῶν ἄλλων Ἀθηναίων [A¹] (from each tribe as *sophronistes,* and from the citizen body as a whole they elect a single *cosmetes*) [syntactical]. The order may be intended to point up the contrast in those eligible for appointment, members of the relevant tribe, and the whole body of male citizens.

42.3: συλλαβόντες [A] δ᾽ οὗτοι τοὺς ἐφήβους [B] πρῶτον μὲν τὰ ἱερὰ [B¹] περιῆλθον [A¹] [syntactical]. εἶτ᾽ εἰς Πειραιέα [A] πορεύονται [B] καὶ φρουροῦσι [B¹] οἱ μὲν τὴν Μουνιχίαν [A¹], οἱ δὲ τὴν Ἀκτήν [A¹] (the cadets assemble under these officers, and first make a tour of the sanctuaries, then proceed to the Peiraeus, where some do guard duty at Munychia and some at Akte) [syntactical]. δίδωσι καὶ εἰς τροφὴν τοῖς μὲν σωφρονισταῖς δραχμὴν [A] ά [B] ἑκάστῳ, τοῖς δ᾽ ἐφήβοις τέτταρας [B¹] ὀβόλους [A¹] ἑκάστῳ (for maintenance one drachma each is provided for the *sophronistae* and four obols for the cadets) [syntactical].

43.2 : αἱ μὲν πρῶται [A] τέτταρες [B], . . . αἱ δὲ ς´ [B¹] αἱ ὕστεραι [A¹] (the first four for thirty-six days each and the remaining six for thirty-five days each) [verbal, syntactical].

43.3,4: καὶ ὅσα δει, . . . οὗτοι [A] προγράφουσι [B]. προγράφουσι [B¹] δὲ καὶ τὰς ἐκκλησίας οὗτοι [A¹] (they prescribe what business, . . . likewise they prescribe the meetings of the assembly) [verbal, syntactical]. The first order refers back to one subject, the βουλή: the reverse order refers forward to another, the ἐκκλησία.

44.1,2: οὗτος [A] δ᾽ ἐπιστατεῖ [B]. . . . τηρεῖ [B¹] δ᾽ οὗτος [A¹] (he is in charge. . . . the same man keeps) [verbal, syntactical]. The first clause is general, the second contains specific functions.

45.1,4: Ἡ δὲ βουλὴ [A] πρότερον μὲν ἦν κυρία [B]. . . . τούτων μὲν οὖν ἄκυρός [B¹] ἐστιν ἡ βουλή [A¹] (formerly the council had full power. . . . in those matters the council does not have final power) [verbal, syntactical]. See chapters 4 and 18, "The Unity of the Ἀθπολ" and "Chapter 45: ἡ βουλή."

45.2–3: ἔφεσις [A] δὲ καὶ τούτοις [B]. . . . νῦν δὲ τούτοις [B¹] ἔφεσις [A¹] (here too there is a reference. . . . there is reference to the jury court in these cases) [verbal, syntactical].

46.2: τῷ τε δήμῳ [A] τοῦτον ἀποφαίνει [B] καὶ καταγνοῦσα παραδίδωσι [B¹] τῷ δικαστηρίῳ [A¹] (it reports him to the people, convicts him and hands him over to a jury court) [syntactical].

Nothing approaching a full-scale study of chiastic order in Greek prose exists: neither the generalized approach of Denniston nor the specific one of Rehdantz[22] leads one to believe that the phenomenon was particularly widespread. To show that chiasmus was so peculiarly an aspect of Aristotle's style as to include it as a criterion in the question of authorship would require that kind of study. This I do not propose. Instead, I will examine Aristotle's use of it in that book of the *Politics*, 5, which is the most "historical" one.[23]

1301A34–5: ἀξιοῦσι [A] μετέχειν [B]. . . . πλεονεκτεῖν [B¹] ζητοῦσιν [A¹] (claim equal participation. . . . seek to get a larger share) [syntactical].

1301B8–9: ἐκ δημοκρατίας [A] ὀλιγαρχίαν [B] ἢ δημοκρατίαν [B¹] ἐξ ὀλιγαρχίας [A¹] (from democracy to oligarchy or from oligarchy to democracy) [verbal, syntactical].

1302A10–2: ἥ τε πρὸς ἀλλήλους [A] στάσις καὶ ἔτι ἡ πρὸς τὸν δῆμον [B]. . . . ἡ πρὸς τὴν ὀλιγαρχίαν [B¹] μόνον, αὐτῷ δὲ πρὸς αὐτόν [A¹] (two factions, one between the oligarchs themselves and one between the oligarchs and the people. . . . against oligarchy; internal faction within a democracy) [verbal, syntactical].

1302A32–3: κέρδος [A] καὶ τίμη [B]. . . . ἀτιμίαν [B¹] φεύγοντες καὶ ζημίαν [A¹] (profit and honor. . . . to avoid dishonor and loss) [verbal, syntactical].

1303A29–30: Τροιζηνίοις [A] Ἀχαιοὶ [B] συνῴκησαν . . . πλείους οἱ Ἀχαιοὶ [B¹] γενόμενοι ἐξέβαλον τοὺς Τροιζηνίους [A¹] (Achaeans were associated with Troezenians. . . . becoming more numerous, they cast out the Troezenians) [verbal, syntactical].

1304A9: ἦρξε [A] τῆς στάσεως [B] καὶ τοὺς Ἀθηναίους [B¹] παρώξυνε [A¹] (he started the faction which spurred Athens into action) [syntactical].

1304A21–24: συντονωτέραν [A] ποιῆσαι [B] τὴν πολιτείαν [C]. . . . τὴν δημοκρατίαν [C¹] ἰσχυροτέραν [A¹] ἐποίησεν [B¹] (to have tightened up the constitution. . . . the Athenian democracy was strengthened) [verbal, syntactical].

1304A22–27: γενόμενος [A] αἴτιος [B]. . . . αἴτιος [B¹] γενόμενος

[A¹] (who had been responsible. . . . responsibility for the victory) [verbal, syntactical].

1308B6–9: ἐν μὲν γὰρ ταῖς ὀλιγαρχίαις [A] καὶ ταῖς πολιτείαις [B]. . . . ἐκ μὲν πολιτείας [B¹] δημοκρατίαν, ἐκ δ᾽ ὀλιγαρχίας [A¹] (in oligarchies and polities. . . . from polity to democracy and from oligarchy) [verbal, syntactical].

1308B27–8: ἀντικεῖσθαι τοὺς ἐπιεικεῖς [A] τῷ πλήθει [B] καὶ τοὺς ἀπόρους [B¹] τοῖς εὐπόροις [A¹] (the respectable sort as contrasted with the generality, and the wealthy as contrasted with the indigent) [syntactical].²⁴

1309A1–3: τοὺς γνωρίμους [A] καὶ τὸ πλῆθος [B]. . . . πᾶσιν ἄρχειν δημοκρατικόν [B¹]. . . . γνωρίμους εἶναι ἐν ταῖς ἀρχαῖς ἀριστοκρατικόν [A¹] (the notables and the multitude. . . . it is democratic that holding office be open to all, aristocratic that the notables should fill them) [syntactical].

1310B19–20: παρεκβαινόντων [A] τὰ πάτρια [B] καὶ δεσποτικωτέρας ἀρχῆς [B¹] ὀρεγομένων [A¹] (deviated from ancestral traditions and were aiming at making their rule more masterlike) [syntactical].

1311A1–2: μηθὲν [A] ἄδικον πάσχωσιν [B]. . . . ὑβρίζηται [B¹] μηθέν [A¹] (against unjust losses, against any ill-treatment) [verbal, syntactical].

1312B17: προσλαβὼν [A] τὸν δῆμον [B], ἐκεῖνον [B¹] ἐκβαλών [A¹] (enlisted popular support; he threw out Dionysius) [verbal, syntactical].²⁵

1313A32: παραδιδοὺς [A] τοῖς υἱέσιν [B] ἢ παρὰ τοῦ πατρὸς [B¹] παρέλαβεν [A¹] (passing the kingdom on to his sons in a lesser state than he had inherited it from his father) [verbal, syntactical].

1314B2–3: ἀπ᾽ αὐτῶν [A] μὲν λαμβάνωσιν [B]. . . . διδῶσι [B¹] δ᾽ ἑταίραις καὶ ξένοις καὶ τεχνίταις [A¹] (gifts are extracted from them. . . . gives to his mistresses, to foreigners, and to his skilled craftsmen) [syntactical].

1315B31–32: ἐν ἔτεσι [A] τριάκοντα καὶ τρισὶν [B] ἑπτακαίδεκα [B¹] ἔτη [A¹] (seventeen years out of thirty-three) [verbal, syntactical].

1315B36–7: Γέλων [A] μὲν γὰρ ἑπτὰ [B] τυραννήσας. . . . δέκα [B¹] δ᾽ Ἱέρων [A¹] (Gelon was tyrant for seven years. . . . Hieron for ten) [verbal, syntactical].

In the same book of the *Politics,* we may compare the interesting text at 1303A27—B3. The passage begins with a general thesis: διὸ ὅσοι ἤδη συνοίκους ἐδέξαντο ἢ ἐποίκους, οἱ πλεῖστοι διεστάσισαν (hence faction has been exceedingly common when the population has included an extraneous element, whether these have joined in the founding or have been taken on later). Thus, action in the first clause leads to a result in the second clause. Aristotle illustrates this thesis with eight examples: in each, the order of the statement of the thesis is followed. Linguistic elements in the first clause are used in each example in a fairly loose structure; a linguistic element from the second clause is used in two examples, but it is not precisely the same (διαστασιάζειν/στασιάζειν) and in the second clauses a much more rigid structure is imposed:

A	συνῴκησαν	ἐξέβαλον	A
A¹	συνοικήσασιν	ἐξέπεσον	B
B	ἔποικοιη	ἐξέπεσον	B¹
C	εἰσδέξαμενοι	ἐξέβαλον	A¹
C¹	ὑποδεξάμενοι	ἐξέπεσον	B²
B¹	ἐποίκους	ἐστασίασαν	C
C²	δεξάμενοι	ἐξέπεσον	B³
B²	ἐποίκους		

Finally, I give a list of examples of the structure in the fragments of the πολιτεῖαι. The obvious theoretical difficulty in this attempt is that it is not possible accurately to tell to what extent the fragments preserve the *ipsissima verba* of Aristotle. This difficulty is compounded by the fact that the largest number of fragments[26] is preserved in a work Ἐκ τῶν Ἡρακλείδου περὶ πολιτειῶν written by one Heracleides Lembos around the middle of the second century B.C.[27] The specific difficulties involved are (1) that Heracleides' work is an epitome, (2) that the manuscript tradition contains an abridgment of Heracleides' original text, and (3) that in at least one way he adapted the word order of his original.[28] The great danger here is the possibility that he may be scrunching together the material of his source and thus giving a false impression of its contents.[29] On the other hand, his language is largely lifted straight from Aristotle, and he can be faithful to his text. Thus, he renders *AP* 18.1: ὁ δ᾽ Ἵππαρχος παιδιώδης καὶ ἐρωτικὸς καὶ φιλόμουσος ἦν. . . . Θέτταλος δὲ νεώτερος πολὺ καὶ τῷ βίῳ θρασὺς καὶ ὑβριστής by *[Exc.* 4] Ἵππαρχος ὁ υἱὸς Πεισιστράτου παιδιώδης ἦν καὶ ἐρωτικὸς καὶ φιλόμουσος, Θέτταλος δὲ νεώτερος καὶ θρασύς. The comparative fidelity of his version provides some grounds for confidence that he is also being careful in reproducing chiastic order.

The alternative orders being A/B/A¹/B¹ and A/B/B¹/A¹, in fragments of other works Heracleides has instances of both:

F3 (*FHG* 3.167–71): κτείνοντες [A] τούτους [B] καὶ συγκλείοντες [A¹] τὰς οἰκίας [B¹] (killing the men and locking up their houses), . . . οὔτε τοῖς ὕδασιν [A] ἦν χρῆσθαι [B] οὔτε τοὺς πόδας [A¹] ἐπὶ γῆν θεῖναι [B¹] (so that they could not have water nor put their feet on the land).

F6: τὸν [A] μὲν ἵππῳ κέλητι [B] νενικηκέναι, τὸν δὲ υἱὸν [A¹] αὐτοῦ. . . . πάλη [B¹] (he won in the horse race, his son in the footrace).

POxy. 11.1367, F 1.17–19: οἵ τε ἄγροι [A] διεφθάρησαν [B] καὶ ἡ οἰκία [A¹] συνέπεσεν [B¹] (the fields were destroyed and the house pulled down).

Outside the *Excerpts,* there is only one pure example of chiasmus, F9:

τελευτήσαντος [A] δ᾽ ᾽Αλεξάνδρου τοῦ Μακεδόνος [B] καὶ τῶν ᾽Αθηναίων [B¹] ἐκπεσόντων [A¹] ὑπὸ Περδίκκου (with the death of Alexander and the expulsion of the Athenians) [syntactical].

There are also two examples of mixed order; F5: ὀρθροβόαν [A] μὲν τὸν ἀλεκτρύονα [B] καλῶν καὶ βροτοκέρτην [A¹] τὸν κουρέα [B¹] καὶ τὴν δραχμὴν [B] ἀργυρίδα [A], τὴν δὲ χοίνικα [B¹] ἡμεροτροφίδα [A¹] καὶ τὸν κήρυκα [B²] ἀπύτην [A²] (calling the cock "dawn-crier," the barber "mortal-shaver," the drachma a "silver bit," the quart-measure "daily-feeder," and the herald "loud-bawler." [tr. Gulick]).

POxy. 11.1367, F1, 3–5, 8–10: [δίκην] [A] ἐπήνεγκαν [B] αὐτῷ ἑκατὸν καὶ ἐνενήκοντα [C] τάλαντα [D]. . . . ἄλλην [A¹] ἐπήνεγκαν [B¹] τάλαντα [D¹] [ἑκατὸν] πεντήκοντα [C¹] (they imposed a penalty of one hundred and ninety talents. . . . another of one hundred and fifty).

The examples of chiastic order I have found in the *Excerpts* are these:

Exc. 1 (Athens): λαβὼν [A] ἐπὶ τῇ θυγατρὶ Λειμώνῃ μοιχόν [B], ἐκεῖνον [B¹] μὲν ἀνεῖλεν [A¹] (after he captured an adulterer with his daughter Leimone, he killed him [tr. Dilts]) [syntactical].

Exc. 10 (Sparta): τὰς ἐκεχειρίας [A] κατέστησε [B] . . . .καθιστᾶσι [B¹] δὲ καὶ ἐφόρους [A¹] (he established [the institution of] armistice. . . . they also appoint ephors) [verbal, syntactical].

Exc. 13: οὐδὲ γὰρ ἄλευρα [A] κομίζουσι [B], σιτοῦνται [B¹] ἄλφιτα [A¹] (for they do not harvest wheat but eat barley meal) [syntactical].

Exc. 15 (Crete): ἀθροίζει [A] αὐτοὺς ὅπου θέλει [B] καὶ ἐπὶ θήραν [B¹] ἐξάγει [A¹] (he musters them wherever he wishes and leads them out to hunt) [syntactical]. ἄρχονται [they begin] τῶν παρατιθεμένων [A] ἀπὸ τῶν ξένων [B], μετὰ δὲ τοὺς ξένους [B¹] τῷ ἄρχοντι διδόασι [A¹] (they begin by serving food to the guests. After the guests, they allot to the ruler) [verbal, syntactical]³⁰ τοὺς Εἵλωτας [A] κατεδουλώσαντό ποτε Λακεδαιμόνιοι [B], Θετταλοὶ [B¹] δὲ τοὺς Πενέστας [A¹] (the Lacedaimonians once enslaved the Helots, the Thessalians the Penestae) [syntactical].³¹

Exc. 18 (Cyrene): τοὺς πολυδίκους καὶ κακοπράγμονας [A] ὑπὸ τῶν ἐφόρων προάγεσθαι [B] καὶ ζημιοῦν [B¹] τούτους [A¹]: ζημιοῦν [A] τούτους [B] καὶ ἀτίμους [B¹] ποιεῖν [A¹] (those who engaged in many lawsuits and in evil deeds were to be brought forward by the Ephors and be punished and deprived of citizenship) [syntactical].

Exc. 20 (Corinth): οὐκ ἐπιτρέπων [A] ἐν ἄστει ζῆν [B], ἔτι δὲ δούλων κτῆσιν καὶ τρυφὴν [B¹] ὅλως ἀφαιρῶν [A¹] (not allowing the people to live in the city, and also by entirely outlawing the possession of slaves and luxuries) [syntactical]. μηδένα τέλος [A] πράσσεσθαι [B] ἀρκεῖσθαι [B¹] τε τῆς ἀπὸ τῆς ἀγορᾶς καὶ τῶν λιμένων [A¹] (not levying a tax on anyone, in being satisfied with a tax on goods from the market and from the harbor) [syntactical].

Exc. 35 (Samos): διατρίβων [A] ἐν ᾽Αθήναις παρ᾽ Εὐριπίδῃ [B] καὶ τὸ γύναιον αὐτοῦ [B¹] διαφθείρων [A¹] (spent time in Athens with Euripides and seduced his wife) [syntactical].

Exc. 43 (Lycia): πωλοῦσι [A] τοὺς ψευδομάρτυρας [B] καὶ τὰς οὐσίας [B¹] αὐτῶν δημεύουσι [A¹] (they sell those convicted of perjury and confiscate their possessions) [syntactical].

Exc. 49 (Samothrace): Σάμιοι κατῴκησαν [A] αὐτὴν [B] . . . καὶ Σαμοθρᾴκην [B¹] ἐκάλεσαν [A¹] (the Samians settled it . . . and called it Samothrace) [syntactical].

Exc. 62 (Locri): τὰς γαλᾶς δάκνειν [A] αὐτὸν [B] καὶ πέρας ἀπορ_οῦντα ἑαυτὸν [B¹] ἀνελεῖν [A¹] (weasels attacked him, and in utter despair he killed himself) [verbal, syntactical].

Exc. 69 (Acragas): ἐφόνευε [A] πολλοὺς [B] ἀλλὰ καὶ τιμωρίαις παρανόμοις [B¹] ἐχρήσατο [A¹] (killed many, but he also resorted to illegal punishments) [syntactical].

The contents of most fragments of other πολιτεῖαι are so exiguous that examples of this structure are unlikely to be found, and a search proved this to be the case. I have discussed one example from a rather longer fragment (Athenaeus 567AB = F 549 R) at Keaney 1980⁴.87.

NOTES

1. The figure is chiasmus, on which see H. Lausberg, *Handbuch der literarischen Rhetorik* 1 (Munich 1960) sections 800–803, whose references show how small a role the figure played in ancient literary analysis. For instance, in the prose passages used by Demetrius, *De elocutione,* to illustrate his theories, the A/B/A¹/B¹ order is pervasive. cf. e.g., (on antithesis) 22–24, 26–27. Only three passages approach chiasmus, and two of these are from Aristotle: ποίαν τοιαύτην πόλιν εἷλον τῶν ἐχθρῶν, οἵαν τὴν ἰδίαν πόλιν ἀπώλεσαν (πόλιν ἐχθρῶν/ἰδίαν πόλιν 28 = F 82R); ἐγὼ ἐκ μὲν Ἀθηνῶν εἰς Στάγειρα ἦλθον διὰ τὸν βασιλέα τὸν μέγαν, ἐκ δὲ Σταγείρων εἰς Ἀθήνας διὰ τὸν χειμῶνα τὸν μέγαν 29 = F 669R; ἐγὼ μὲν σὲ ἔσωσα καὶ σὺ μὲν δι' ἐμὲ ἐσώθης ἐγὲ δὲ διὰ σὲ ἀπωλόμην 213 = Ctesias 688 F 8aJ).

2. 1.2, 16.8, 20.1, 20.3, 24.2, 36.1, 38.1, and 40.1.

3. Cf. chapter 6, "Methods and Purposes."

4. N.b. that this word is taken from Solon's vocabulary: 12.3 and 4, 14.2.

5. Eustathios *ad* B 763: cf. S. E Bassett, "Ὕστερον πρότερον Ὁμηρικῶς," *HSCP* 31 (1920) 39–62 at 47–51.

6. Cf. chapter 16.

7. In chapters 20ff. the rigid formula A/B/C/C¹/B¹/A¹ is occasionally relaxed to produce, e.g., A/B/C/B¹/A¹/C or A/B/C/C¹/A¹/B¹. Sometimes the reason for this is clear—it is for the sake of emphasis—(cf. below at 27; 34–35 and 38.4) at other times it is quite unclear.

8. Cf. chapter 4, "The Unity of the Ἀθπολ."

9. Cp. the thematically related 3.5 (of the archons): κύριοι δ ἦσαν καὶ τὰς δίκας αὐτοτελεῖς κρίνειν καὶ οὐχ ὥσπερ νῦν προανακρίνειν.

10. Rhodes (46) has stated that according to the principle whereby the outer elements of a complex ring frame are the more important, "it could as well be argued from his [sc., Keaney.1963.124] analysis of 2.1–5.1 that the political background is enclosed within, and thus shown to be less important than, the economic background." There would be more justice to this remark if the first sentence of chapter 5 had ended with τοῖς ὀλίγοις, that is, with the economic connotation.

11. The second is τῶν δὲ πολιτῶν ἐνίους.

12. For the πόλις in Solon's poetry, cf. 12.4 and F 4, 9, 19 West.

13. The chiastic structure also forms the first half of a complex ring structure with 34.3: see chapter 8, "Vertical Structure: Ring Composition."

14. Cf. chapter 10, "The Politics of Institutions versus the Politics of Personality."

15. Cf. chapter 17, "The Dating Formula."

16. On the unusual function of δοκῶν here, cf. chapters 11 "The δοκεῖν Formula;" and 14 "Aristotle and Theramenes."

17. There may be a pun in ἀνεῖλεν and περιεῖλε, and there surely is ironic word-play in ἀνεῖλεν and the death of Ephialtes, ἀνῃρέθη. . . . δολοφονηθείς.

18. Aristotle apparently thought it so important to use this structure here that, by doing so, he broke one of his usual rules of word order. In the Ἀθπολ, when one verb is used with two nonverbal elements joined by μέν-δέ, the verb precedes. Cf., e.g., (subject) 17.4, 43.2; (object) 8.5, 23.3, 53.4; (indirect object) 24.1, 62.2. When this practice is not followed, as here, it is more often than not posssible to see why. 11.2 ὁ μὲν γὰρ δῆμος ᾤετο . . . οἱ δὲ γνώριμοι. Both subjects are put in the initial emphatic position, supplementing (γάρ) their antecedents (τὰς στάσεις ἀμφοτέρας) in the preceding clause. 16.9: τοὺς μὲν γὰρ ταῖς ὁμιλίαις τοὺς δὲ ταῖς εἰς τὰ ἴδια βοηθείαις προσηγέτο. This is again a case of a supplementing clause with antecedents in the preceding clause (τῶν γνωρίμων καὶ τῶν δημοτικῶν).

19. For discussion, see chapter 6, "Methods and Purposes."

20. Cf. chapter 14, "Aristotle and Theramenes."

21. A reader for the Press points out that the "abnormal" order is found at Dem 19.58: τρίτη ἐπὶ δέκα τοῦ σκιροφοριῶνος μηνός and τῇ ἕκτῃ ἐπὶ δέκα ἐγίγνετο τοῦ σκιροφοριῶνος. The fact of a narrative context may have had some effect here, but it is to be noted that the orator has intended or chanced upon a chiastic order: in section 57 we have ἐλαφηβολιῶνος ἐνάτη ἐπὶ δέκα.

22. J. D. Denniston, *Greek Prose Style* (Oxford 1952) 74–77; C. Rehdantz, *Demosthenes' Neun Philippische Reden* 2.2 (Leipzig 1886) 29–30. Unfortunately, the chapter on "Chiasmus in Ancient Greek and Latin Literatures" in J. W. Welch, ed., *Chiasmus in Antiquity* (Hildesheim 1981) 250–68 contains little of relevance.

23. Cf. the brief remarks on chiastic order in Newman 3.164–65 and his references in 4.702, s.v. "Chiasmus."

24. Compare the transition from economic to political terminology at *AP* 5.1.

25. ἐκεῖνον refers to Dion.

26. That is, of *politeiai* other than the Ἀθπολ. Of that work, the main source were the *Lexeís* of Harpocration.

27. Cf. H. Bloch, "Heraclides Lembos and his *Epitome* of Aristotle's *Politeiai*," *TAPA* 71 (1940) 17–39. I cite from the edition of M. Dilts, *Greek Roman and Byzantine Monograph* 5: Durham 1971.

28. This is his habit of taking a word out of its original order to make it serve as an introductory lemma: cf. Bloch 34–35.

29. Thus, of the two sentences of *Exc.* 3, the first is from *AP* 6.1 and the second from 11.1.

30. There may be paronomasia in ἄρχονται/ἄρχοντι.

31. The same material is found in a fuller version: ὡς Ἀριστοτέλης ἐν Συρακοσίων πολιτείᾳ, ὅμοιοι τοῖς παρὰ Λακεδαιμονίοις εἵλωσι, καὶ παρὰ Θεσσαλοῖς πενέσταις καὶ παρὰ Κρησὶ κλαρώταις (Photius, s.v. Καλλικύριοι = F 586 R).

10

The Politics of Institutions versus the Politics of Personality

Near the beginning and near the end of his treatment of Peisistratus Aristotle brings him into contact with Solon; the second passage (17.1) reports a tradition that there existed an erotic relationship between the two: this Aristotle denied, using a chronological argument based on archon dates.[1]

The first text contains an anecdote about Solon's vocal opposition on the occasion of the future tyrant's first attempt to seize power (14.2). The anecdote is no more likely to be historically true than the erotic relationship. It is, however, ethically consistent with Solon's character. This is not, however, the main reason Aristotle had for accepting it and choosing to include it, for that character had already been established. Rather, his reasons were based on content and structure. The first text, positively, and the second text, negatively, were chosen to point up a contrast between Solon and Peisistratus. Both texts are explicit in content and both are consistent with, and a clue to, the existence of a series of implicit contrasts between the two men. The contrast, or dichotomy, may most simply be described as the clash between the politics of personality and the politics of institutions. This is a theme which begins with the careers of Solon and Peisistratus and is most prominent in their activities, but it is also present in the rivalry between Pericles and Cimon.

Before these terms are defined more precisely, it may be pointed out that the peculiar nature of this dichotomy is reflected in the peculiar structure of the narrative of Peisistratus' career (13.5–17) and that of his sons. The narrative is distinguished by five features. First, it is largely[2] written in what Rhodes (44)[3] has called the "sequential style." This is distinguished from a more analytic style, characterized especially by ring composition, and this is one (negative) way in which these chapters differ from the rest of the narrative. A second (positive) difference is the presence of another kind of cohesive factor. The analytical style articulates the narrative into separate segments: here the narrative is tied together by repetition:

A (13.4): δημοτικώτατος εἶναι δοκῶν
A (14.1): δημοτικώτατος δ' εἶναι δοκῶν

B (14.3): διώκει τὰ κοινά, πολιτικῶς μᾶλλον ἢ τυραννικῶς

Ba (16.2): διώκει δ᾽ ὁ Πεισίστρατος, ὥσπερ εἴρηται, τὰ περὶ τὴν πόλιν μετρίως καὶ μᾶλλον πολιτικῶς ἢ τυραννικῶς

C (15.3): παρελόμενος τοῦ δήμου τὰ ὅπλα

Ca (15.4): παρείλετο δὲ τοῦ δήμου τὰ ὅπλα τόνδε τὸν τρόπον

D (16.7): συνέβη γὰρ ὕστερον διαδεξαμένων τῶν υἱέων πολλῷ γενέσθαι τραχυτέραν τὴν ἀρχήν.

D (19.1): συνέβαινεν πολλῷ τραχυτέραν εἶναι τὴν τυραννίδα·

An allied feature is structure. The Solon-connection frames the beginning and end of the portion dealing with Peisistratus himself. The fourth feature is a matter of language and the fifth one of placement. At 16.1 Aristotle says: ἡ μὲν οὖν Πεισιστράτου τυραννὶς ἐξ ἀρχῆς τε κατέστη τοῦτον τὸν τρόπον καὶ μεταβολὰς ἔσχεν τοσαύτας (the tyranny of Peisistratus was set up in this way from the beginning and had this number of changes). There follows directly the repeated passage just designated as Ba, at which point we get a description of Peisistratus' ways of governing. Three points are to be made about the language here. First, μὲν οὖν shows that we are at the end of a structural unit. Second, ἐξ ἀρχῆς is the phrase Aristotle used at the beginning of many of the πολιτεῖαι, and, if we are to trust Heraclides Lembos,[4] it was used near the beginning of the ᾽Αθπολ. Third, when Aristotle sums up the constitutional development of Athens before he describes the contemporary constitution, the summary (ch. 41) is in terms of μεταβολαί. In other words, the structure of the narrative of Peisistratus is a replica of the structure of the ᾽Αθπολ as a whole. As chapter 41 is the dividing line between the narrative of the development of the constitution into democracy and the description of that democracy, so 16.1 is the dividing line between the narrative of Peisistratus' acquisition of power and the description of how he used that power. This replication means that the material on tyranny is different from the rest of the narrative, can be treated as a separate unit, and that the tyranny is not so integral to the development of the Athenian democracy as some other μεταβολαί/ καταστάσεις.

To return to our dichotomy: by the politics of personality I mean a political style in which goals, decisions, and actions are determined in the absence of or outside of a written institutional code; institutional politics is a style which works through institutional processes, e.g., a written law code, deliberative assemblies, responsible magistrates, law courts etc.

We have seen that Aristotle explicitly divorces Solon from Peisistratus in two passages, and, as he did with the anecdotes about Solon and Peisistratus, Aristotle has chosen to select from his sources the kind of material illustrative of these contrasts and to arrange that material in such a way as to bring them out.[5] Perhaps the clearest way to show this is to follow the structure of Aristotle's treatment of Solon and juxtapose the apposite material about Peisistratus (A = before coming to power, B = in power, C = character):

A: chosen by both sides (5.2)   seizes power (14.1)
neutral (5.2)   favors one στάσις (13.5, 14.1)

B: social measures (6.1)
legal measures (6.1, 7.1)
institutional measures (7, 8, 9, 10)
use of arms in civil war (8.5)
C: honesty (6.2–4)
personal epithets:
μέτριος (6.3)
κοινός

encourages agriculture (16.2)
none
one (16.5)
disarms citizens (15.4)
deceit (14.1, 14.4, 15.3)
personal epithets:
δημοτικώτατος (13.4; 14.1)
φιλάνθρωπος (16.2)
πρᾷος
συγγνωμικός
δημοτικός (16.8)
φιλάνθρωπος

Although not all of these contrasts are of the same weight nor of the same immediate relevance, it is clear that Solon acted for the good of the πατρίς and Peisistratus out of self-interest. Solon operated through laws and institutions and thus had a permanent effect on the development of the Athenian constitution; Peisistratus depended upon the power of his person, operated extrainstitutionally and extralegally and thus had only minor effects on the constitution.

The most salient contrasts are five:

1. Institutions: (a) Solon set up a whole πολιτεία, Peisistratus was responsible for one institution, οἱ δικασταὶ οἱ κατὰ δήμους. The establishment thereof was not a personally neutral action, for it was in support of and a result of his politico-economic policy.[6]

(b) Peisistratus granted ἀτέλεια to the farmer on Mt. Hymettus. The implicit contrast here is that a private individual grants a privilege which in later times would have been granted through a ψήφισμα of the ἐκκλησία.

(c) When summoned before the court of the Areopagus on a charge of murder, Peisistratus αὐτὸς μὲν ἀπήντησεν ὡς ἀπολογησόμενος, ὁ δὲ προσκαλεσάμενος φοβηθεὶς ἔλιπεν (16.8) (he showed up to make his defence, but his accuser, through fear, failed to appear).

The overt point of the story is that Peisistratus ἐβούλετο πάντα διοικεῖν κατὰ τοὺς νόμους, οὐδεμίαν ἑαυτῷ πλεονεξίαν διδούς (wished to manage everything according to the laws, giving no advantage to himself).[7] The relevant point of the story is that the institution, the court of the Areopagus, was ineffective because it was not powerful enough to guarantee the safety of the prosecutor.[8]

2. Laws: Theophrastus (F 99 Wimmer = 23 Szegedy-Maszak) ascribed to Peisistratus a νόμος ἀργίας,[9] which is not mentioned by Aristotle but is consistent with his account of the agricultural policy of Peisistratus. Apart from the statement of 16.5, the ᾿Αθπολ (22.1) says only that τοὺς μὲν Σόλωνος νόμους ἀφανίσαι τὴν τυραννίδα διὰ τὸ μὴ χρῆσθαι (the tyranny obscured the laws of Solon by failure to use them). The fact that Aristotle could have specified a Peisistratean νόμος but failed to do so is further support of the thesis.

3. Tyranny: Peisistratus was a tyrant, aided in his first accession and first restoration by factional politics (14.1, 4) and in his second restoration by foreign help (15.2–3). Solon had the opportunity to become tyrant by using factions but rejected that option (6.3, 11.2).

4. Reception: at one or more times Solon chose, in reference to rich and poor, ἀμφοτέροις ἀπεχθέσθαι, and his reforms caused such dissatisfaction among rich and poor that he chose voluntary exile (11.1–2). By contrast, Peisistratus got the good will of both γνώριμοι and δημοτικοί, with the result that πρὸς ἀμφοτέρους ἐπεφύκει καλῶς (16.9).

5. Language: finally, it is interesting to note two sets of parallels in the language which Aristotle uses. The form μέγιστον is found twice in the 'Aθ-πολ, in similar contexts. After describing Solon's reforms, Aristotle sums them up in chapter 9, beginning πρῶτον μὲν καὶ μέγιστον τὸ μὴ δανείζειν ἐπὶ τοῖς σώμασιν (first and most important was that loans were not made with persons as sureties). After describing Peisistratus' policies and character, he sums up and begins (16.8): μέγιστον δὲ πάντων ἦν τῶν εἰρημένων τὸ δημοτικὸν τῷ ἤθει καὶ φιλάνθρωπον (the most important of all the qualities I have mentioned was the democratic humanity of his character).

The second parallel involves largely the same context. Solon's measures are called δημοτικώτατα (9.1) and δημοτικά (10.1): Peisistratus is called δημοτικώτατος (13.4, 14.1) and δημοτικός (16.8). This is the single epithet shared by the two and it well encapsulates the dichotomy I have been describing: δημοτικός (like μέγιστον) refers in the first instance (neuter gender) to institutions, in the second instance (masculine) to a person.

II

I have been concerned to show that one set of contrasts between Solon and Peisisratus, as Aristotle conceived it, was the different attitude of each toward the creation and maintenance of political institutions. That contrast resulted in a dichotomy between personality and institutions which now becomes a theme: this theme initially helps to explain one passage (A: 17.3) which has not seemed to require explanation, and contributes to the understanding of another passage (B: 22.1) which seems not only to contradict Herodotus and Thucydides but a passage in the 'Aθπολ as well. It will become clear that, when Aristotle chose to exploit this theme, the choice entailed certain other choices of material for inclusion.

A: 17.3. On the death of Peisistratus, κατεῖχον οἱ υἱεῖς τὴν ἀρχήν, προάγοντες τὰ πράγματα τὸν αὐτὸν τρόπον (his sons held the rule, carrying forward matters in the same way). What is the function of this passage and what precisely does the last clause mean? The answer to the first question seems clear enough: the whole passage effects the transition from the rule of Pesistratus to that of his sons. That answer, however, is not quite complete, for the passage is the first of two to perform the same function. The transition from the death of Peisistratus to the *activity* of his sons is effected in another passage, formally marked by a small repetition, τὰ πράγματα being picked up at the beginning of 18:ἦσαν δὲ κύριοι τῶν πραγμάτων . . . Ἵππαρχος καὶ Ἱππίας. This type of introduction, one marked by repetition, occurs only twice elsewhere, and both instances are in the introduction to Peisistratus:

13.4: δημοτικώτατος preview
14.1: δημοτικώτατος action
14.3: πολιτικῶς μᾶλλον ἢ τυραννικῶς preview
16.2: μᾶλλον πολιτικῶς ἢ τυραννικῶς action

The latter set (πολιτικῶς . . .) is formally parallel to 18: the words in 16.2 are followed by a list of Peisistratos' personal qualities: φιλάνθρωπος ἦν καὶ πρᾶος καὶ τοῖς ἁμαρτάνουσι συγγνωμικός κτλ. So, in 18 a list of the qualities of Hippias and Hipparchus follows directly: πρεσβύτερος δὲ ὢν Ἱππίας καὶ τῇ φύσει πολιτικὸς καὶ ἔμφρων κτλ. The parallelism connecting Peisistratus and his sons suggests that προάγοντες τὰ πράγματα τὸν αὐτὸν τρόπον refers to a continuation of the politics of personality.

B: For the period immediately after (τούτων δὲ γεωομένων) Cleisthenes, Aristotle begins: 22.1:καὶ γὰρ συνέβη τοὺς μὲν Σόλωνος νόμους ἀφανίσαι τὴν τυραννίδα διὰ τὸ μὴ χρῆσθαι, καινοὺς δ' ἄλλους θεῖναι τὸν Κλεισθένη στοχαζόμενον τοῦ πλήθους, ἐν οἷς ἐτέθη καὶ ὁ περὶ τοῦ ὀστρακισμοῦ νόμος.

> Many of Solon's laws had been consigned to oblivion by the tyranny, through not being used, and Cleisthenes enacted other new laws in his bid for popular support, among them the law about ostracism.[10]

On the face of it, the passage seems to contradict 16.8, as well as both of Aristotle's main sources for the tyranny, Herodotus and Thucydides.[11] If both passages from the Ἀθπολ are historically correct, it is not difficult to reconcile them on a factual level,[12] but to operate on the factual level in this context is not to use the correct approach.

We must again consider the phenomenon of repetition. At 16.8, Aristotle introduces the specific anecdote about Peisistratus' appearance before the court with a general comment, ἔν τε γὰρ τοῖς ἄλλοις, he wished to conduct things legally; here we have καινοὺς δ' ἄλλους, a generalization followed by a particular instance of legislation.

The notion, then, that Solonian laws vanished for lack of use under the tyranny should not stand on its own two feet. It is there to serve a function, and that function is to create an opportunity for Cleisthenian legislation.[13] Apart from the law on ostracism, Aristotle does not mention any other Cleisthenic law, none is known from other sources and Cleisthenes did not have a reputation as a lawgiver. I am prepared to believe that Aristotle made up this statement to create the parallel with 16.8 and thereby to have another example of the dichotomy.

III

We have seen that Peisistratus' appearance before the court was an instance of the politics of a law-abiding individual. When Cleisthenes, according to Aristotle, made new laws, he made them στοχαζόμενος τοῦ πλήθους. The difference in the approach of Cleisthenes to achieve support is that it was institutional, through law. We may observe that the course ultimately taken by Cleisthenes is the opposite of the one which he originally adopted: (20.1): ἡττώμενος δὲ ταῖς ἑταιρείαις ὁ Κλεισθένης προσηγάγετο τὸν δῆμον (failing to get the support of political groups, he attracted the demos). The failure of the politics of personal associations turned Cleisthenes toward the δῆμος.[14]

IV

Once this contrast is established, a further observation is called for. There is a paratext in the rivalry between Cimon and Pericles. Cimon's advantages were personal (he allowed his fellow demesmen to use the produce of his orchards) and institutional: τὰς κοινὰς λητουργίας ἐλητούργει λαμπρῶς (he performed brilliantly the "regular public services").[15] The response of Pericles (27.4): ἐπεὶ τοῖς ἰδίοις ἡττᾶτο, διδόναι τοῖς πολλοῖς τὰ αὐτῶν (since his private resources could not match Cimon's, he gave to the masses what belonged to them).

As distinct from the versions of the dichotomy we have seen (Solon/Peisistratus; Cleisthenes), this version is different in two ways. The first is that Pericles is not creating a new institution but tampering with an existing one; the second is that Cimon's politics are both personal and institutional; further, as Aristotle expresses it, Cimon's personal policy was limited to his fellow-demesman, a small portion of the civic population.

In a previous chapter,[16] we have observed that Aristotle skewed the chronology of chapter 27 for thematic reasons. In connection with the considerations of this chapter, let us focus the question a little more sharply: why does Aristotle mention the δικαστήρια μισθοφόρα after he has mentioned the attack on Cimon and after he has alluded to the outbreak of the Peloponnesian War. I will argue that the reasons are thematic, that they are connected with the personality/institutions dichotomy and that this dichotomy underlies an important facet of Aristotle's conception of the development of the Athenian constitution.

The particular connection to which I refer is the collapse of the dichotomy or, perhaps more precisely, the fusion and incorporation of its terms into a single body, the active δῆμος. The collapse takes place through a process which begins with Peisistratus and can be traced in a series of parallel texts. When Peisistratus disarmed the δῆμος, he told its members not to be amazed or dispirited (15.5),

A: ἀλλ᾽ ἀπελθόντας ἐπὶ τῶν ἰδίων εἶναι, τῶν δὲ κοινῶν αὐτὸς ἐπιμελήσε-
σθαι πάντων

but to go off to their private concerns, he himself would attend to all public matters.

The purpose of Peisistratus' agricultural policy was (16.3):

B: ἵνα μήτε ἐν τῷ ἄστει διατρίβωσιν ἀλλὰ διεσπαρμένοι κατὰ τὴν χώραν,
καὶ ὅπως εὐποροῦντες τῶν μετρίων καὶ πρὸς τοῖς ἰδίοις ὄντες μήτ᾽
ἐπιθυμῶσι μήτε σχολάζωσιν ἐπιμελεῖσθαι τῶν κοινῶν

so that they would not spend time in the city but scattered throughout the countryside, and that, being well off in a moderate way and with private concerns, they
would have neither desire nor time to attend to public matters.

The purpose of his single institutional measure, the creation of the δικασταὶ
κατὰ δήμους, was (16.5):

C: ὅπως μὴ καταβαίνοντας εἰς τὸ ἄστυ παραμελῶσι τῶν ἔργων;

so that they would not come into the city and neglect to work their farms;

Years later, when the city was confident and a lot of money had been collected,
Aristeides advised the Athenians to lay hold of hegemony (24.1) and:

D: καταβάντας ἐκ τῶν ἀγρῶν οἰκεῖν ἐν τῷ ἄστει;

to come in from the fields and dwell in the city;

There follows in the same chapter a list of civil and military functionaries
supported by the τροφή from the Delian League: this in turn is followed by a
similar list from after the beginning of the Peloponnesian War.

It was observed that the personal politics of Cimon and the institutional politics of Pericles were different from, and diminished in comparison to, the
politics of Solon, Peisistratus, and Kleisthenes. The process we have been through
does much to explain why. Income from the empire made Peisistratus' agricultural policy irrelevant for many Athenians, and the number of Athenians engaged in civic functions shows that the institutions of the city were strong and
functioning. On the political side, as Aristotle says in chapter 27, the fact of
Athens becoming a naval power made confident τοὺς πολλούς and embold-
ened them ἅπασαν τὴν πολιτείαν μᾶλλον ἄγειν εἰς αὐτούς. Thus, when
Pericles made the δικαστήρια μισθοφόρα, he was not creating a new institution, and when Damonides advised him, by this measure, διδόναι τοῖς
πολλοῖς τὰ αὐτῶν, the advice was only a recognition of economic and political reality.

If this is correct, one reason for the chronological oddity of chapter 27 is to
underline the (comparative) lack[17] of innovation, and the oddity is reinforced
by a rhetorical device. In the sentence before Pericles' measure is introduced,
Aristotle said that after the outbreak of the Peloponnesion War the Athenians
grew accustomed (συνεθισθείς) μισθοφορεῖν. Then, we have Pericles'

measure: ἐποίησε δὲ καὶ μισθοφόρα τὰ δικαστήρια. A normal interpretation of καί would be that the measure was part of a process already long in existence when, in fact, it was near the beginning of that process.

The sentence containing the reference to μισθοφορία also shows the collapse of the dichotomy and the fusion of its terms. Its structure is impressive, although it is not immediately clear why Aristotle fashioned it in this way:

[A] μετὰ δὲ τὴν ἐν Σαλαμῖνι ναυμαχίαν ἑνὸς δεῖ πεντηκοστῷ ἔτει
[B] ἐπὶ Πυθοδώρου ἄρχοντος
[C] ὁ πρὸς Πελοποννησίοις ἐνέστη πόλεμος,
ἐν ᾧ κατακλεισθεὶς ὁ δῆμος ἐν τῷ ἄστει καὶ
συνεθισθεὶς ἐν ταῖς στρατιαῖς μισθοφορεῖν
τὰ μὲν ἑκὼν
τὰ δὲ ἄκων
προῃρεῖτο τὴν πολιτείαν διοικεῖν αὐτός.

Four features of this sentence call for comment. The first is the mention of the battle of Salamis. This is not for the sake of chronology, for here, as in the two passages shortly to be mentioned, there is an archon date: its purpose is thematic. This is the third passage in which a military victory is used in a dating context; each marks a decisive step and each is marked by Athenian confidence:

(a) 22.3: victorious in the battle at Marathon, θαρροῦντος ἤδη τοῦ δήμου, they first used ostracism.
(b) 23.4–24.1: after the sea battle in Salamis, Aristeides imposed the first tribute on the allies: thereafter, θαρρούσης ἤδη τῆς πόλεως, he advised them to seize hegemony.
(c) 27.1–2: the naval power, as a result of which θαρρήσαντας τοὺς πολλούς, turning the *politeia* to themselves. After the battle of Salamis. . . .[18]

The second feature is the repetition of the phrase ἐν τῷ ἄστει, an allusion to the development from the politics of personality to the politics of institution. The third is the chiastic arrangement, with ἑκών taking up συνεθισθείς and ἄκων κατακλεισθείς.

The final feature is the choice of the verb προαιρεῖσθαι. It is surprising that its use here has not evoked comment. The verb is familiar from the ethical and political writings of Aristotle, but whether it be used of a legislator[19] or of an ethical choice, the verb is always used of an individual moral agent, never, as here, of a collective body. What Aristotle has done has been to personalize the δῆμος and put it in the position of making choices. Here is the point at which the terms of our dichotomy are fused: the δῆμος, as person, is now in control of its choices, directions, and policies, although some of these will be wrong.[20] It is one of the purposes of the following chapters to show that the δῆμος, when making these choices, is not acting as a totally free moral agent. The δῆμος was corrupted (διαφθείρειν) by Cleon (28.3) and deceived (ἐξαπατᾶν) by Cleophon (28.3, 34.1), Callicrates (28.3) and οἱ παροργίσαντες

(34.1): in voting in the oligarchic regimes of the Four Hundred and the Thirty, it was falsely persuaded (συμπείθειν: 29.1)[21] and the victim of compulsion (ἀναγκάζειν: 29.1, 34.3).

The imperfect tense of προῃρεῖτο implies that Aristotle is talking about a process of turning ἅπασαν τὴν πολιτείαν toward οἱ πολλοί. The process is not a steady one, for it was twice interrupted. Aristotle signals one of these interruptions by a familiar structural device. The sentence of 27.2 set out above in ABC form is balanced by framing ring composition at 32.2:

C¹: ἡ μὲν οὖν ὀλιγαρχία τοῦτον κατέστη τὸν τρόπον

B¹: ἐπὶ Καλλίου μὲν ἄρχοντος,

A¹: ἔτεσιν δ᾽ ὕστερον τῆς τῶν τυράννων ἐκβολῆς μάλιστα ἑκατόν.[22]

The structure is intended to contrast the parallel triumphs of A/A¹ over against the dissimilar political results of C/C¹.

The final stage in the fusion of the terms of the dichotomy may be seen in two balancing sentences of chapter 41:

41.1: τότε δὲ κύριος ὁ δῆμος γενόμενος τῶν πραγμάτων ἐνεστήσατο τὴν νῦν οὖσαν πολιτείαν . . . δοκοῦντος δὲ δικαίως τοῦ δήμου λαβεῖν τὴν πολιτείαν διὰ τὸ ποιήσασθαι τὴν κάθοδον δι᾽ αὑτοῦ.

at that time, the δῆμος, gaining control of affairs, set up the government which exists now . . . the δῆμος seems justly to have taken over the government, since it effected its return by itself.

41.2: ἁπάντων γὰρ αὐτὸς αὑτὸν πεποίηκεν ὁ δῆμος κύριον, καὶ πάντα διοικεῖται ψηφίσμασιν καὶ δικαστηρίοις, ἐν οἷς ὁ δῆμός ἐστιν ὁ κρατῶν.

for the δῆμος has put itself in control of everything, and everything is managed through decrees and law courts, in which the δῆμος has the power.

In both passages, the δῆμος is acting as a subject, and two details of the language suggest that it is almost as a human subject. For the phrase κύριος τῶν πραγμάτων, one may compare its use of Solon (6.1) and the Peisistratids (18.1). More striking is the use of the reflexive pronoun. Until this chapter it has been used of individuals, whether acting singly or together,[23] but the collective use of αὐτὸς αὑτόν is anticipated in the chapter in which the dichotomy began to break down (27.1, 4): τοὺς πολλοὺς ἅπασαν τὴν πολιτείαν μᾶλλον ἄγειν πρὸς ἑαυτούς, and Damonides advised Pericles διδόναι τοῖς πολλοῖς τὰ αὑτῶν, with its unusual and striking use of the reflexive.

If, then, the δῆμος is one of the fused terms of our dichotomy, the other term, the institutions, is not far to seek: it is represented by ψηφίσματα and δικαστήρια.

NOTES

1. 17.2. The conclusion is not necessarily supported by his chronological evidence: Rhodes 24.

2. But not exclusively. The term is accurate for chs. 14–16 (17 is of the nature of a long footnote) and 18: the style of 19 is mixed (cf. chapter 8, "Vertical Structure: Ring Composition").

3. Rhodes instances chapter 22 as an example and does not use the term of these chapters.

4. *Exc.* 1 Dilts: Ἀθηναῖοι τὸ μὲν ἐξ ἀρχῆς ἐχρῶντο βασιλείᾳ.

5. It hardly need be said that this allusive form of contrasting narrative is unique to the treatment of Solon and Peisistratus.

6. It was also an impermanent institution, for it fell into desuetude after the tyranny and had to be reestablished in 453/1 (26.3).

7. This point is made in a reference to the same event at *Pol.* 5.1315B21–2, where no allusion is made to the failure of the accuser to appear.

8. It is noteworthy that these two points are made in anecdotes about Peisistratus. That form of expression was chosen, I think, to attach a certain personal and ephemeral quality to the events.

9. For the correct interpretation of this as a νόμος ἀ-εργασιας = a law to keep the land worked. Cp. *AP* 16.4: ἐξεργαζομένης τῆς χώρας and 16.6: σκάπτοντα καὶ ἐργαζόμενον. Cf. A. Dreizehnter, "νόμος ἀργίας. Ein Gesetz gegen Müssigang?" *Acta Antiqua* 26 (1978) 371–86.

10. A paratext for καινοὺς δ' ἄλλους νόμους is 7.1 (of Solon): νόμους ἔθηκεν ἄλλους.

11. Herod. 1.59.6: Πεισίστρατος ἦρχε Ἀθηναίων, οὔτε τιμὰς τὰς ἐούσας συνταράξας οὔτε θέσμια μεταλλάξας, ἐπί τε τοῖσι κατεστεῶσι ἔνεμε τὴν πόλιν κοσμέων καλῶς τε καὶ εὖ (Peisistratus was the ruler of Athens, without disturbing existing magistracies or changing legal provisions and managed the city on the basis of established procedures, ordering it attractively and efficiently); Thuc. 6.54.6: τὰ δὲ ἄλλα αὐτὴ ἡ πόλις τοῖς πρὶν κειμένοις νόμοις ἐχρῆτο (in other respects the city used the laws previously established).

12. Cf. Rhodes 219.

13. Rhodes (262) comments: "the subject of ostracism is raised, only to be dropped without adequate explanation and then resumed [in sect. 3]." The comment misses Aristotle's stylistic tactic. The point of the sentence is to focus attention on ostracism, the main topic of the chapter. The "subject is dropped" because the arrangement of the chapter is chronological. Aristotle is here illustrating a thesis, that there was a process by which the πολιτεία became δημοτικωτέρα. That process involved discrete chronological actions; and ostracism, in both its theoretical and applied aspects, is treated under the year in which it was first acted upon.

14. For want of any evidence to the contrary, it is generally assumed that Cleisthenes, as a private citizen, was able to get his reforms passed as ψηφίσματα in the ἐκκλησία.

15. Tr. von Fritz and Kapp. The phrase is untranslatable because there is both redundancy and paronomasia involved. A λητουργία is ἰδία because it is provided by an individual citizen and κοινή because it is for the benefit of the political community. For the use of these terms in the structure of 27, cf. chapter 13, "Aristotle and Theopompus."

16. Cf. chapter 6, "Methods and Purposes."

17. The fact that it was not particularly innovative does not mean that it was not important.

18. On the pattern of victory, confidence, and reversal found in these and other passages, cf. Keaney 1984.

19. Solon: *Pol.* 2.1274A2: Lycurgus:1271A32.

20. 3 4.1–2: deceived by Cleophon, they reject peace overtures but recognized their error (ἔγνωσαν τὴν ἁμαρτίαν); 41.2: the city committed many errors (ἁμαρτάνειν) because of the demagogues.

21. For the connotation of deceit in this word, cf. 14.1 and 20.2

22. A[1] is taken from Thuc. 8.68.4.

23. With ποιήσασθαι τὴν κάθοδον δι'αὐτοῦ compare the Alcmeonids of 19.3 who δι' αὐτῶν οὐκ ἐδύναντο ποιήσασθαι τὴν κάθοδον.

11

The δοκεῖν Formula

A traditionally Greek way of describing the opposition between Solon and Peisistratus would be to see in the former an example of ἔργον, in the latter an
example of λόγος. A similar dichotomy between appearance and reality underlies a repeated pattern which I describe as the δοκεῖν formula and which operates as follows.

It is a characteristic feature of the *AthPol* that, before political figures play a
major role in Athenian constitutional history, Aristotle alludes to the fact that
they already have some kind of favorable reputation. He does this by use of a
formula, the repeated element of which is a subordinate verb with the root δοκ-
. Words with this root can be ambiguous, since appearance may not coincide
with reality. I first quote the texts with appropriate comment and then treat
larger issues.[1]

13.4: Πεισίστρατος, δημοτικώτατος εἶναι δοκῶν. (Peisistratus, a man
who seemed most inclined to democracy.)

14.1: δημοτικώτατος δ᾽ εἶναι δοκῶν ὁ Πεισίστρατος καὶ σφόδρα
εὐδοκιμηκὼς ἐν τῷ πρὸς Μεγαρέας πολέμῳ. (. . . and won high distinction in the war against Megara).

Given what we have seen in the last chapter, it may be significant that the
first clear use of the formula is of Peisistratus, since that also is true, as we
will see, of the constitutional formula. Highly relevant in this connection is a
passage in *Pol.* 5.1305A18–24:

> ἔτι δὲ διὰ τὸ μὴ μεγάλας εἶναι τότε τὰς πόλεις, ἀλλ᾽ ἐπὶ τῶν ἀγρῶν
> οἰκεῖν τὸν δῆμον ἄσχολον ὄντα πρὸς τοῖς ἔργοις, οἱ προστάται του δήμου,
> ὅτε πολεμικοὶ γένοιντο, τυραννίδι ἐπετίθεντο. πάντες δὲ τοῦτο ἔδρων
> ὑπὸ τοῦ δήμου *πιστευθέντες*, ἡ δὲ *πίστις* ἦν ἡ ἀπέχθεια ἡ πρὸς τους
> πλουσίους, οἷον ᾿Αθήνησί τε Πεισίστρατος στασιάσας πρὸς τοὺς
> πεδιακούς.

> a further reason is that cities were smaller in those days and the people lived all
> over the countryside, busy with their labors there; so their champions, if they were
> military men, used to aim at tyranny. They would all do this because they had the
> confidence of the people, a confidence based on hostility to the rich. At Athens,
> for example, Peisistratus led a revolt against the dwellers on the plain.[2]

23.1: ἡ ἐν ᾿Αρείῳ πάγῳ βουλή . . . οὐδενὶ δόγματι λαβοῦσα τὴν
ἡγεμονίαν ἀλλὰ διὰ τὸ γενέσθαι τῆς περὶ Σαλαμῖνα ναυμαχίας αἰτία

(the Council of the Areopagus . . . acquired its predominance not by any formal decision but through being responsible for the battle of Salamis). The passage is discussed in chapter 12, "A Constitutional Formula."[3]

23.3: ἦσαν δὲ προστάται τοῦ δήμου κατὰ τούτους τοὺς καιροὺς Ἀριστείδης ὁ Λυσιμάχου καὶ Θεμιστοκλέους ὁ Νεοκλέους, ὁ μὲν τὰ πολέμια ⟨δοκῶν⟩, ὁ δὲ τὰ πολιτικὰ δεινὸς εἶναι καὶ δικαιοσύνη τῶν καθ᾽ ἑαυτὸν διαφέρειν (the champions of the people at this time were Aristeides the son of Lysimachus and Themistocles the son of Neocles: Themistocles practiced the military arts, while Aristeides was skilled in the political arts and was outstanding among his contemporaries for his uprightness).[4]

25.1: γενόμενος τοῦ δήμου προστάτης Ἐφιάλτης ὁ Σοφωνίδου, δοκῶν καὶ ἀδωροδόκητος εἶναι καὶ δίκαιος[5] πρὸς τὴν πολιτείαν (Ephialtes son of Sophonides became champion of the people, a man who appeared to be uncorrupt and upright in political matters). This latter quality was soon belied: the πολιτεία was that προεστώτων τῶν Ἀρεοπαγιτῶν (in which the Areopagus was dominant), and, Aristotle continues, Ephialtes ἐπέθετο τῇ βουλῇ (attacked the council [of the Areopagus]).

27.1: πρὸς τὸ δημαγωγεῖν ἐλθόντος Περικλέους καὶ πρῶτον εὐδοκιμήσαντος ὅτε κατηγόρησε τὰς εὐθύνας Κίμωνος στρατηγοῦντος νέος ὤν.[6] (Pericles took on the leadership of the people; he had first distinguished himself when, as a young man, he prosecuted Cimon in the examination after his generalship).

28.1: πρῶτον γὰρ τότε προστάτην ἔλαβεν ὁ δῆμος οὐκ εὐδοκιμοῦντα παρὰ τοῖς ἐπιεικέσιν. (it was then that the people first took a champion who was not of good repute among the better sort).

28.3: Κλέων ὁ Κλεαινέτου, ὃς δοκεῖ μάλιστα διαφθεῖραι τὸν δῆμον ταῖς ὁρμαῖς (Cleon son of Cleaenetus who, it seems, more than anyone else corrupted the people by his wild impulses).

28.5: δοκοῦσι δὲ βέλτιστοι γεγονέναι τῶν Ἀθήνησι πολιτευσαμένων μετὰ τοὺς ἀρχαίους Νικίας καὶ Θουκυδίδης καὶ Θηραμένης. . . . δοκεῖ μέντοι τοῖς μὴ παρέργως ἀποφαινομένοις οὐχ ὥσπερ αὐτὸν διαβάλλουσι πάσας τὰς πολιτείας καταλύειν ἀλλὰ πάσας προάγειν ἕως μηδὲν παρανομοῖεν κτλ.[7] (it appears that the best of the Athenian politicians after the older ones were Nicias, Thucydides and Theramenes. . . . however, the judgment of those who are not superficial critics is that he did not destroy all regimes, as his detractors allege, but supported all as long as they did nothing unlawful).

34.3: ἄλλως δὲ δοκοῦντες οὐδενὸς ἐπιλείπεσθαι τῶν πολιτῶν τὴν πάτριον πολιτείαν ἐζήτουν· ὧν μὲν ἦν καὶ Ἀρχῖνος καὶ Ἄνυτος καὶ Κλειτοφῶν καὶ Φορμίσιος καὶ ἕτεροι πολλοί, προειστήκει δὲ μάλιστα Θηραμένης (in other respects seemed inferior to none of the citizens had as their objective the traditional constitution: these last included Archinus, Anytus, Cleitophon, Phormisius and many others, but their particular champion was Theramenes).

40.2: καὶ δοκεῖ τοῦτό τε πολιτεύσασθαι καλῶς Ἀρχῖνος (it seems that Archinus' policy was good both in this matter).

41.1: δοκοῦντος δὲ δικαίως τοῦ δήμου λαβεῖν τὴν πολιτείαν διὰ ποιήσασθαι τὴν κάθοδον δι' αὐτοῦ τὸν δῆμον (the people's taking power seems justifiable, since it was the people themselves who achieved their return).

I discuss chapter 28 and the passages following it in chapter 14, "Aristotle and Theramenes." I note here only that there is a marked difference in Aristotle's use of the pattern beginning at chapter 28 and carrying through thereafter. Prior to that chapter, the δοκ-formula was used before the figure appeared and thus left open the possibilities that there would be a discordance between reputation and action. The new usage reverses that order: now, δοκ- is coincident with or follows the action, and there is no possibility of discordance.

SOURCE AND PURPOSE

The ultimate extant source (chronologically and thematically) of this pattern would seem to be Herodotus. Compare especially 1.59.4 (of Peisistratus): πρότερον εὐδοκιμήσας ἐν τῇ πρὸς Μεγαρέας γενομένῃ στρατηγίῃ (having gained distinction in his military leadership against the Megarians); 6.132 (of Miltiades): καὶ πρότερον εὐδοκιμέων παρὰ ᾿Αθηναιοίσι τότε μᾶλλον αὔξετο (formerly enjoying a good reputation among the Athenians, after that his distinction increased), as well as his frequent use of the adjective δόκιμος the first time a person is mentioned (1.65.10, 96.6, 114.11, al.). Others used the idiom as well: Thuc. 1.79.2 (first appearance of Archidamus): ἀνὴρ καὶ ξυνετὸς δοκῶν εἶναι καὶ σώφρων (a man by reputation both intelligent and moderate); Plato, Gorg. 515C7: δοκοῦσιν ἀγαθοὶ πολῖται (reputedly good citizens); 515E11: τὸ μὲν πρῶτον ηὐδοκίμει Περικλῆς;[8] (in the first place Pericles had distinction); and Theopompus 115 F 89 (of Cimon): ηὐδοκίμει καὶ πρῶτος ἦν τῶν πολιτῶν (had distinction and was first among the citizens). Diodorus (and/or his source) made his own little formula out of it: 8.30.2 (Demonax): συνέσει καὶ δικαιοσύνῃ δοκῶν διαφέρειν (by reputation superior in intelligence and uprightness); 13.38.2 (Theramenes): φρονήσει δοκῶν διαφέρειν τῶν ἄλλων; (reputedly superior to the rest in wisdom); 13.70.1 (Lysander): δοκοῦντι στρατηγίᾳ διαφέρειν τῶν ἄλλων (. . . in leadership) and 13.102.2 (Diomedon): δικαιοσύνῃ τε καὶ ταῖς ἄλλαις ἀρεταῖς δοκῶν διαφέρειν (. . . and in the other virtues).

The only prominent figure not introduced by means of this formula is Cleisthenes, but that omission is only apparent. In this case, Aristotle was faced with a unique problem: he shared the common ancient ignorance of the career of Cleisthenes before the confrontation with Isagoras[9] and after his legislation. He solved the problem by splitting the activity of Cleisthenes into two parts. First came references to his Alkmeonid background, framing his initial activity in an elaborate ring structure.[10] This is closed off by (21.1) διὰ μὲν οὖν ταύτας τὰς αἰτίας ἐπίστευον ὁ δῆμος τῷ Κλεισθένει (for these reasons the people placed their trust in Cleisthenes). The sentence functions as a substitute for the δοκ- formula, in the sense that the following sentence introduces the description of Cleisthenes' constitutional activity in chapter 21 but chronologically takes us back to the events of chapter 20: τότε δὲ τοῦ πλήθους προεστηκώς, ἔτει τετάρτῳ μετὰ τὴν τῶν τυράννων κατάλυσιν ἐπὶ Ἰσαγόρου ἄρχοντος[11] (then, as champion of the masses, in the fourth year after the overthrow of the tyrants, the archonship of Isagoras).

One purpose of the use of his formula is that it enabled Aristotle to avoid irrelevant biographical detail. Momigliano[12] stated that "readers of his *Athenaion Politeia* know that its anecdotes—such as that on Peisistratus and the Hymettus farmer—are told for their own sakes. They are not really part of an argument." If my remarks about Solon, Peisistratus, and the βουλή of chapter 45 are correct, this statement is seriously flawed. Anecdotes have their place but only as part of an argument, and anecdotes are best used in an argument which does not need explicit expression.

The final purpose for the use of this formula is to be sought, I suggest, in the way in which Aristotle's deployment of δοκ- differs from that of his successors. δοκ- as used in this way by Herodotus and Thucydides does not connote ambiguity: the appearance matches the reality. The presence of this ambiguity enables Aristotle to exploit the tension between expectation and performance, and ultimately to reinforce the conception of Theramenes he wants to recommend.

NOTES

1. At 5.3, Aristotle says ἦν δ' ὁ Σόλων τῇ μὲν φύσει καὶ τῇ δόξῃ τῶν πρώτων (Solon was by birth and repute one of the leading citizens), but this is one of only two (26.1) occurrences of δόξα in the text, and it is not formulaic. In Plutarch (and, presumably, his source) *vitSol* 1.1, Solon is ἔνδοξος καὶ μέγας before his political career begins, but we don't know if Solon was treated in the lost beginning of the Ἀθπολ.

2. For "the men of the plain," cf. *AthPol* 13.4. One ironic effect of this pattern is that the career of Peisistratus—δημαγωγὸς καὶ στρατηγὸς ὢν τύραννος κατέστη (who from being popular leader and general had made himself tyrant)—produced the popular institution of ostracism.

3. Cf. *Pol.* 5.1304A20–21: οἷον ἡ ἐν Ἀρείῳ πάγῳ βουλὴ εὐδοκιμήσασα ἐν τοῖς Μηδικοῖς συντονωτέραν ποιῆσαι τὴν πολιτείαν (the Council of the Areopagus, after having been greatly in esteem during the Persian Wars, was considered to have tightened up the constitution).

4. This is one of two exceptions to the general rule I enunciated at the beginning of the chapter. Aristeides was mentioned in another context, a list of *ostracisés* at 22.7, and Themistocles' advice on the disposition of the money from the mines in the same place. The mention of Aristeides at 22 is determined by the dominant topic of the chapter, ostracism and its victims. Themistocles had no reputation before this appearance on the scene: Herod. 8.142.1: ἀνὴρ ἐς πρώτους νεωστὶ παριών (a man having recently advanced to the forefront). The second exception is Pericles, whose citizenship law is mentioned (26.4) before he comes on the scene. The self-evident importance of the law made its inclusion necessary, but it was not relevant to (and therefore not

included within) those aspects of Pericles' career which were of structural and thematic importance.

5. Only the first of these qualities is attested in the Ephialtes tradition: Aelian, *VH* 11.9, 13.39.

6. For discussion, cf. chapter 6, "Methods and Purposes," and chapter 13, "Aristotle and Theopompus."

7. In Keaney 1979[2] I have argued that this passage and A's picture of Theramenes were influenced by Plato's *Apology*.

8. On the texts from Plato and Theopompus, cf. chapter 14, "Aristotle and Theramenes." E. Badian has recently called this phrasing "ironic.": "Thucydides and the Peloponnesian War," in J. Allison, ed., *Conflict, Antithesis, and the Ancient Historian* (Columbus 1990) 46–91, at p. 68.

9. Unknown details included the fact that he held the archonship while Peisistratus was in power: *Hesperia* 32 (1963) 187–208; *M & L* 6.

10. Cf. chapter 8, "Vertical Structure: Ring Composition."

11. Cp. 20.1: καταλυθείσης δὲ τῆς τυραννίδος (when the tyranny had been overthrown).

12. A. Momigliano, *The Development of Greek Biography* (Cambridge, Mass. 1971).

12

A Constitutional Formula

In a passage (23.1) we saw but did not discuss in the foregoing chapter, Aristotle says that after the Persian Wars the Council of the Areopagus grew powerful again and was managing the state, having gotten the leadership through no *dogma*, οὐδενὶ δόγματι λαβοῦσα τὴν ἡγεμονίαν, but because of its responsibility for the sea battle at Salamis. Although most scholars have concerned themselves with the historicity of the first part of the statement,[1] that question does not affect the aspects that concern me here. Those are the process alluded to and the terminology involved. Commentators and translators agree that Aristotle is talking about a decision through a decree: "formal decree" (Kenyon, Warrington, von Fritz, and Kapp), "förmel Beschluss" (Kaibel/ Kiessling, Gigon), "by no definite resolution" (Rackham), "por ningun decreto" (Tovar), "sans aucun decision regulière" (Mathieu), "not because it was voted the position" (Moore). The assumption makes sense only if the passage is considered over against some paratexts: this kind of consideration it has, in fact, received, but only partially.

The distinguished commentator on the *Politics*, W. Newman[2] thought that the clause was an intentional contrast to the description of the appointment of the Four Hundred (29.1) and of the Thirty (34.3). Rhodes (287) doubts this and believes that the clause is a preparation for the view that the powers of the Areopagus revoked by Ephialtes were ἐπίθετα (25.2). The two views are not mutually exclusive. It is not necessarily an argument against Rhodes that we do not know of a single function appropriated by the Areopagus in the intervening period, but it is at least as possible that some of the ἐπίθετα were picked up before the Persian Wars. Newman's view is correct, but it does not go far enough. It is not so much that there is a contrast between the Areopagus and the Four Hunded/Thirty as that this passage is part of two formulaic patterns. The first is the δοκ- pattern which is used to introduce newly important entrants on the political scene,[3] and it is this, as we shall see, which explains the use of δόγμα. The second is a constitutional formula—found in different subtexts—according to which the institution of a nondemocratic regime is accomplished through democratic forms.

There are four instances of this pattern. The list:

A. 14.1: Peisistratus seized the Acropolis with the bodyguards he had requested from the *demos*, Ἀριστίωνος γράψαντος τὴν γνώμην[4] (the proposal was made by Aristion).

B. 23.1: οὐδενὶ δόγματι λαβοῦσα τὴν ἡγεμονίαν.

C. 29.1: the Athenians were compelled to dissolve the democracy and establish the regime of the Four Hundred, εἰπόντος τὸν μὲν πρὸ τοῦ
ψηίσματος λόγον Μηλοβίου, τὴν δὲ γνώμην γράψαντος Πυθοδώρου
τοῦ Ἀναφλυστίου. . . . [29.3] Κλειτοφῶν δὲ τὰ μὲν ἄλλα καθάπερ
Πυθόδωρος εἶπεν. . . . [32.1] ἐπικυρωθέντων δὲ τούτων ὑπὸ τοῦ
πλήθους, ἐπιψηφίσαντος Ἀριστομάχου (the speech introducing the
decree was made by Melobius, and the motion stood in the name of Pythodorus of Anaphlystus. . . . Cleitophon moved that in other respects
Pythodorus' decree should be followed. . . . it was ratified by the masses,
at an assembly under the presidency of Aristomachus).

D. Under pressure from Lysander (34.3), καταπλαγεὶς ὁ δῆμος ἠναγκάσθη
χειροτονεῖν τὴν ὀλιγαρχίαν.⁵ ἔγραψε δὲ τὸ ψήφισμα Δρακοντίδης
Ἀφιδναῖος (the people were intimidated and compelled to decide in
favor of the oligarchy. The author of the decree was Dracontides of
Aphidna).

Some features of this pattern seem to call for comment. All of these passages
concern the formal institution of non-δῆμος regimes: although opportunities
for its application to a δῆμος regime existed,⁶ it was not so used. Although
Aristotle will have found the material for the formula in various of his sources,
no source will have used this material in the formulaic way he did. His general
purpose is obvious enough: it is to set up an ironic contrast between a δῆμος
process and an anti-δῆμος result. This is most clear in passage D: χειροτονεῖν
is used only here in the narrative but occurs eighteen times in the documentary
section as part of the normal democratic process.

This general purpose may go some way to explain one anomaly in N, the
amount of space devoted to the constitutional maneuverings of 411. Indeed,
the most complete description in the *AP* of how the assembly decides an issue
is in 29.1ff.: a speech before the motion for the vote, the motion, the content
of the decree, a rider, and the results. The elaborated account seems out of
proportion to the historical importance of a short-lived regime, and the tension
between process and result does not seem to be a sufficient justification for this
kind of treatment. It may be that the special attention is due to Aristotle's
admiration for the regime (more on this below). It may be that this regime
represented the last serious threat in the historical progression toward radical
democracy. *Non liquet.*

οὐδενὶ δόγματι: to claim that this passage is an instance of the constitutional formula runs into one obvious difficulty. The vocabulary of the other
instances is γνώμη and ψήφισμα. δόγμα sits uneasily here. In epigraphic
usage, it refers only to decrees of allies.⁷ While it can refer to a decree τῆς
πόλεως,⁸ that use is rare, not elsewhere in Aristotle's works and not an obvious choice. That it belongs and how it belongs to the pattern is shown by
two paratexts. The leadership of the Areopagus after the Persian Wars was due
to its responsibility (αἰτία) for the financial support of men to fight the battle
of Salamis: διὰ ταύτην δὴ τὴν αἰτίαν παρεχώρουν αὐτῆς τῷ ἀξίωματι

(23.2). After Aristotle described Cleisthenes' background and his opposition to the tyrants, he says (21.1): διὰ μὲν οὖν ταύτας τὰς αἰτίας ἐπίστευον ὁ δῆμος τῷ Κλεισθένει. We have seen that because of the peculiar facts of Cleisthenes' life, Aristotle used this phrasing as a substitute for the δοκ- formula. I suggest that an analogous process is going on here, and that in the phrase οὐδενὶ δόγματι there is a conflation of two formulae. One is the δοκ- formula introducing an important[9] factor on the political scene; the second is the constitutional formula introducing a non-δῆμος regime. If this be correct, δόγματι is a superb example of paranomasia, and it is impossible to translate.

A final comment. Passages B and C above introduce regimes of which Aristotle approved, and the approval is expressed in language which is similar but not identical. Of the Areopagus (23.2):

> καὶ ἐπολιτεύθησαν Ἀθηναῖοι καλῶς καὶ κατὰ τούτους τοὺς καιρούς. συνέβη γὰρ αὐτοῖς περὶ τὸν χρόνον τοῦτον τά τε εἰς τὸ πόλεμον ἀσκῆσαι καὶ παρὰ τοῖς Ἕλλησιν εὐδοκιμῆσαι καὶ τὴν τῆς θαλάττης ἡγεμονίαν λαβεῖν. . . .

the city was well governed at this time. During this period they trained themselves for war, gained a good reputation among the Greeks, and acquired the leadership at sea. . . .

Of the "intermediate regime" of the Five Thousand (33.2):

> δοκοῦσι δὲ καλῶς πολιτευθῆναι κατὰ τούτους τοὺς καιρούς, πολέμου τε καθεστῶτος καὶ ἐκ τῶν ὅπλων τῆς πολιτείας οὔσης.

The Athenians seem to have been well governed at this time, when they were at war and the constitution was based on the hoplites.

In the first text we have the simple ἐπολιτεύθησαν, in the second the qualified δοκοῦσι πολιτευθῆναι. Is there a difference? If my arguments about these two formulae are correct there should be, and I suggest that there is. The question is, in what does the difference consist? It is not in the matter of opinion versus reality: nothing shows that Aristotle did not agree with the opinion expressed in 33.2.[10] There is, however, another way in which these statements may differ, namely, if the qualified statement represents an opinion which Aristotle inherited and shared, while the simple statement represents his own invention. As it happens, the qualified statement of 33.2 repeats[11] a similar statement of Thucydides 8.97.2: καὶ οὐχ ἥκιστα δὴ τὸν πρῶτον χρόνον ἐπί γε ἐμοῦ Ἀθηναῖοι φαίνονται εὖ πολιτεύσαντες (it was during the first period of this regime that the Athenians seem to have had the best government, at least in my time). On the other hand, the only parallel to the unqualified statement at 23.2 is in Aristotle's own *Politics*.[12] Whence Aristotle derived the notion of an Areopagite hegemony after the Persian Wars is a thorny problem, and one for which we have no precise evidence whatsoever. It is possible that it was his own inference from the attacks of Ephialtes and thus that the unqualified statement was his own conception.

Once Aristotle had decided to create a pattern to introduce non-δῆμος regimes, the ἡγεμονία of the Areopagus had to be included because it was that kind of regime. Why then did he not use the language of the formula, e.g., by writing οὐδενὶ ψηφίσματι? I suggest that the regime of the Areopapus differed from the others in two ways: (1) unlike the others, its accession to leadership was untainted by deceit (14.1, 29.1: συμπείθειν) or compulsion (29.1, 34.3: ἀναγκάζειν) and (2) Aristotle admired this regime (23.1) as he did not the others. Thus, by a kind of negative (οὐδενί) variation of the pattern, he was able to include the Areopagites within the pattern and, at the same time, distinguish their regime from the other instances.

NOTES

1. The majority doubt: cf. Rhodes *ad loc.*
2. *CR* 5 (1891) 163–64.
3. Cf. chapter 11, "The δοκεῖν Formula."
4. In Aristotle's source (Androtion): Plut. *vitSol* 30.2 and 3: ᾿Αριστίωνος γράψαντος. . . . τὸ ψήφισμα.
5. A subtext is the source of Diodorus 14.3.7: δῆμος καταπλαγεὶς ἠναγκάζετο χειροτονίᾳ καταλῦσαι τὴν δημοκρατίαν (frightened, the people were compelled to dissolve the democracy by vote).
6. One assumes the normal assembly procedure in the restoraton of the democracy at 34.1. Cf. Thuc. 8.97.: ἐκκλησίαν ξυνέλεγον. . . . ἐν ᾗ ἧπερ καὶ τοὺς τετρακοσίους καταπαύσαντες κτλ. (they collected the assembly in which they put down the Four Hundred) and at 38.1.
7. *IG* II² 4, 96, 97, 103. This usage is also found in literature: Xen. *Hell.* 5.2.37 al; Dem. 17.27 al; Aesch. 2.32 al.
8. Philochorus 328 F 5 quotes a verse inscribed by officials: βουλῆς καὶ δήμου δόγμασι πειθόμενοι (in obedience to the decrees of council and people). Other examples are Xen. *Hell.* 6.2.2, [Dem.] 12.16, Dem. 51.22, and Aesch. 3.43.
9. Of the figures/institutions to whom the δοκεῖν- formula is attached, Peisistratus, Cleisthenes, Areopagus, Aristeides, Ephialtes, and the *demos* are in the summary of μεταβολαὶ πολιτειῶν of chapter 41.
10. The paratexts here are δοκοῦσι and δοκεῖ of 28.5.
11. "Though with a different slant": Rhodes 414.
12. *Politics* 1304A20–21

13

Aristotle and Theopompus

Modern interest in the relationship between Aristotle and Theopompus' excursus on the Athenian demagogues in book 10 of his *Philippica* may be said to have had at least a chronological beginning with an article by Wade-Gery in 1938.[1] Wade-Gery thought that, although Aristotle was writing later than the date of the excursus (350s), it was not used by him,[2] and he posited a common source, the oligarchic revolutionary, Critias. Connor[3] opted for the same conclusion but thought it pointless to attempt to identify this source. Raubitschek[4] and Ruschenbusch,[5] on the other hand, believed that Theopompus was a source for Aristotle.[6] Most recently, Ferretto[7] has resolutely refused to face the question and has stressed instead the ideological and methodological divergence between the two authors.[8] It is, again, surprising that the major texts to be considered have received only superficial analysis, and a closer examination should make it clear that the position of Raubitschek is closest to the truth, although he never really argued for his conclusion.

I begin by discussing that chapter in which is it abundantly clear that there is a connection between Aristotle and Theopompus' *Philippica,* a connection which, if the evidence allowed more precise analysis, would doubtless be seen to underlie chapter 28 as well. In 27.2, Aristotle says that the *demos* προῃρεῖτο τὴν πολιτείαν διοικεῖν αὐτός (chose to administer public affairs themselves). One of the ways in which it was able to do this was through its control of the courts. Aristotle continues (27.3–4):

A: ἐποίησε δὲ καὶ μισθοφόρα τὰ δικαστήρια Περικλῆς πρῶτος, ἀντιδημαγωγῶν πρὸς τὴν Κίμωνος εὐπορίαν ὁ γὰρ Κίμων, ἅτε τυρρανικὴν ἔχων οὐσίαν, (Pericles was the first man to provide payment for jury service, as a political measure to counter the generosity of Cimon. Cimon was as rich as a tyrant:) [private means]

B: πρῶτον μὲν τὰς κοινὰς λητουργίας ἐλητούργει λαμπρῶς, (he performed the public liturgies lavishly;) [public generosity]

C: ἔπειτα τῶν δημοτῶν ἔτρεφε πολλούς. (and he maintained many of his fellow demesmen.) [private generosity]

C¹: ἐπεὶ τοῖς ἰδίοις [sc., Pericles] ἡττᾶτο (Pericles' property was insufficient for this kind of service) [lack of private means]

B¹· διδόναι τοῖς πολλοῖς τὰ αὐτῶν (give the people their own property;) [public generosity],

A¹: κατεσκεύασε μισθοφορὰν τοῖς δικασταῖς. (and so he devised payment for the jurors).

With this we may contrast Aristotle's basic subtext which is represented by the lengthy fragment of Theopompus preserved by Athenaeus.

καίτοι ὁ πατὴρ αὐτῶν Πεισίστρατος μετρίως ἐχρῆτο ταῖς ἡδοναῖς· ὅς γε οὐδ᾽ ἐν τοῖς χωρίοις οὐδ᾽ ἐν τοῖς κήποις φύλακας καθίστα, ὡς Θεόπομπος ἱστορεῖ ἐν τῇ πρώτῃ καὶ εἰκόστῃ [F 135], ἀλλ᾽ εἴα τὸν βουλόμενον εἰσιόντα ἀπολαύειν καὶ λαμβάνειν ὧν δεηθείη· ὅπερ ὕστερον ἐποίησεν καὶ Κίμων μιμησάμενος αὐτόν. περὶ οὗ καὶ αὐτοῦ ἱστορῶν ἐν τῇ δεκάτῃ τῶν Φιλιππικῶν Θεόπομπός φησι·[X] Κίμων ὁ Ἀθηναῖος ἐν τοῖς ἀγροῖς καὶ ἐν τοῖς κήποις οὐδένα τοῦ καρποῦ καθίστα φύλακα, ὅπως οἱ βουλόμενοι τῶν πολιτῶν εἰσιόντες ὀπωρίζονται καὶ λαμνβάνωσιν εἴ τινος δέοιντο τῶν ἐν τοῖς χωρίοις. ἔπειτα τὴν οἰκίαν παρεῖχε κοινὴν ἅπασιν ὡς δεῖπνον αἰεὶ εὐτελὲς ἀνθρώποις καὶ τοὺς ἀπόρους προσιόντας τῶν Ἀθηναίων δειπνεῖν. ἐθεράπευεν δὲ καὶ τοὺς καθ᾽ ἑκάστην ἡμέραν αὐτοῦ τι δεομένους [X], καὶ [Y] λέγουσιν ὡς περιήγετο μὲν ἀεὶ νεανίσκους δύ᾽ ἢ τρεῖς ἔχοντας κέρματα τούτοις τε διδόναι προσέταττεν, ὁπότε τις προσέλθοι αὐτου δεόμενος [Y]. καί φασι [Z] μὲν αὐτὸν εἰς τάφην εἰσφέρειν. ποιεῖν δὲ καὶ τοῦτο πολλάκις, ὅποτε τῶν πολιτῶν τινα κακῶς ἠμφιεσμένον, κελεύειν αὐτῷ μεταμφιέννυσθαι τῶν νεανίσκων τινὰ συνακολουθούντων αὐτῷ. ἐκ δὴ τούτων ἁπάντων ηὐδόκιμει καὶ πρῶτος ἦν τῶν πολιτῶν[Z]. (Athenaeus 12.533 A–C = Theopompus 115 F 89 J)

and yet their father Peisistratus was moderate in his pleasures. He didn't put guards in his properties and gardens, as Theopompus narrates in book 21, but allowed anyone who wanted to enter to take and enjoy what he needed. Cimon later did the same, imitating him. Of him Theopompus in Book 10 of the *Philippica* says: [X] "Cimon of Athens put no guard over his produce in his fields and gardens so that any of the citizens who wanted could enter, enjoy and take whatever they needed of the things on the properties. Secondly, he opened his house to all, and an inexpensive meal was always ready for many, and poor Athenians came in and ate. He also took care of those who each day asked him for something [X]. As he walked around [Y], they say, he instructed two or three young men to give coins to these people, whenever someone would approach him and ask [Y]. They say [Z] that he also contributed to burial expenses. Whenever he saw one of the citizens poorly clothed, it was his frequent practice to bid that one to exchange clothing with one of the young men in his company. As a result of all of this, he enjoyed a good reputation and was first among the citizens [Z]."[9]

There are five parallel passages:
1. Plutarch, *vitPer* 9.2:

πρὸς τὴν Κίμωνος δόξαν ἀντιταττόμενος ὑπεποιεῖτο τὸν δῆμον, ἐλαττούμενος δὲ πλούτῳ καὶ χρήμασιν, ἀφ᾽ ὧν ἐκεῖνος ἀνελάμβανε τοὺς πένητας, δεῖπνόν τε καθ᾽ ἡμέραν τῷ δεομένῳ παρέχων Ἀθηναίων καὶ τοὺς πρεσβυτέρους ἀμφιεννύων, τῶν δὲ χωρίων τοὺς φραγμοὺς ἀφαιρῶν ὅπως ὀπωρίζωσιν οἱ βουλόμενοι, τούτοις ὁ Περικλῆς καταδημαγωγούμενος τρέπεται πρὸς τὴν τῶν δημοσίων διανομήν, συμβουλεύσαντος αὐτῷ ⟨Δάμωνος τοῦ⟩ Δαμωνίδου Οἴηθεν, ὡς Ἀριστοτέλης ἱστόρηκε. καὶ ταχὺ θεωρικοῖς καὶ δικαστικοῖς λήμμασιν ἄλλαις τε μισθοφορίαις καὶ χορηγίαις συνδεκάσας τὸ πλῆθος κτλ.[10]

setting himself up against the reputation of Cimon, he tried to get the *demos* on his side, although not up to this level in wealth and possessions: with this base, Cimon was winning over the poor, providing daily a meal to any Athenian who wanted it and clothing the elderly, taking fences off his properties so that those who wanted could enjoy them. Trying to get *demos* support in the face of these measures, Pericles turned to the distribution of public funds, on the advice of Damon, son of Damonides, of the deme Oia, as Aristotle narrated. And quickly bribing the masses with money for attendance at theater and law court and with other payments for public service and theatrical productions. . . .

2. Plutarch, *vitCim* 10.1–2:

ἤδη δ᾽ εὐπορῶν ὁ Κίμων. . . . τῶν τε γὰρ ἀγρῶν τοὺς φραγμοὺς ἀφεῖλεν ἵνα καὶ τοῖς ξένοις καὶ τῶν πολιτῶν τοῖς δεομένοις ἀδεῶς ὑπάρχῃ λαμβάνειν τῆς ὀπώρας καὶ δεῖπνον οἴκοι παρέχων λιτὸν μέν, ἀρκοῦν δὲ πολλοῖς, ἐποιεῖτο καθ᾽ ἡμέραν, ἐφ᾽ ὃ τῶν πενήτων ὁ βουλόμενος εἰσῄει καὶ διατροφὴν εἶχεν ἀπράγμονα, μόνοις τοῖς δημοσίοις σχολάζων. ὡς δ᾽ Ἀριστοτέλης φησίν, οὐχ ἁπάντων Ἀθηναίων ἀλλὰ τῶν δημοτῶν αὐτοῦ Λακιαδῶν παρεσκευάζετο τῷ βουλομένῳ τὸ δεῖπνον. αὐτῷ δὲ νεάνισκοι παρείποντο συνήθεις ἀμπεχόμενοι καλῶς, ὧν ἕκαστος, εἴ τις συντύχοι τῷ Κίμωνι τῶν ἀστῶν πρεσβύτερος ἠμφιεσμένος ἐνδεῶς, διημείβετο πρὸς αὐτὸν τὰ ἱμάτια. . . .

Cimon was by now wealthy. . . . he removed the fences from his fields so that both foreigners and citizens in need had the opportunity to take from the produce without fear; at his house he daily made available a meal, simple but sufficient for many to which any poor man who wanted came and had nurture without trouble, reserving his time and effort only for civic activitites. As Aristotle says, he did not provide a meal for any and every Athenian who wanted it, but for his fellow demesmen. Well-dressed young men habitually accompanied him, each of whom, if Cimon ran into any elder of the citizens poorly dressed, would exchange clothing with him. . . .

3. Σ BD to Aelius Aristeides, *On the Four* 46.118 (3.446 Dindorf):

δύο δὲ ἦσαν Ἀθήνησι πολιτεῖαι· οἱ μὲν γὰρ ἦσαν καλοὶ καὶ ἀγαθοί, οἱ καλούμενοι ὀλιγαρχικοί, οἱ δὲ δημοτικοί· καὶ τούτων μὲν προΐστατο Κίμων, πολλὰ διανέμων καὶ συγχωρῶν ἐκ τῶν χωρίων ὀπωρίσασθαι τοῖς βουλομένοις, καὶ ἱμάτια διανέμων τοῖς πένησι. τῶν δὲ ὀλιγαρχικῶν προΐστατο Περικλῆς.

there were two political factions at Athens; one group was the beautiful people, called oligarchics; the others were supporters of democracy. Cimon was the leader of the latter, distributing much, allowing those who waned to take produce from his properties and distributing clothing to the poor. Pericles was the leader of the oligarchics[11]

4. Nepos, *Vita Cimonis* 4.1–3:

fuit enim tanta liberalitate cum compluribus locis praedia hortosque haberet, ut numquam in eis custodem imposuerit fructus servandi gratia, ne quis impediretur, quominus eius rebus quibus quisque vellet frueretur. semper enim pedisequi cum nummis sunt secuti, ut, si quis opis eius indigeret, haberet quod statim daret, ne differendo videretur negare. saepe, cum aliquem offensum fortuna videret minus bene vestitum, suum amiculum dedit. cotidies sic cena ei coquebatur, ut, quos invocatos vidisset in foro, omnis devocaret, quod facere nullo die praetermittebat. nulli fides eius, nulli opera, nulli res familiaris defuit: multos locupletavit, complures pauperes mortuos, qui unde efferentur non reliquissent, suo sumpto extulit.
. . .

He was of such generosity, since he had estates and gardens in many places, that he never put a guard in them to protect the produce, lest anyone who wanted be prevented from enjoying his things. Attendants with coins always followed him so that, if anyone needed his resources, he would have something to give him immediately lest he seem to refuse him by putting him off. Often, when he saw one of fate's victims less well clothed, he gave him his own cloak. Daily dinner was prepared for him under circumstances such that whomever he saw in the forum without dinner invitations he called them in: he didn't miss a day in this. His loyalty, his assistance, his personal wealth failed no one. Many he enriched; not a few of the poor when they died he buried at his own expence since they left nothing to pay for their burial. . . .

5. Cicero, *De officiis* II.18.64:

Theophrastus quidem scribit Cimonem Athenis etiam in suos curiales Laciadas hospitalem fuisse; ita enim instituisse et uilicis imperauisse, ut omnia praeberentur, quicumque Laciades in uillam suam deuertisset.

Theophrastus indeed writes that at Athens Cimon was hospitable to his own demesman, the Lakiads. For he arranged and so instructed his bailiffs that everything be provided for any Lakiad who visited his country home.

It is clear that only Plutarch knew the accounts both of Theopompus and of Aristotle, and he alone draws attention to a difference in detail between the two *(Cim)*, namely, that Aristotle restricted Cimon's largesse to his fellow demesmen. That detail is important, but not as important as it can be made to be and perhaps less important than other differences between the two accounts. It is initially useful in separating out exactly what Theopompus said and how he said it.

The following statements will be unobjectionable. Theophrastus, whose view is known from Cicero, followed Aristotle: that would be expected. The account of Nepos, based only on Theopompus whether directly or indirectly, contains much rhetorical exaggeration. The account of Σ Aristeides is based only on Theopompus.

That much said, the basic question must now be faced: what is the relationship between Aristotle and Theopompus? The options are three: (1) a common source which Aristotle reported more correctly than did Theopompus, (2) Aristotle corrected Theopompus through a source unknown to the latter, (3) Aristotle used Theopompus and adjusted that account *sua sponte* for reasons involved with his own choice of presentation. Due to our ignorance, (1) and (2) cannot absolutely be ruled out. I hope to show that, on the evidence we have, (3) is correct.

To show that, it is necessary first to discern what Theopompus said. In his influential article Wade-Gery stated that the details of the opposition between Cimon and Pericles, as found in Aristotle, are due to Theopompus; but Wade-Gery's statement involved a methodological flaw. He assumed that the material in Plutarch was basically Theopompan, with the single divergence about the nature of the group with access to the produce, the divergence which Plutarch noted in Aristotle. But the fact that Plutarch used Aristotle does not mean that he used him only in noting this divergence: it does mean that the account in Plutarch is contaminated, and that the only way to recover what Theopompus said is to use those versions of the events which are uncontaminated. These are the versions of Athenaeus, Nepos and Σ Aristeides. What is in Aristotle and Plutarch but not in these is

1. Cimon engaged in acts of public generosity.[12]
2. Cimon's private largesse was limited to his fellow demesmen.
3. Their rivalry[13] expressed itself in financial outlays.
4. On Pericles' part, the outlay consisted of making the law courts μισθο-φόρα.

Given the contrasting facts that, on the one hand, there is no evidence that Theopompus said anything about the Athenian law courts and, on the other hand, that the development of the law courts was a central theme in the Ἀθ-πολ, it is easy to see how Aristotle took a narrative of Theopompus and revised it to incorporate that theme. The revisions involve selection of content, vocabulary, and structure, all three of which are intertwined.

Regarding selection of content, it has not, I think, been noticed that Athenaios' version of Theopompus has him speaking with two or three voices. The first segment (X) is in his own voice (Θεόπομπός φησι) and extends down to αὐτοῦ τι δεομένους. The next segment (Y) begins with λέγουσιν, and the last segment (Z) begins with φασι: in Y and Z Theopompus is recording the statements of others.[14]

This segmentation is blurred by Plutarch. His main source for *vitPer* is Aristotle, but he includes one item from Z (τοὺς πρεσβυτέρους ἀμφιεννύων): in *vitCim* the main source is Theopompus, and details from all three segments are found.

In Aristotle, however, the distinction is observed: his borrowing is restricted to segment X. There could be various reasons for this. He may have thought the views of others reported by Theopompus less credible than the *ipsissima verba* of Theopompus, but he didn't think those words particularly accurate. I suspect that the reason is one of scale: Aristotle was not writing even a mini-biography of Cimon, and from Theopompus he took only what sufficed to assist the points he wanted to make.

The structure of 27.3–4 is informed by ring composition.

A (27.3): ἐποίησε δὲ καὶ μισθοφόρα τὰ δικαστήρια Περικλῆς πρῶτος.
. . ..
B (27.3): ὁ γὰρ Κίμων. . . . πρῶτον μὲν τὰς κοινὰς λητουργίας
ἐλητούργει λαμπρῶς,
C (27.3): ἔπειτα τῶν δημοτῶν ἔτρεφε πολλούς. . . .
C¹ (27.4): ἐπεὶ τοῖς ἰδίοις ἡττᾶτο [sc., Pericles],
B¹ (27.4): διδόναι τοῖς πολλοῖς τὰς αὐτῶν,
A¹ (27.4): κατεσκεύασε μισθοφορὰν τοῖς δκασταῖς. . . .

The structure has two effects: (1) it puts the rivalry between Cimon and
Pericles within a specific context; the rivalry led to payment for jury duty and
thus made more members of the lower class interested in serving as dicasts; (2)
it serves sharply to demarcate the public/private sides of the acts of Cimon and
Pericles. It is (2) which explains one curious feature of Aristotle's language.

We have seen that there are two major discrepancies in the accounts of Aristotle and Theopompus, Aristotle's reference to public benefactions of Cimon
and the number of beneficiaries of his private benefactions. Aristotle describes
the first as follows: τὰς κοινὰς λητουργίας ἐλητούργει λαμπρῶς. The
alliterative phrase is both traditional and new. It is traditional in that the
genus λητουργία and its species χορηγέω/ία are frequently found qualified by
λαμπρ-.[15] It is new in that κοιναὶ λητουργίαι is Aristotle's coinage. The
result is pleonastic: every λητουργία, by definition, is κοινή. Since pleonasm
is not a readily recognized feature of Aristotle's style, it must be asked why he
resorted to it. The answer is clear: the κοιναὶ λητουργίαι are at the opposite
pole from the financial status of Pericles, who τοῖς ἰδίοις ἡττᾶτο.

The other change introduced by Aristotle concerned the number of beneficiaries. Now, part of what Theopompus said about Cimon is a doublet of what
he said about Peisistratus:

Πεισίστρατος	Κίμων
οὐδ'. . . φύλακας ἐφίστα	οὐδένα . . . καθίστα φύλακα
τὸν βουλόμενον	οἱ βουλόμενοι
εἰσιόντα	εἰσιόντες
ἀπολαύειν	ὀπωρίζονται
λαμβάνειν ὧν δεηθείη	λαμβάνωσιν εἴ τινος δέοιντο.[16]

If Cimon's generosity thoroughly imitated that of Peisistratus, it would not
have been restricted to demesmen: that restriction is not mentioned in the text,
and the deme in the time of Peisistratus was not of sufficient socio-political
importance for such a restriction to make sense. It is necessary, then, to conclude that Theopompus is here exaggerating the scope of Cimon's generosity,
as scholars now agree.[17] To produce the corrected version also suited Aristotle's purposes: to reduce the scale of Cimon's largesse is to make of it more
a private than a public activity, and thus to keep the structural difference between public and private, if it be true to say that there is a sense in which
benefactions with a larger number of recipients are more public than those with
a smaller number.

NOTES

1. H. T. Wade-Gery, "Two Notes on Theopompus, *Philippika, X,*" *AJP* (60) 129–34 = *Essays in Greek History* (Oxford 1958) 233–38.

2. This conclusion was stated but not supported by argument.

3. W. R. Connor, *Theopompus and Fifth-Century Athens* (Cambridge, Mass. 1968) 110.

4. A. E. Raubitschek, "Theopompus on Thucydides the Son of Melesias," *Phoenix* 14 (1960) 81–94.

5. E. Ruschenbusch, "Theopompea II: Theopomps Hellenika als Quelle in Aristotelis AP," *ZPE* 45 (1982) 91–94. Ruschenbusch's method (in which he had been partially preceded by Raubitschek) is basically linguistic. He sought to isolate vocabulary ἅπαξ or rare in Aristotle but relatively common in Theopompus. Given the fragmentary nature of the evidence, certainty is unattainable, but some conclusions are suggestive. For example, if ἀντιπολιτεύεσθαι (ἅπαξ: cf. Theopompus F 91 and 261; Connor 41–42; Ruschenbusch 81) of *Pol.* 1274A14 is borrowed by Aristotle, this part of Theopompus' work was in circulation before Aristotle returned to Athens in 335/4.

6. The latter believed that Aristotle knew Theopompus through the mediation of Androtion.

7. C. Ferretto, *La città dissipatrice* (Genova 1984) 39 with n. 43.

8. She does, however, entertain the possibility of personal contact between the two at the court of Philip (p. 46).

9. This last phrase may contain an allusion to Thucydides' remark of Cimon's rival, Pericles, that Athens under his leadership (2.65.9) ἐγίγνετό τε λόγῳ μὲν δημοκρατία, ἔργῳ δὲ ὑπὸ τοῦ πρώτου ἀνδρὸς ἀρχή (it was called democracy but in reality it was the rule of the leading man).

10. The expanded list of Periclean benefits may result from a confused memory of Plato, *Gorgias* 515E5–6.

11. The alleged political allegiances of both Cimon and Pericles are strange, but not of immediate concern. Cf. Connor, *Theopompus* 37.

12. Plutarch's version of this is (*vitCim*) μόνοις τοῖς δημοσίοις σχολάζων.

13. In these sources, the rivalry is found only in Σ Aristeides, an anonymous account (i.e., not attributed to Theopompus). I think this can stand as Theopompan, since other details in Σ clearly go back to him.

14. This segmentation does not help with the problem of sources for the relevant divergence between Aristotle and Theopompus is confined to X.

15. Cf. Antiphon, *Tetr.* 1.2.12; Isoc., *Ad Nicoclem* 56; Aristotle, *NE* 1122B23 (metaphorically, *Protr.* 2.8 Düring). The verbal association is so familiar that Thucydides can use it to indulge in wordplay: cf. 3.16.3 (speech of Alcibiades): ὅσα αὖ ἐν τῇ πόλει χορηγίαις ἢ ἄλλῳ τῳ λαμπρύνομαι (the many ocasions of personal pride acquired by *khoregiai* or in some other way).

16. Aristotle's remark about Cimon, ἅτε τυραννικὴν ἔχων οὐσίαν, is doubtless an allusion to this text.

17. Cf. J. K. Davies, *Athenian Propertied Families* (Oxford 1971) 333; and D. Whitehead, *The Demes of Attica* (Princeton 1986) 307.

14

Aristotle and Theramenes

Critical evaluation of the actions, character, and motives of the Athenian politician Theramenes began during his lifetime, continued at some level of passion in the years immediately after his death, and is still with us.[1] Aristotle's judgment (28.5) of him, it is well known, was unambiguously favorable: why that should have been so is a question I cannot answer,[2] and I turn instead to an examination of the (largely unexamined) panoply of techniques with which Aristotle so shaped his narrative as to justify his judgment of Theramenes to the mind of his reader. I will argue that he used two methods, a deliberately and unusually highly articulated structure designed, especially in chapter 28, to highlight Theramenes, and a pattern of suggestions and associations, the purpose of which is to link Theramenes with Solon and other popular leaders.

I. THE STRUCTURE OF 28

It is necessary to have the complete text of chapter 28 before us.

> A. Ἕως μὲν οὖν Περικλῆς προειστήκει τοῦ δήμου βελτίω τὰ κατὰ τὴν πολιτείαν ἦν, τελευτήσαντος δὲ Περικλέους πολὺ χείρω. πρῶτον γὰρ τότε προστάτην ἔλαβεν ὁ δῆμος οὐκ εὐδοκιμοῦντα παρὰ τοῖς ἐπιεικέσιν· ἐν δὲ τοῖς πρότερον χρόνοις ἀεὶ διετέλουν οἱ ἐπιεικεῖς δημαγωγοῦντες.
> B. ἐξ ἀρχῆς μὲν γὰρ καὶ πρῶτος ἐγένετο προστάτης τοῦ δήμου Σόλων, δεύτερος δὲ Πεισίστρατος τῶν εὐγενῶν καὶ γνωρίμων, καταλυθείσης δὲ τῆς τυραννίδος Κλεισθένης τοῦ γένους ὢν τῶν Ἀλκμεωνιδῶν, καὶ τούτῳ μὲν οὐδεὶς ἦν ἀντιστασιώτης, ὡς ἐξέπεσον οἱ περὶ τὸν Ἰσαγόραν. μετὰ δὲ ταῦτα τοῦ μὲν δήμου προείστηκει Ξάνθιππος, τῶν δὲ γνωρίμων Μιλτιάδης, ἔπειτα Θεμιστοκλῆς καὶ Ἀριστείδης· μετὰ δὲ τούτους Ἐφιάλτης μὲν τοῦ δήμου, Κίμων δ᾽ ὁ Μιλτιάδου τῶν εὐπόρων· εἶτα Περικλῆς μὲν τοῦ δήμου, Θουκυδίδης δὲ τῶν ἑτέρων, κηδεστὴς ὢν Κίμωνος.
> C. Περικλέους δὲ τελευτήσαντος τῶν μὲν ἐπιφανῶν προείστηκει Νικίας ὁ ἐν Σικελίᾳ τελευτήσας, τοῦ δὲ δήμου Κλεὼν ὁ Κλεαινέτου, ὃς δοκεῖ μάλιστα διαφθεῖραι τὸν δῆμον ταῖς ὁρμαῖς, καὶ πρῶτος ἐπὶ τοῦ βήματος ἀνέκραγε καὶ ἐλοιδορήσατο καὶ περιζωσάμενος ἐδημηγόρησε τῶν ἄλλων ἐν κόσμῳ λεγόντων. εἶτα μετὰ τούτους τῶν μὲν ἑτέρων Θηραμένης ὁ Ἅγνωνος, τοῦ δὲ δήμου Κλεοφῶν ὁ λυροποιός, ὃς καὶ τὴν διωβελίαν ἐπόρισε πρῶτος· καὶ χρόνον μέν τινα διεδίδου, μετὰ δὲ ταῦτα κατέλυσε Καλλικράτης Παιανιεύς, πρῶτος ὑποσχόμενος ἐπιθήσειν πρὸς τοῖν δυοῖν ὀβόλοιν ἄλλον ὀβολόν. τούτων μὲν οὖν ἀμφοτέρων θάνατον κατέγνωσαν

ὕστερον· εἴωθεν γάρ, κἂν ἐξαπατηθῇ, τὸ πλῆθος ὕστερον μισεῖν τούς τι προαγαγόντας ποιεῖν αὐτοὺς τῶν μὴ καλῶς ἐχόντων. ἀπὸ δὲ Κλεοφῶντος ἤδη διέδεχοντο συνεχῶς τὴν δημαγωγίαν οἱ μάλιστα βουλόμενοι θρασύνεσθαι καὶ χαρίζεσθαι τοῖς πολλοῖς πρὸς τὸ παραυτίκα βλέποντες.

D. δοκοῦσι δὲ βέλτιστοι γεγονέναι τῶν Ἀθήνησι πολιτευσαμένων μετὰ τοὺς ἀρχαίους Νικίας καὶ Θουκυδίδης καὶ Θηραμένης. καὶ περὶ μὲν Νικίου καὶ Θουκυδίδου πάντες σχεδὸν ὁμολογοῦσιν ἄνδρας γεγονέναι οὐ μόνον καλοὺς κἀγαθοὺς ἀλλὰ καὶ πολιτικοὺς καὶ τῇ πάσῃ πόλει πατρικῶς χρωμένους, περὶ δὲ Θηραμένους διὰ τὸ συμβῆναι κατ' αὐτὸν ταραχώδεις τὰς πολιτείας ἀμφισβήτησις τῆς κρίσεώς ἐστι. δοκεῖ μέντοι τοῖς μὴ παρέργως ἀποφαινομένοις οὐχ ὥσπερ αὐτὸν διαβάλλουσι πάσας τὰς πολιτείας καταλύειν, ἀλλὰ πάσας προάγειν ἕως μηδὲν παρανομοῖεν, ὡς δυνάμενος πολιτεύεσθαι κατὰ πάσας, ὅπερ ἐστὶν ἀγαθοῦ πολίτου ἔργον, παρανομούαις δὲ οὐ συγχωρῶν ἀλλ' ἀπεχθανόμενος.

A. While Pericles was champion of the people, the constitution was not in too bad a state, but after his death it became much worse. It was then that the people first took a champion who was not of good repute among the better sort, whereas previously it was always men of the better sort who were popular leaders.

B. To begin at the beginning, Solon was the first champion of the people, the second was Peisistratus, [who was from] the well-born and notable; after the overthrow of the tyranny came Cleisthenes, of the Alcmeonid family, and he had no opponent, since Isagoras's party was expelled. After this, Xanthippus was champion of the people and Miltiades of the nobles: then Themistocles and Aristeides [respectively]; after them Ephialtes was champion of the people and Thucydides, a relative of Cimon, champion of the others.

C. After Pericles' death the distinguished were championed by Nicias, who died in Sicily, and the people by Cleon, son of Cleainetus: Cleon, it seems, more than anyone else corrupted the people by his wild impulses, and was the first man, who, when on the platform, shouted, uttered abuse and made speeches with his clothes hitched up, while everyone else spoke in an orderly manner. Next, after them, Theramanes son of Hagnon was champion of the others and Cleophon the lyre maker champion of the people. Cleophon was the first man to provide the two-obol grant: for a while it continued to be paid, then it was abolished by Callicrates of Paeania, after he had first promised to add another obol to the two. Both Cleophon and Callicrates were subsequently condemned to death by the Athenians: the masses generally come to hate those who have led them on to do anything wrong, particularly if they have deceived them. Since Cleophon there has been an unending succession of popular leaders whose chief desire has been to be outrageous and to gratify the masses, looking only to considerations of the moment.

D. It appears that the best of the Athenian politicians after the older ones were Nicias, Thucydides and Theramenes. As far as Nicias and Thucydides are concerned, almost everyone agrees that they were not only gentleman but were public-spirited and behaved like fathers toward the whole city; but the verdict on Theramenes is disputed, because in his time there was constitutional upheaval. However, the judgment of those who are not superficial critics is that he did not destroy all regimes, as his detractors allege, but supported all as long as they did nothing unlawful (since he was able to take part in politics under all regimes, as a good citizen should), but when they broke the law did not acquiesce but earned their enmity.

Since the text I print differs in spots from that of the most recent commentary and edition, I first attempt to justify it. There follow some general remarks about structure, particular points being reserved to their place in the wider treatment.

B. Πεισίστρατος τῶν εὐγενῶν καὶ γνωρίμων: the text has been variously emended; Rhodes prefers, and Chambers prints, one of three suggestions of Gomme,[3] εὐγενῶν καὶ γνωρίμων ⟨Λυκοῦργος⟩. The stated assumption behind the emendation is that Aristotle is giving pairs of leaders, and one of the texts behind the assumption is the last part of the statement about Cleisthenes, καὶ τούτῳ μὲν οὐδεὶς ἦν ἀντιστασιώτης. The assumption cannot totally be true, for Solon has no rival, and, at the end of the list, Cleophon and Callicrates have no rivals. The statement on Cleisthenes is, in fact, opposed to Gomme's assumption: it points up that period of his activity in which he had no rival, and it will be suggested below that this is the salient point of the inclusion of the leaders of segment A. The reference then will be to the period after Peisistratus' second restoration, in which, according to Aristotle, he enjoyed the good will of both sides. The point of including the phrase εὐγενῶν καὶ γνωρίμων is that Peisistratus' background has not hitherto been mentioned. Compare 5.3 on Solon: τῇ μὲν φύσει καὶ τῇ δόξῃ τῶν πρώτων (by birth and repute one of the leading citizens).

B. ἔπειτα Θεμιστοκλῆς καὶ Ἀριστείδης. The same assumption of Gomme's operates here (Rhodes 349), to the effect that Themistocles and Aristeides were rivals, the first as προστάτης τοῦ δήμου, the second as προστάτης τῶν γνωρίμων. The fact that this result is in blatant contradiction to 23.3, at which both are called προστάται τοῦ δήμου κατὰ τούτους τοὺς καιρούς, is acknowledged but ignored[4] But this fact alone suffices to guarantee their inclusion in the list, since all previous προστάται τοῦ δήμου are repeated therein, as well as all the opposed leaders. The pair of 23.3 is unique and uniquely treated in 28.

Further, Aristotle makes clear his intention here by a stylistic device. Every other instance of rival politicians in this list is marked by the use of δήμου and a polar genitive (γνωρίμων vel. sim.). Both genitives are missing here, and the resulting options are two: both men are τοῦ δήμου or both τῶν γνωρίμων. Since we have already been told that they are the first, that is what they are.

C. Καλλικράτης Παιανιεὺς πρῶτος ὑποσχόμενος. Van Leeuwen emended the reading of the papyrus to πρῶτον. I retain πρῶτος[5] because it is a recurring element of a pattern involving Cleon, Cleophon and, from chapter 27, Pericles and Anytus.[6]

D. μετὰ τοὺς ἀρχαίους. According to Rhodes (358), "it is not clear where the line is to be drawn." Since, of the comparandi to Theramenes, Thucydides is from segment B and Nicias from segment C (and no small reason for their inclusion is the fact that they are from precisely those segments), it should be clear that οἱ ἀρχαῖοι are the inhabitants of segment A.

II. THE SUBTEXTS OF CHAPTER 28

The first sentence of the chapter proposes a thesis, the second sentence begins to prove the thesis by means of a formula (δοκ-) we have previously encountered, and the rest of the chapter, by way of continuing the proof, contains a list of politicians from Solon to Cleisthenes and ends with an *apologia pro Theramene*. Many questions should be raised by the contents (though they rarely have been) and by the structure (these never have been) of this chapter: the most pressing are (1) why a list of political leaders at all and why here? (2) when the listing of rival leaders begins, with Xanthippus and Miltiades, the order is τοῦ δήμου . . . τῶν γνωρίμων: with the pair Nikias/Cleon the order is reversed: why? (3) why the concentration, unparalleled in the chapter, on Theramenes in its last segment? (What, indeed, does this segment have to with the original thesis?)

Structural considerations provide an initial basis for dealing with these questions, and we may begin here. The chapter has two halves, and each half, like Plato's divided line, is further divided into two segments: ἕως μὲν . . . βελτίω. . . . τελευτήσαντος δὲ Περικλέους πολὺ χείρω.[7] The second half is introduced by a chiastic repetition of part of this sentence; Περικλέους δὲ τελευτήσαντος.[8] The division of the first three segments is effected by the repetition of the idea of προστασία: (A) πρῶτος ἐγένετο προστάτης τοῦ δήμου Σόλων; (B) τοῦ μὲν δήμου *προειστήκει* Ξάνθιππος; (C) τῶν μὲν ἐπιφανῶν *προειστήκει* Νικίας. The fourth segment is connected to the third by another repetition, which takes up the δοκ-motif of the introduction to the chapter; (C) ὃς δοκεῖ μάλιστα, (D) δοκοῦσι δὲ βέλτιστοι, but is also clearly demarcated from the preceding three by the difference of its contents.[9]

One further element to be noted of this structure is its balance: in A and D there are only single politicians, without rivals,[10] while B and C contain lists of rivals.

The main thesis of 28 (the first sentence) is substantiated by the thesis contained in the next sentence (πρῶτον—δημαγωγοῦντες), the first part of which is illustrated by C and the second part by AB. It is to be noted that segment D has no overt connection with the thesis and that the fullness of of A and B was not necessary to it. Although we may be fairly confident that Thucydides was the source (immediate or mediated) of the introductory thesis of 28, he was not responsible for the devices which Aristotle used to express his version of that thesis. We know also that the main thesis was sustained (in different ways) by several writers between Thucydides and Aristotle,[11] and it is worth asking what relationship might obtain between Aristotle and these predecessors. A simplistic approach is adopted by Rhodes 346: ''probably the list is not *A.P.*'s own compilation but he is summarizing what he found at length in an earlier work.'' In fact, the list of the Ἀθπολ does not overlap with that of any of his sources/ models we know of, and we are justified in examining the question more deeply.

(1a) Thuc. 2.65.10–11: οἱ δὲ ὕστερον (sc. than Pericles) ἴσοι μᾶλλον αὐτοί, πρὸς ἀλλήλους ὄντες καὶ ὀρεγόμενοι πρῶτος ἕκαστος γίγνεσθαι ἐντράποντο καθ᾽ ἡδονὰς τῷ δήμῳ καὶ τὰ πράγματα ἐνδιδόναι . . . κατὰ τὰς ἰδίας διαβολὰς περὶ τῆς τοῦ δήμου προστασίας (those later were more on the same level and each desired to be at the top. They were concerned with what pleased the *demos,* and they handed over control to it . . . in reference to their personal quarrels about their leadership of the *demos*).

(1b) 8.89.3: ἦν δὲ τοῦτο μὲν σχῆμα πολιτικὸν τοῦ λόγου αὐτοῖς, κατ᾽ ἰδίας δὲ φιλοτιμίας οἱ πολλοὶ αὐτῶν τῷ τοιούτῳ προσέκειντο, ἐν ᾧπερ καὶ μάλιστα ὀλιγαρχία ἐκ δημοκρατίας γενομένη ἀπόλλυται· πάντες γὰρ αὐθήμερον ἀξιοῦσιν οὐχ ὅπως ἴσοι, ἀλλὰ καὶ πολὺ πρῶτος αὐτὸς ἕκαστος εἶναι (this was the political *schema* put forward in their speeches, and through their personal ambitions most of them adhered to something like this, especially at the moment at which the oligarchy which had arisen from the democracy was being dissolved. For all at once claim not that they should be equal but each that he should be on top).

(2a) Plato, *Gorg.* 502E4–6: στοχαζόμενοι, ὅπως οἱ πολῖται ὡς βέλτιστοι ἔσονται διὰ τοὺς αὐτῶν λόγους, ἢ καὶ οὗτοι πρὸς τὸ χαρίζεσθαι τοῖς πολίταις ὡρμημένοι, καὶ ἕνεκα τοῦ ἰδίου τοῦ αὐτῶν ὀλιγωροῦντες τοῦ κοινοῦ κτλ. (and aim to make the citizens as good as possible by their speeches? Or do they too concentrate on gratifying the citizens, despising the common interest for their own private interest? [tr. Irwin]).

(2b) 503C1–3: Θεμιστόκλεα οὐκ ἀκούεις ἄνδρα ἀγαθὸν γεγονότα καὶ Κίμωνα καὶ Μιλτιάδην καὶ Περικλέα τουτονὶ τὸν νεωστὶ τετελευτηκότα, οὗ καὶ σὺ ἀκήκοας; (don't you hear it said that Themistocles proved himself a good man, and Cimon and Miltiades, and Pericles? He's lately died and you've heard him speak yourself).

(2c) 515C7–D1: εἰ ἔτι σοι δοκοῦσιν ἀγαθοὶ πολῖται γεγονέναι Περικλῆς καὶ Κίμων καὶ Μιλτιάδης καὶ Θεμιστοκλῆς (whether you still think that they have proved themselves good citizens—Pericles, Cimon, Miltiades, Themistocles).

(2d) 517B3–C2: ἀλλά μοι δοκοῦσι τῶν γε νῦν διακονικώτεροι γεγονέναι καὶ μᾶλλον οἷοί τε ἐκπορίζειν τῇ πόλει ὧν ἐπεθύμει. ἀλλὰ γὰρ μεταβιβάζειν τὰς ἐπιθυμίας καῖ μὴ ἐπιτρέπειν, πείθοντες καὶ βιαζόμενοι ἐπὶ τοῦτο ὅθεν ἔμελλον ἀμείνους ἔσεσθαι οἱ πολῖται, ὡς ἔπος εἰπεῖν οὐδὲν τούτων διέφερον ἐκεῖνοι· ὅπερ μόνον ἔργον ἐστὶν ἀγαθοῦ πολίτου (no: I think they've proved to be better servants than the present people, and more capable of supplying the city with what it had an appetite for. But for forcing change in their appetites, not indulging them, persuading and forcing them towards what will make the citizens better—here they were virtually no different from people now—and that's the only work for a good citizen).

(2e) 526A6–B3: ἐπεὶ καὶ ἐνθάδε καὶ ἄλλοθι γεγόνασι, οἶμαι δὲ καὶ ἔσονται, καλοὶ κἀγαθοὶ ταύτν τὴν ἀρετὴν τὴν τοῦ δικαίως διαχειρίζειν ἃ ἄν τις ἐπιτρέπῃ, εἰς δὲ καὶ πάνυ ἐλλόγιμος γέγονεν καὶ εἰς τοὺς ἄλλους Ἕλληνας, Ἀριστείδης ὁ Λυσιμάχου (but they have appeared here and elsewhere and I think they will—men fine and good in this virtue of justly managing what is entrusted to them. And one of them has become widely famous among the rest of the Greeks too, Aristeides the son of Lysimachus).

(3a) Isocrates, *De pace* 75: ἡ μὲν τοίνυν πολιτεία τοσούτῳ βελτίων καὶ κρείττων ἡ τότε τῆς ὕστερον καταστάσης, ὅσωπερ Ἀριστείδης καὶ Θεμιστοκλῆς καὶ Μιλτιάδης ἄνδρες ἀμείνους ἦσαν Ὑπερβόλου καὶ Κλεοφῶντος καὶ τῶν νῦν δημηγορούντων (well, the constitution of that time was better and stronger than the one established later to the same extent that Aristeides and Themistocles were better than Hyperbolus and Cleophon and the *demos* politicians now).

(3b) *Antidosis* 232–34: ἐκεῖνός τε γὰρ προστάτης τοῦ δήμου καταστάς . . . μετὰ δὲ ταῦτα Κλεισθένης . . . τοὺς τυράννους ἐξέβαλε . . . ἐπὶ δὲ τούτῳ Θεμιστοκλῆς . . . τὸ δὲ τελευταῖον Περικλῆς κτλ. (for he [sc., Solon] was established as the first leader of the *demos* . . . after this Cleisthenes . . . expelled the tyrants . . . thereupon Themistocles . . . finally, Pericles. . . .

(4) Theopompus, *Philippica* 10: the text is preserved only in fragments. The book had the subtitle Περὶ δημαγωγῶν (115 F 95).[12] In it he discussed Athenian politicians from Themistocles to Euboulos in the third quarter of the fourth century, including Cimon, Thucydides, Cleon and Hyperbolus. The work also seems to have discussed rivalries between politicians (F 261).

The elements common to Aristotle and the others can be divided into names and themes (Table 14-1).

Table 14-1 Common Elements: *AP* and Other Sources

AP	Thucydides	Plato	Isocrates	Theopompus
Names				
Solon			x	
Peisistratus				x
Cleisthenes			x	
Xanthippus				
Miltiades		x	x	
Aristeides		x	x	
Themistocles		x	x	x
Thucydides				x
Cimon		x		x
Ephialtes				
Pericles	x	x	x	
Nicias				
Cleon	x			x
Theramenes	x			
Cleophon			·x	
Themes				
Solon first προστάτης			x	
Pericles as cut-off point	x	x	x	
Death of Pericles	x	x[13]		

The most important element which is not shared is that of rival politicians, and in this the influence of Theopompus may have been greater than can be suggested by Table 14-1.[14] On the basis of the table, however, I want to suggest that in this chapter Aristotle is exploiting a motif—political degeneration after Pericles—and that his subtexts are Thucydides, the *Gorgias* and Theopompus.

Thucydides makes three claims: (1) that there was degeneration in the political leadership of Athens after Pericles (it is implied that he, and he alone, is the basis of comparison); (2) that the successors of Pericles were all of a piece (ἴσοι πρὸς ἀλλήλους); and (3) that the successors were motivated (and, by implication, motivated solely) by personal ambition.

Aristotle subverts these claims in various ways.[15] For the first, he lessens the intensity of focus Thucydides had placed on Pericles by widening the field of *comparandi* in two directions, going further back than Pericles to Solon and forward to beyond the point at which Thucydides had stopped his account. Thus, Pericles retained his traditional centrality as a cutting-off point but was no longer the single term of comparison. With this maneuver, Aristotle exploited the freedom inherent in his lack of genre in a way in which Thucydides could not because of his self-imposed limitations.[16]

The second claim is partially allowed to stand, partially rejected. It is allowed to stand in that Theramenes is pictured as acting in concert with others (32.2, 33.2, 34.3). It is partially rejected in that Theramenes stands alone (and, by implication, acts in a manner superior to others) in his opposition to the Thirty.

Aristotle's way of defending against the third claim is to deflect it, in two ways. The first way we have just seen: Theramenes acting with others. The second way, if it is proper to look at the text in this light, is to paint Theramenes as subject to the law. By this I mean that, when Aristotle puts Theramenes in an adversary position, that position is principled and directed against policies or actions, not against individuals: indeed, no opponent of Theramenes is identified.[17] Once Aristotle adopted this narrative strategy and used it consistently, it allowed him to pass over Critias by name,[18] but it did not prevent him from alluding to Critias, as we shall see.

The most effective way by which Aristotle undercuts the general force of Thucydides' thesis is to mediate it through Plato. Thucydides and Plato agree in that the posteriors to Pericles were motivated by personal ambition (ἰδίας φιλοτιμίας; ἐκ τοῦ ἰδίου) and that their measures were advocated to please the people (καθ᾽ ἡδονὰς τῷ δήμῳ; χαρίζεσθαι τοῖς πολλοῖς). The language each uses for this idea is different, and it is Plato's language which Aristotle selects to characterize the demagogues after Cleophon.

The small coincidence of language provokes a closer look at the relation between the *Gorgias* and the *AP*. The strongest indication that a relation exists is the language Aristotle uses to sum up the political activity of Theramenes: ὡς δυνάμενος πολιτεύεσθαι κατὰ πάσας [sc., πολιτείας], ὅπερ ἐστὶν ἀγαθοῦ πολίτου ἔργον. The language is so close to 2b: ὅπερ μόνον ἔργον ἐστὶν ἀγαθοῦ πολίτου[19] that we must conclude that Aristotle had Plato's work[20] in mind when he was talking about Theramenes.[21]

This conclusion is supported by the incidence of thematic and (less importantly) linguistic parallels between the two texts. The first group includes the death of Pericles (2a),[22] the list of four names (2b, 2c), the courting of the people's favor (2a) and the general theme of political decline (2e). The linguistic parallels include (2a) βέλτιστοι (36.1: μεταδοῦναι δὲ τῶν πραγμάτων τοῖς βελτίστοις); (2d) καλοὶ κἀγαθοί (28.5: καλοὺς κἀγαθούς); (2d) ἀρετή (36.2; τῆς ἀρετῆς ὡρισμένης); (2c) ἀγαθὸς πολίτης (28.5); (2c, 2e) δοκοῦσι, (2b, 2c, 2d, 2e) γεγον- (28.5; δοκοῦσι δὲ βέλτιστοι γεγονέναι; γεγονέναι).

We may, then, conclude that Aristotle was certainly using Thucydides[23] and the *Gorgias*:[24] he may have used Isocrates and Theopompus, but it is clear that he took over none of these totally. Apart from his use of Plato to mitigate the harshness of Thucydides' judgment, can another purpose be discerned? I believe so: it is that by taking the trouble to use more than one source and making it clear that he is using more than one source to get at what he conceives to be the truth about a controversial figure, Aristotle is classing himself with those μὴ παρέργως ἀποφαινομένοις.[25]

The explanation for Aristotle's list and its insertion at this point in his narrative is that the list as a whole, and, more narrowly, specific segments of it provide the contexts in which Aristotle intended that Theramenes be judged. I am not only suggesting, with Wilamowitz (1.126), that Aristotle's vindication of Theramenes (28.5) was introduced "gewissermassen als anweisung, wie die folgende erzählung der beiden revolutionen beurteilt werden solle" (to some extent as a direction as to how the following narrative is to be evaluated) but that the first three segments of 28 introduce a certain kind of Theramenes, a Theramenes for whom the claims made in 28 can be supported and justified in the narrative following. Mario Levi[26] has noted that the list of 28 constitutes a type of recapitulation which closes one phase of the democracy to begin another. The comment was made with reference to the change in leadership after Pericles and is only true as so interpreted. Otherwise, it is too narrowly focused, and the chapter, as summary and transitional, should be read in the light of other chapters like it.

III. SEGMENT D

Thus, as segments A, B, and C form an introduction to D, so D is an introduction to the further narrative of Theramenes. The thematic relevance, however, of the three segments does not end with chapter 28 but carries over into the narrative, and it will be necessary occasionally to switch back and forth between the introduction of a theme and its later application.

In segment D, many phrases are of special interest. I begin with two related ones: δοκοῦσι δὲ βέλτιστοι and δοκεῖ μέντοι τοῖς μὴ παρέργως ἀποφαινομένοις. The use of δοκ- verbs with reference to Theramenes is continued at 32.2: Peisander, Antiphon and Theramenes, ἀνδρῶν καὶ γεγενημένων εὖ καὶ συνέσει καὶ γνώμῃ δοκούντων διαφέρειν (men who were well-born and appeared outstanding in intelligence and judgment) and, describing Archinus, Anytus, Cleitophon, Phormisius and Theramenes, ἄλλως δὲ δοκοῦντες οὐδενὸς ἐπιλείπεσθαι τῶν πολιτῶν (34.3) (in other respects seemed inferior to none of the citizens).[27] Combined with εὐδοκιμοῦντα at the beginning of the chapter, this usage shows that we are in the context of the δοκ- formula considered before, and I am going to suggest that the formula is in essence one of the rhetorical ploys which Aristotle uses to make his case for Theramenes. The formulaic quality of the references will not disguise the fact that Aristotle is using it very differently in this chapter. The differences are that (1) the referent of οὐκ εὐδοκιμοῦντα is not immediately identified, as it was heretofore; (2) δοκοῦσιν and δοκεῖ are main verbs,[28] elsewhere the formula employs subordinate verbs, usually participles;[29] (3) elsewhere the subject is found in the immediate vicinity of, and usually preceding, the verb; here, it is delayed, for rhetorical effect; (4) δοκ- is applied to more than one named individual in the last three passages printed above; (5) only in these passages[30] does the use of the formula not lead immediately and directly to an account of the individual's activity: after 28, three and one-half chapters intervene before Theramenes is mentioned again; (6) with two exceptions, only in 32 and 34 is the formula used of individuals after an activity of theirs is mentioned.[31]

These variations from the previous use of the formula are deliberate and are one of a number of literary devices intended to underscore the importance of Theramenes: (1) εὐδοκιμοῦντα is not attached to a person, partly because it could not be since the person(s) to whom it applies did not have the good reputation, partly because the word is used to introduce a general theme.[32] (2) Hitherto, the participles have been subordinate and introductory to a described activity, laying the groundwork for the acceptance of an individual by the political public. Here, a main verb is used because this verb is itself the focus of the topic, the reputation of Theramenes. The verb functions analogously to the way it functioned before, but with the difference that now the public is not the political one acting in history but the reading audience. (4) The minicatalogs of 32.2 (Πεισάνδρου καὶ Ἀντιφῶντος καὶ Θηραμένους)[33] and 34.3 (Ἀρχῖνος καὶ Ἄνυτος καὶ Κλειτοφῶν καὶ Φορμίσιος καὶ.Θηραμένης) are intended to create a kind of virtue by association, linking Theramenes with two different groups, each of which is characterized in highly complimentary terms. Formally, these lists are similar to the three names at the beginning of D: all three lists end with Theramenes and all are in praise of him. (5–6) The delay in describing the activity of Theramenes and the concomitant suspense are formally unique.

Finally, it was earlier noted that δοκ- is inherently ambiguous, and there was no guarantee that the reputation of the individual would accord with his actions. By placing the formula, in 32.2 and 34.3, after the event described, Aristotle is implying that there is now no ambiguity in the term. Opinion/ reputation, insofar as it is placed after an activity, is based on that activity and will not be belied by future activity. If this is correct, the passages in 32 and 34 are thematic doublets of 28.5, and the doublets have a unique feature: only of Theramenes is δοκ- used of an individual before and after he appears on the scene.

In this connection, a pattern of association is created, if we bring to bear some paratexts:

9.1: δοκεῖ δὲ τῆς Σόλωνος πολιτείας τρία ταῦτ᾽ εἶναι τὰ δημο-τικώτατα (the following seem to be the three most democratic features of Solon's constitution)

10.1: ἐν μὲν οὖν τοῖς νόμοις ταῦτα δοκεῖ θεῖναι δημοτικά (those appear to be the democratic features in Solon's laws)

33.2: δοκοῦσι δὲ καλῶς πολιτευθῆναι κατὰ τούτους τοὺς καιρούς (the Athenians seem to have been well governed at this time)

40.2: δοκεῖ τοῦτό τε πολιτεύσασθαι καλῶς Ἀρχῖνος (it seems that Archinus' policy was good both in this matter)

40.2: δοκοῦσιν κάλλιστα δὴ καὶ πολιτικώτατα. . . . χρήσασθαι (the Athenians reacted better and more public-spiritedly)

41.1: δοκοῦντος δὲ δικαίως λαβεῖν τὴν πολιτείαν (the people's taking political power seems justifiable)

41.2: καὶ τοῦτο δοκοῦσι ποιεῖν ὀρθῶς (the people seem to be right to follow this line).

With the exception of 41.1, δοκ- is a main verb, as in 28. Although Thera-menes is explicitly connected with only one of these texts (33.2), the implica-tions place him squarely in a demotic context, beginning with the measures of Solon and ending with the Athenian δῆμος. We will see that this is the first of three such associations.

At this point, other features of Aristotle's method begin to emerge, with specific reference to our first question. Once he had decided to rank Thera-menes with "good" politicians of the past, he had to select from those men-tioned earlier in the text. This had effects both positive and negative. Posi-tively, the criteria of excellence are the ἀρχαῖοι, Solon, Peisistratus and Cleisthenes, and it is no surprise that each of these had been given fairly full and favorable treatment. Negatively, it meant that the denizens of B and C were comparatively less important and required less treatment. Thus, we are told of Xanthippus only that he was ostracized (22.6), have heard nothing hith-erto of Thucydides, and chapter 28's opposed pair of Thucydides and Pericles sits uneasily with the rivalry of Pericles and Cimon in 27.[34]

The decision to include segment A, in the context of Thucydides' thesis, entailed segments B and C: C, because the rejection of that thesis as it applied to Theramenes needed names to serve as a counterpoint to him; B, since the existence of A and C would have made a lacuna of the politicians between Cleisthenes and Pericles intolerable.[35]

The statement is immediately qualified: καὶ περὶ μὲν Νικίου καὶ Θουκυδίδου πάντες σχεδὸν ὁμολογοῦσιν[36] ἄνδρας γεγονέναι οὐ μόνον καλοὺς κἀγαθούς, ἀλλὰ καὶ πολιτικοὺς καὶ τῇ πόλει πάσῃ πατρικῶς χρωμένους. The purpose of the qualification is double. First, to include Ther-amenes in company otherwise agreed to be καλοὶ κἀγαθοί at once puts him on a level with the pre-Periclean leaders in terms of social status and approval παρὰ τοῖς ἐπιεικέσιν, and looks forward to the characterization of him in

32.4.[37] Second, the social acceptability of Theramenes just achieved is paralleled on the political level: πολιτικοὺς καὶ τῇ πόλει πάσῃ χρωμένους.

What Aristotle says here has been curiously misinterpreted, but his meaning can be divined from internal evidence. The analogs to πολιτικούς are (1) Peisistratus διῴκει τὰ κοινὰ πολιτικῶς μᾶλλον ἢ τυραννικῶς (14.3) (Peisistratus administered public affairs more like a citizen than like a tyrant); (2) διῴκει . . . τὰ περὶ τὴν πόλιν μετρίως καὶ μᾶλλον πολιτικῶς ἢ τυραννικῶς (16.2) (moderately and more); (3) Hippias was τῇ φύσει πολιτικὸς καὶ ἔμφρων (18.1) (was public-spirited and sensible in character); (4) Aristotle, in mentioning the amnesty and the joint repayment (ἀπέδοσαν κοινῇ) of the oligarchs' debt to the Spartans, says (40.2): δοκοῦσιν κάλλιστα δὴ καὶ πολιτικώτατα ἁπάντων καὶ ἰδίᾳ καὶ κοινῇ χρήσασθαι ταῖς προγεγενημέναις συμφοραῖς (the Athenian reacted to their previous misfortunes, both individually and together, better and more public-spiritedly, than anyone else at any other time).

The implications of these passages with reference to Theramenes are (a) to act πολιτικῶς is different from acting τυραννικῶς; (b) to act πολιτικῶς can be to act in a reconciliatory (i.e., nonfactional) way. The connection with Theramenes (a) is that, though he began as a member both of the Four Hundred and of the Thirty, he broke with them when they began to act τυραννικῶς.[38]

Implication (b) is exemplified especially in τῇ πάσῃ πόλει of τῇ πόλει πάσῃ πατρικῶς χρωμένους, a phrase again frequently misunderstood. Commentators and translators almost[39] unanimously assume that πατρικῶς is to be connected to πατήρ, and the results are occasionally bathetic.[40] When one notes that the three figures of segment D are considered best μετὰ τοὺς ἀρχαίους, that Theramenes is associated by Aristotle with Cleitophon who proposed (29.3): προσαναζητῆσαι . . . τοὺς πατρίους νόμους, οὓς Κλεισθένης ἔθηκεν, ὅτε καθίστη τὴν δημοκρατίαν (search out the traditional laws which Cleisthenes enacted when he set up the democracy), and that Theramenes was the leader of the group who (34.3) τὴν πάτριον πολιτείαν ἐζήτουν, (had as their objective the traditional constitution), it would seem to be beyond dispute that the phrase means "treating the city as a whole in the ancestral way."

The basis of the comparison of Theramenes to the "ancients" is not to be found in any specific constitutional or institutional proposals or goals. It is rather a general attitude which he shares with his predecessors, that of nonfactional political activity. This attitude is explicitly ascribed to Solon (6.3) ἀμφοτέροις ἀπεχθέσθαι, (11.2) πρὸς ἀμφοτέρους ἀπεχθέσθαι (accepted the hatred of both sides), but is also predicated of Peisistratus (16.9) ἐβούλοντο γὰρ καὶ τῶν γνωρίμων καὶ τῶν δημοτικῶν οἱ πολλοί . . . καὶ πρὸς ἀμφοτέρους ἐπεφύκει καλῶς (he had many supporters both among the notables and among the ordinary people. . . . he behaved honorably to both), and is the point of the remark made of Cleisthenes at 28.2: καὶ τούτῳ μὲν οὐδεὶς ἦν ἀντιστασιώτης, ὡς ἐξέπεσον οἱ περὶ τὸν Ἰσαγόραν (and he had no opponent, since Isagoras' party was expelled).

The text continues (28.5):

περὶ δὲ Θηραμένους, διὰ τὸ συμβῆναι κατ' αὐτὸν ταραχώδεις τὰς πολιτείας, ἀμφισβήτησις τῆς κρίσεώς ἐστι. δοκεῖ μέντοι μὴ παρέργως ἀποφαινομένοις οὐχ ὥσπερ αὐτὸν διαβάλλουσι πάσας τὰς πολιτείας καταλύειν, ἀλλὰ πάσας προάγειν ἕως μηδὲν παρανομοῖεν, ὡς δυνάμενος πολιτεύεσθαι κατὰ πάσας, ὅπερ ἐστὶν ἀγαθοῦ πολίτου ἔργον, παρανομούσαις δὲ οὐ συγχωρῶν, ἀλλ' ἀπεχθανόμενος.

Three elements of this passage especially call for comment. The first is the phrase πάσας τὰς πολιτείας καταλύειν. This is doubtlesss taken from attacks[41] on Theramenes, but there is an unnoticed nuance in Aristotle's use of the verb. In the *AthPol,* the verb is always used of the dissolution of a nondemocratic form of government: the Peisistratid tyranny (19.2, 20.1 = 28.2), the Four Hundred (33.1), the Thirty (36.1; 38.1, 2)) and the Ten (38.3). The nuance allows Aristotle to admit the partial truth of the accusation[42] and at the same time to turn it to Theramenes' advantage.

Allied to this element is a structural feature characteristic of the transitional chapters, namely, that they contain statements later to be proved or illustrated. A good case in point is the statement in 41.2 about the κρίσεις τῆς βουλῆς coming into the jurisdiction of the δῆμος, a statement not illustrated until chapter 45. Here, Aristotle states about Theramenes that (1) he was καλὸς κἀγαθός, that (2) he did not destroy all forms of government, that (3) he advanced all forms of government as long as they were not lawless, and that (4) he did not yield to lawlessness. The activities to prove these statements are found in (1) 32.2, (2) 32.2, (3) 33.2, and (4) 36–37.

Finally, I remarked above that one implication of the word πολιτικῶς is that of nonfactional activity. The definition of the good citizen given at the end of the chapter, to be able to engage in political activity under any kind of regime, is nowhere to be found in the *Politics:* one would not expect it to be, for that was not the kind of question with which the work was concerned. But, as has often been noted,[43] one passage of the work is especially relevant to Theramenes. This is 4.1294A3–1296B12, at which is discussed the desirability of a constitution peopled with a strong (economically) middle class. Theramenes' support of the Five Thousand[44] and opposition to the restricted oligarchy of the Thirty made him, in those circumstances, an advocate of what Aristotle would call a μέση πολιτεία. It is characteristic of this constitution that it alone is ἀστασίαστος (1296A7). More will be said on constitutional matters in section V below.

IV. THERAMENES: A POTENTIAL προστάτης τοῦ δήμου?

The second question I originally asked was why the order γνώριμοι–δῆμος, operative in segment B, is reversed in segment C. One reason for this is the same as the chiastic arrangement in the references to Pericles' death: the reversed order here reflects the reverse in Athenian political fortunes. A second reason; in segment C, nothing is said about the figures in the left-hand column, so to speak: it is the figures in the right-hand column who are damned for character (Cleon) or for action (Cleophon, Callistratus). By merely listing the former, Aristotle highlights what he says about the latter.

A third reason, and the most important one, is that it is the left-hand column which has the προστάται τοῦ δήμου. It is the theme of προστασία τοῦ δήμου which generates this chapter and is its main unifying device. Outside the list in 28, the phrase is used first of Solon (2.2), then of Cleisthenes (20.4), Aristeides and Themistocles (23.2), and Ephialtes (25.1). After 28, it is used once (36.1), the Thirty φοβηθέντες μὴ προστάτης γενόμενος [sc., Theramenes] τοῦ δήμου καταλύσῃ τὴν δυναστείαν (afraid that he might become champion of the people and overthrow the ruling clique). Aristotle's choice of language[45] here is odd and surely suggestive. It is easy to interpret the phrase as referring simply to the moment by the process (a) the *demos* was against the Thirty, (b) Theramenes was against the Thirty, (c) therefore, Theramenes was implicitly an ally of the *demos* and potentially its leader. Doubtless this is true but it does not go far enough. When one considers that the spectrum covered by the phrase προστάτης τοῦ δήμου is wide enough to contain figures so disparate in intention and operation as Solon on the one hand and Themistocles and Ephialtes on the other, I think that Aristotle's use of the phrase here and his placement in the left column reinforce the comparison of Theramenes to the ἀρχαῖοι, each of whom was a προστάτης τοῦ δήμου. The action of the Thirty made unrealizable the actualization of a potentiality: we cannot know how genuine a potentiality that was.

V. THE CONSTITUTIONAL BACKGROUND

When Aristotle descibes the geo-political situation in Attica before Peisistratus, he uses this structure:

A (13.4): μία [sc., στάσις] μὲν τῶν παραλίων, ὧν προειστήκει
Μεγακλῆς ὁ Ἀλκμέωνος, οἵπερ ἐδόκουν μάλιστα διώκειν τὴν μέσην
πολιτείαν· (one the men on the coast, led by Megacles, the son of
Alcmeon, whose particular object seemed to be the middle form of constitution);

B (13.4): ἄλλη δὲ τῶν πεδιακῶν, οἳ τὴν ὀλιγαρχίαν ἐζήτουν· ἡγεῖτο
δ᾽ αὐτῶν Λυκοῦργος· (another the men of the plain, whose aim was
oligarchy, and who were led by Lycurgus);

C (13.4): τρίτη δ᾽ ἡ τῶν διακρίων, ἐφ᾽ ᾗ τεταγμένος ἦν Πεισίστρατος,
δημοτικώτατος εἶναι δοκῶν. (and the third, the men of the Diakria,
whose leader was Peisistratus, a man who seemed most inclined to democracy).

According to Aristotle, one of the terms of the peace treaty offered by Sparta was that the Athenians would be governed by the ancestral constitution (ἐφ᾽ ᾧ τε πολιτεύσονται τὴν πάτριον πολιτείαν), but the form of that constitution was disputed:

C¹ (34.3): οἱ μὲν δημοτικοὶ διασῴζειν ἐπειρῶντο τὸν δῆμον, (the democrats tried to preserve the democracy);

B¹ (34.3): τῶν δὲ γνωρίμων οἱ μὲν ἐν ταῖς ἑταιρείαις ὄντες καὶ τῶν φυγάδων οἱ μετὰ τὴν εἰρήνην κατελθόντες ὀλιγαρχίας ἐπεθύμουν, (of the notables those who belonged to the clubs and the exiles who had returned after the peace treaty were eager for oligarchy);

A¹ (34.3): οἱ δὲ ἐν ἑταιρείᾳ οὐδεμιᾷ συγκαθεστῶτες, ἄλλως δὲ δοκοῦντες οὐδενὸς ἐπιλείπεσθαι τῶν πολιτῶν, τὴν πάτριον πολιτείαν ἐζήτουν· ὧν ἦν μὲν καὶ Ἀρχῖνος καὶ Ἄνυτος καὶ Κλειτοφῶν καὶ Φορμίσιος καὶ ἕτεροι πολλοί, προειστήκει δὲ μάλιστα Θηραμένης. (those who did not belong to any club and who in other respects seemed inferior to none of the citizens had as their objective the traditional constitution: these last included Archinus, Anytus, Cleitophon, Phormisius and many others, but their particular champion was Theramenes.

That this is an intentional allusion to 13.4 is shown by the familiar structure, by the obvious (political) echoes of language and by the (perhaps) not so obvious links: ὧν and προειστήκει in A and A¹.

The other major source for the event makes the conflict bipartite (Diod. 14.3), between oligarchs and democrats, but sufficient evidence for a tripartite division exists to show that Aristotle did not invent it.[46] Unfortunately, that evidence says nothing about the "constitutional" coloration of the groups.

At any rate, the language Aristotle uses—τὴν πάτριον πολιτείαν ἐζήτουν—reveals his belief that only the stance adopted by Theramenes met this term of the peace, but he does not say what this constitution was like. Reference to 13.4 shows a match between oligarchy and oligarchy, democracy and democracy, and πάτριος πολιτεία and μέση πολιτεία. If we then ask two questions: is this list of constitutions meant to be exhaustive (in the historical contexts)? and which of these constitutions most resembles the Solonian one? The answer to the first is yes, the answer to the second—if only because oligarchy is excluded and democracy is impossible—is the μέση πολιτεία.[47] I suggest, then, that the structure suggests two allusions, one to Megacles the Alcmaeonid (who at one stage was driven by faction to cooperate with the tyrant), the other to Solon.

There are two further allusions to the past here. Aristotle divided the γνώριμοι into two groups, those ἐν ταῖς ἑταιρείαις and those—the Theramenean group—ἐν ἑταιρείᾳ οὐδεμιᾷ. It is not mistaken to think of another γνώριμος who failed to get the support of the ἑταιρεῖαι, Cleisthenes. The second allusion is through another member of the group, Cleitophon. It was he who in 411 added to the motion of Pythodorus a rider suggesting that they "search into the ancestral laws which Cleisthenes enacted when he set up the democracy"—προσαναζητῆσαι . . . τοὺς πατρίους νόμους οὓς Κλεισθένης ἔθηκεν ὅτε καθίστη τὴν δημοκρατίαν (29.3).[48]

Other members of the Theramenean group are interesting in a different way. Archinus: one of the terms of the reconciliation at the end of the war was that supporters of the Thirty could emigrate to Eleusis if they so registered within a certain period. When Archinus saw that many eligibles were delaying, he truncated the registration period, so that many were compelled to remain in the city, unwillingly, until they got confidence,[49] an action praised by Aristotle. From other sources, it is known that he was with the democrats at Phyle[50] as was Anytus. Phormisius cannot be placed there, but he was with the democrats at the return from the Peiraeus.[51] Rhodes has two interesting comments on Archinus: "It is surprising to find a man remembered in the fourth century as one of the principal heroes of Phyle praised as an associate of Theramenes" (431). Again, "It is not obvious why Archinus, of the leaders of the returning democrats, should be singled out for particular commendation" (474). On the other hand, when we recall that both the action of Archinus and the return of the *demos* were parts of the pattern of "demotic" associations we noted earlier, it is clear that his association with Theramenes is responsible for the singling out.

VI. THERAMENES: *ALTER SOLON*

To make the claim that Aristotle intended to suggest that Theramenes was a "democrat" of some kind entails a question: which kind? The analysis of chapter 28 leads perforce to the conclusion that he is compared to the ancients in general. Closer analysis of structure and vocabulary enables us to refine that conclusion and make the specific focus of comparison Solon.

I have earlier[52] argued that one model for the portrait of Theramenes in the *AP* is the portrait of Socrates in the *Apology*. That association was a comparatively easy one for Aristotle. Socrates and Theramenes were contemporaries and implicated (albeit differently) in the same socio-political milieu. Secondly, a passage from Diodorus (14.5) shows that the association had been made before Aristotle. We may be confident, however, that the selection of many details to produce Aristotle's portrait was his own. This, his Theramenes shared with Socrates' character (refusal to tolerate παρανομία),[53] context (opposition to the Thirty),[54] and circumstance (victims of διαβολή[55] and ἀπέχθεια).[56]

To effect a similar comparison with Solon was a task of a different order. The fact that the protagonists were products of widely diverse societies limited some opportunities of portrait assimilation. On the other hand, the fact that this association originated (as far as we can tell) with Aristotle itself allowed some creativity. The first link in this association is one we have just observed with Socrates, for Solon too was a victim of διαβολή (6.2: unjustified) and ἀπέχθεια (6.3; 11.1, 2: self-chosen). This further similarity does not lessen the significance of such associations. It rather suggests that Aristotle is going a little distance toward creating a model of moral activity in a political context,[57] and that, in the *AP*, Solon and Theramenes are the only examples of this model.

One important feature of this activity must be put in context. At 28.2, Aristotle says that ἐξ ἀρχῆς μὲν γὰρ καὶ πρῶτος ἐγένετο προστάτης τοῦ δήμου Σόλων (to begin at the beginning, Solon was the first champion of the people).

The main clause repeats the first item of information we get about Solon (3.2): οὗτος δὲ πρῶτος ἐγένετο τοῦ δήμου προστάτης. The latter clause functions as part of an introduction to Solon, the former as a part of an introduction to Theramenes, for he is the last person to be termed a προστάτης τοῦ δήμου. The functional utility of ἐξ ἀρχῆς we have seen in another context,[58] and there is another beginning in which Solon is involved for with him ἀρχὴ δημοκρατίας ἐγένετο. Theramenes was precluded from potential participation in the final stage of this process by his assassination.

But there remains one final activity of which Solon is the first participant and Theramenes the last (and only other): this is vocal opposition to tyranny (14.2) and the moral degradation (ἀσέλγεια) of its practitioners (36.1). That Aristotle intended this connection to be made is shown by one detail of his language, a detail which, again, has gone unnoticed. At 36.1, Aristotle says Θηραμένης ἀγανακτῶν ἐπὶ τοῖς γιγνομένοις αὐτοῖς παρῄνει παύσασθαι (Theramenes, annoyed at what was happening, urged the Thirty to abandon their outrageous behavior). It is not so much the fact that the verb παραινεῖν is elsewhere used only of Solon in the *AP*:[59] it is the fact that the verb is used by Aristotle only of poetic advice.[60] That the "abnormal" application of the verb to Theramenes suggests an allusion to Solon is supported by the antityrant context in which the verb is used and by another allusion to Solon. This is Aristotle's choice of the word ἀσέλγεια.[61] At *Rhet.* 1375B31– 34 he quotes Κλεοφῶν, who κατὰ Κριτίου τοῖς Σόλωνος ἐλεγείοις ἐχρήσατο, λέγων ὅτι πάλαι ἀσελγὴς ἡ οἰκία· οὐ γὰρ ἄν ποτε ἐποίησε Σόλων

> εἰπεῖν μοι Κριτίᾳ πυρρότριχι πατρὸς ἀκούειν [F 22a1 West]

(used the elegies of Solon against Critias, saying that his family had long been licentious, for [otherwise] Solon would never have written,

> "please tell red-haired Critias to listen to his father").

If this is correct, there will also be an allusion to Theramenes' opponent, Critias, whose apparent absence from the *AP* has caused surprise (cf. Rhodes 429–30).

NOTES

1. Recent publications include P. Harding, "The Theramenes Myth," *Phoenix* 28 (1974) 101–11; A. Andrewes, "The Arginousai Trial," *ibid.* 112–22 A papyrus containing fragments of a speech purportedly delivered sometime after the death of Theramenes initially excited interest. Still valuable is R. Merkelbach, "Egoistic and Altruistic Motivation in Historiography: An Excursus to the Papyrus of Theramenes," in J. H. D'Arms and J. W. Eadie, eds. *Ancient and Modern: Essays in Honor of Gerald F. Else* (Ann Arbor 1977), but it is probably a late rhetorical invention and of no independent historical value. Cf. G. E. Pesely, "The Origin and Value of the Theramenes Papyrus," *The Ancient History Bulletin* 3 (1989) 29–35.

2. A final evaluation is an historical question, and I agree with Harding (103) that this is a matter "incapable of an objective solution." The mystery would be solved if it were possible to see a reference to Theramenes in the εἷς ἀνήρ of the tantalizing passage of *Pol.* 4.1296A32–40: ἔτι δὲ καὶ τῶν ἐν ἡγεμονίᾳ γενομένων τῆς Ἑλλάδος πρὸς τὴν παρ' αὑτοῖς ἑκάτεροι πολιτείαν ἀποβλέποντες οἱ μὲν δημοκρατίας ἐν ταῖς πόλεσι καθίστασαν οἱ δ' ὀλιγαρχίας, οὐ πρὸς τὸ τῶν πόλεων συμφέρον σκοποῦντες ἀλλὰ πρὸς τὸ σφέτερον αὐτῶν, ὥστε διὰ ταύτας τὰς αἰτίας ἢ μηδέποτε τὴν μέσην γίνεσθαι πολιτείαν ἢ ὀλιγάκις καὶ παρ' ὀλίγοις· εἷς γὰρ ἀνὴρ συνεπείσθη μόνος τῶν προτέρων ἐφ' ἡγεμονίᾳ γενομένων ταύτην ἀποδοῦναι τὴν τάξιν (also those [i.e., Athenians and Spartans] who came to exercise leadership among the Greek states installed democracies or oligarchies in them according to the constitution which each had at home, looking entirely to their own advantage, not to that of the states themselves. So for these reasons the middle constitution has never occurred anywhere, or only seldom and sporadically. Only one of a long succession of leaders was prevailed upon to allow a system of this kind). If ἐφ' ἡγεμονίᾳ refers to the external imposition of a constitution, i.e., if τῆς Ἑλλάδος is to be understood Theramenes is ruled out. So G. Huxley, *On Aristotle and Greek Society* (Belfast 1979) 55–6, If it does not (so Newman 1.470–71; 4.220), he is a strong candidate for the "one leader." I suggest in section V the strong possibility that Aristotle suggested that the πάτριος πολιτεία championed by Theramenes and his allies at 35.3 was a μέση πολιτεία.

3. A. W. Gomme, *HSCP* Suppl. Vol. 1 (1940) 238 n. 2.

4. That they are linked is underscored by the chiastic structure of 23.3: cf. above chapter 9, "Horizontal Structure: Chiasmus."

5. For the construction, πρῶτος + part., cp. *Met.* 1086A11; *Poet.* 1456A29; *Pol.* 1271B32, 1274A26, and 1311B32.

6. Cf. chapter 6, "Methods and Purposes."

7. The comparative βελτίω occurs only here, and χείρω only elsewhere at 27.4, again in a context of post-Periclean degeneration.

8. It is not fanciful to suggest that the chiastic order underscores the reversal in the Athenian political situation.

9. On the chiastic arrangements of the phrase προστάτης τοῦ δήμου, cf. chapter 9 "Horizontal Structure: Chiasmus."

10. This is implicit for Solon and Peisistratus, of whom no rivals are named, and explicit for Cleisthenes, to whom οὐδεὶς ἦν ἀντιστασιώτης.

11. There is a convenient list in Rhodes 345–46. It is conceivable that Aristotle drew on other works, e.g., the Socratic dialogs of Aeschines of Sphettos or the essay on Athenian politicians by Antisthenes (F 43 Caizzi).

12. For discussion, cf. chapter 13, "Aristotle and Theopompus."

13. It is not clear why Plato refers to this. The purpose is not to establish a dramatic date for the dialog, for those indications in the work are contradictory: E. R. Dodds, *Plato: Gorgias* (Oxford 1959) 18–19.

14. Rivalry is specifically attested only between Thucydides and Pericles (F 261; Connor 39–40) and may be assumed between Cimon and Pericles, *if* Σ BD Aristeides (Connor 36) go back to Theopompus. Since it will be argued that Aristotle has more than one subtext for 28, it is evident that he may easily have extended a structural principle found in one of them (and the only one in which it is found is Theopompus).

15. See also "The Deconstruction of Pericles" in chapter 6, "Methods and Purposes."

16. The closest Thucydides could come to Aristotle's approach was to use the first

major appearance of Pericles (1.127 and 139ff.) to frame his digression on Themistocles and thus to invite comparison of the two figures.

17. 33.2: οὐ συναρεσκόμενοι τοῖς ὑπὸ τοῖς τριακισίων γιγνομένοις (dissatisfied with their conduct); 36.1: ἀγανακτῶν ἐπὶ τοῖς γιγνομένοις (annoyed at what was happening); 36.2: ἐπιτιμᾷ καὶ τούτοις (objected again to this). Attention has been drawn (Sandys 137; Rhodes 414) to the apparent oddity of the Greek of 33.2. The use of γιγνομένοις (instead of the normal πραττομένοις) may have been influenced by 36.1.

18. Rhodes (430) attributes the absence of Critias to Platonic influence.

19. In classical literature, similar phraseology is found only at Lysias 14.4: πολίτου χρηστοῦ καὶ δικαστοῦ δικαίου ἔργον (the task of a worthwhile citizen and a just juryman); and Xenophon, *Mem.* 4.6.14: τί ἐστιν ἔργον ἀγαθοῦ πολίτου (what is the task of a good citizen?); cp. also (for which I thank C. Reichmann) Lys. 33.3: ἔργα. . . .ἀνδρὸς δὲ ἀγαθοῦ καὶ πολίτου πολλοῦ ἀξίου (the tasks. . . . of a good man and citizen of much worth).

20. Cf. Keaney 1979[2] on the influence of the *Apology* in the same context.

21. I would like to see in this allusion to the language of the *Gorgias* some kind of challenge to Plato's conception of the ἀγαθὸς πολίτης, and I suspect that it is connected with the theoretical speculation of *Politics* 3.1276B16ff. about the ἀρετή of the ἀνὴρ ἀγαθός and the πολίτης σπουδαῖος, but I cannot be more precise.

22. It is not exactly clear why a special point is made of Pericles' death in 2b (cf. n. 12 above) It had the obvious advantage, in the immediate context, of making the date of Pericles' death a cut-off point, thereby precluding mention of others, some of whom (e.g., Nicias) the fictional Socrates will not have wanted to offend.

23. For other uses of Thucydides in the vicinity, cp. 32.2, ἔτεσιν δ' ὕστερον τῆς τῶν τυράννων ἐκβολῆς μάλιστα ἑκατόν, with Thuc. 8.68.4: ἐπ'ἔτει ἑκατοστῷ μάλιστα ἐπειδὴ οἱ τύραννοι κατελύθησαν, and my remarks in Keaney 1980.51–56.

24. It is possible that Aristotle's use of the πρῶτος- idiom in 27 and 28 was influenced by *Gorgias* 515E6–7: εἰς μισθοφορίαν πρῶτον καταστήσαντα.

25. He does this anyway by providing an accurate summary in 28 of Theramenes' actions later to be described.

26. *Commento storico* 2.272.

27. As in 28, when Theramenes is grouped with others, he is always named last.

28. As also in 40.1 of Archinus, 40.2 and 41.2 of the Athenians. Note also the form πολιτικώτατα used of the Athenians in 40.2.

29. As of Theramenes and others at 32.2 and 34.3, and of the *demos* at 41.1.

30. There is a parallel, of δοκ- applied to Aristeides and Themistocles, *if* Kenyon's emendation of 23.3 is correct: the London papyrus has ασκων: the emendation is δοκῶν ⟨ἀσκεῖν⟩.

31. The exceptions are Themistocles, whose advice on how to use the revenue from the silver mines is mentioned (22.7) before the formula is applied to him (28.3), and Pericles, whose citizenship law is noted (26.4) shortly before the formula. The first mentions are accompanied by archon dates, and this means that chronological considerations were determinative.

32. A similar device involving a negative is used at 45, at which Aristotle lists functions in which the βουλή is ἄκυρος instead of κυρία.

33. 32.2 is a revised version of Thuc. 8.86: for a suggestion as to why Aristotle omitted Phrynichus, cf. Keaney 1980[1] 53–54.

34. We recall, however, that for Theopompus, Pericles and Thucydides were rivals (F 91).

35. It would also have produced a lack of symmetry. There are three politicians mentioned in A and three in D.

36. General agreement like this is noted only of one other figure, Solon (5.3) ἔκ τε τῶν ἄλλων ὁμολογεῖται (the other evidence agrees on this); 6.4: οἱ ἄλλοι συνομολογοῦσι πάντες (everyone else agrees); 12.1: οἵ τ' ἄλλοι συμφωνοῦσι πάντες (everyone else agrees).

37. In D, Theramenes is mentioned first in the company of two others, and then attention is focused on him alone. As the narrative continues, he is mentioned in concert with two others (32.2), next with one other (33.2), with four others (34.3), and finally he stands alone (37). It is to be noted that no individual, save Theramenes, is a member of more than one of these groups: presumably this fact is a doublet, on the personal-political level, of the statement that he was δυνάμενος πολιτεύεσθαι κατὰ πάσας (πολιτείας).

38. 32.2: the Thirty ἅπαντα γὰρ δι' αὐτῶν ἔπραττον; 35.4: οὐδενὸς ἀπέχοντο τῶν πολιτῶν κτλ. I develop the antityrant stance of Theramenes below.

39. Exceptions are Levi, *Commento storico* 284 "il loro rispetto alle tradizioni;" and A. Tovar, *Aristoteles, La Constitucion de Atenas* (Madrid 1948) 119: "que serviron a toda la ciudad conforme a la tradicion."

40. "In a manner worthy of their ancestry," "paternally," "as a father rules his household." This is not to deny that πατρικῶς can mean "like a father": it is to deny that it has that meaning here.

41. Cf. Lysias 13.17 and Critias *ap.* Xenophon, *Hell.* 2.3.28.

42. Cf. 33.2: αἰτιώτατοι δ' ἐγένοντο τῆς καταλύσεως Ἀριστοκράτης καὶ Θηραμένης.

43. Cf. B. Keil, *Die solonische Verfassung in Aristoteles Verfassungsgeschichte Athens* (Berlin 1892) 204–6.

44. Cf. 33.2: δοκοῦσι δὲ καλῶς πολιτευθῆναι κατὰ τούτους καιρούς, πολέμου τε καθεστῶτος καὶ ἐκ τῶν ὅπλων τῆς πολιτείας οὔσης. (the Athenians seem to have been well governed at this time, when they were at war and the constitution was based on the hoplites).

45. I think he is taking it from Thucydides' account of the events of 411 (8.89.4): ἠγωνίζετο οὖν εἰς ἕκαστος αὐτὸς πρῶτος προστάτης τοῦ δήμου γενέσθαι.

46. Lysias 12.43–47; 75–76: Rhodes 428.

47. Cf. note 2 above.

48. It is Aristotle's comment on this that Cleitophon assumed (ὡς with accusative absolute) that Cleisthenes' πολιτεία was not δημοτική but similar to Solon's.

49. ἕως ἐθάρρησαν. Given the "democratic" overtones of θαρρεῖν in the *AP* (22.3, 24.1, 27.1), the implication is that these people would accept the democratic regime.

50. Rhodes 431.

51. Rhodes 432–33.

52. Keaney 1979.[2]

53. 28.5; 32B4–7.

54. 36; 32C8–D8

55. 28.5; 18D2; 19B3 al.

56. 28.5; 23A1; 24A7 al.

57. 28.5: ἔργον ἀγαθοῦ (moral) πολίτου (political): cp. *Apol.* 28B9: ἀνδρὸς ἀγαθοῦ ἔργα.

58. Cf. chapter 10.

59. 5.2: παραινεῖ καταπαύειν and 5.3: παραινῶν τοῖς πλουσίοις, both in poetic contexts (ἐλεγεία, ποιήματα).

60. The evidence: *NE* 1109A31–32: καθάπερ καὶ ἡ Καλυψὼ παραινεῖ, followed by a quotation of *Od.* 12.219–20; 1177B31–33: οὐ χρὴ δὲ κατὰ τοὺς παραινοῦντας φρονεῖν ἄνθρωπον ὄντα οὐδὲ θνητὰ τὸν θνητόν (there is no need [to obey] those who advise us as humans to have human thoughts and mortals mortal). Translators and commentators illustrate with tags from various of the poets, but the sharpest discussion is that of F. Dirlmeier, *Aristoteles' Nikomakische Ethik* (= *Aristoteles' Werke in deutscher Übersetzung* [Berlin 1956]) 233 with n. 7, who translates "den Dichtern folgen, die un mahnen" "to follows the poets, who admonish us," and cites many of the parallels to Soph. F 590 Radt = Pearson. The fragment begins θνητὰ φρονεῖν χρὴ θνητὴν φύσιν.

61. The root is comparatively rare in the corpus: *Pol.* 1304B21; 1305B40.

15

The Series in Chapter 41

It has been observed that the basic structure of chapter 41 is that of ring composition,[1] but further questions involving structure and content suggest themselves. A summary (41.2):

1. πρώτη	genitive absolute	comment
2. δευτέρα	μετὰ ταύτην ἐπὶ Θησέως	comment
3. τρίτη	μετὰ τὴν στάσιν ἐπὶ Σόλωνος	comment
	(ἀφ᾽ ἧς ἀρχὴ δημοκρατίας)	
4. τετάρτη	ἐπὶ Πεισιστράτου τυραννίς	
5. πέμπτη	μετὰ κατάλυσιν ἡ Κλεισθένους	comment
6. ἕκτη	μετὰ τὰ Μηδικά	genitive absolute
7. ἑβδόμη	μετὰ ταύτην Ἀριστείδης/Ἐφιάλτης	comment
8. ὀγδόη	ἡ τῶν τετρακοσίων κατάστασις	
9. ἐνάτη	μετὰ ταύτην ἡ δημοκρατία παλιν	
10. δεκάτη	ἡ τῶν τριάκοντα καὶ ἡ τῶν δέκα τυραννίς	
11. ἑνδεκάτη	μετὰ . . . κάθοδον	long comment
	(ἀφ᾽ ἧς διαγεγένηται μέχρι τῆς νῦν)	

The series gives rise to some questions:

(a) why only two genitives absolute and why here?
(b) why is ἐπί used in (2), (3), and (4) but not elsewhere?
(c) why comments after some καταστάσεις but not after others?[1]
(d) why is there no μετά- phrase in (4), (8), and (10)?
(e) what is the significance, if any, of the fact that there is only one repetition: ἀφ᾽ ἧς [3, 11], in the qualifying phrases/clauses?

To some of these questions it may be thought that the author's desire for variety of expression is a simple and adequate answer. Yet the variety here is not total, there is some repetition, this answer may be simplistic, and others can be found. The order of treatment will proceed from suggestions in which I have more, to those in which I have less, confidence.

In the only treatment of question (b),[2] von Fritz (83) concluded: "Aristotle appears to use the formula with ἐπί in those cases in which a new constitution can be designated by the name of a man because he is representative of it, although it cannot be said that the whole political order existing under or start-

153

ing with him is his work.'' The truth of this conclusion is not obvious, it came into existence as an attempt to answer a false question,[3] and it is entangled in false assumptions.[4]

There are some facts which lead to a better answer. The first is that ἐπί + genitive is not interchangeable with the genitive alone. This is because, although chapter 41 begins as a list of μεταβολαὶ πολιτειῶν, the first noun is replaced by an expression using or implying the result of change/μεταβολή, a κατάστασις. Thus, the phrase ἡ ἐπὶ Θησέως γενομένη means "the change which took place in the time of Theseus": ἡ Θησέως γενομένη would be meaningless. The second fact is that ἐπί + genitive is used in a series. The third fact is that the final use of the phrase coincides with the change from μεταβολή to κατάστασις: ἡ ἐπὶ Πεισιστράτου τυραννίς. Since one would expect ἡ Πεισιστράτου τυραννίς,[5] I suggest that ἐπί is combined with τυραννίς to signal the transition to κατάστασις.

The repetition raised in question (e) comes near the beginning and at the end of the whole series, and its purpose is obvious: it is to link the beginning (ἀρχή) of the process which led to democracy with the end of that process.[6]

The three changes which are not accompanied by a μετά- phrase (4, 8, 10) raised in question (d) resulted in oligarchy or tyranny, each in a different sense an antithesis of democracy. Since chapter 41 sums up those parts of the *AP* which show that and how the constitution developed into a democracy, (4), (8), and (10) are included because they are part of the historical process, but they made no contribution to what may be called the organic process, and I suggest that this is underlined by the omission of the μετά- phrase.

It may be objected that the same is true of (6), the hegemony of the Areopagus, which does have a μετά- phrase. I would reply that this hegemony was ambivalent: it existed but (25.1) ὑποφερομένη κατὰ μικρόν (though it gradually declined) throughout the period. It was during this hegemony that Athens became a naval power (23.2) and it was this (27.1) ναυτικὴ δύναμις, ἐξ ἧς συνέβη θαρρήσαντας τοὺς πολλοὺς ἅπασαν τὴν πολιτείαν μᾶλλον ἄγειν πρὸς αὑτούς. (naval power, so that the common people grew confident and increasingly attached to themselves complete control of the state).

Question (c) is the other side of the coin represented by (d): comments are attached to those constitutional changes which formed part of the organic process: here, (6) has no comment because, like the more avowedly antidemocratic regimes, it contributed nothing to the democracy.

As for (a), the single feature apparently shared by (1) and (6) is a lack of a clear indication of political coloration. The constitution in the time of Ion was clearly a βασιλεία[7] but, because of the institution of the tribe kings, it was not precisely the same as that which preceded it nor as that which followed it, μικρὸν παρεγκλίνουσα τῆς βασιλικῆς (which deviated slightly from monarchy). The authority of the leaders will have somehow been different in each of the stages. So, the hegemony of the Areopagus will not have differed *institutionally* from the preceding regime of its predecessor. Whether these phenomena have any connection to the original question, I do not know.

NOTES

1. Cf. chapter 8, "Vertical Structure: Ring Composition."

2. K. von Fritz, "The Composition of Aristotle's *Constitution of Athens*," *CP* 49 (1954) 73–93.

3. Why ἐπί in the phrase ἡ ἐπὶ Δράκοντος (41.2)? The question is false, since the choice of ἐπί here was influenced by other instances of the preposition in the immediate vicinity.

4. The assumptions are (a) that the Ἀθπολ does not attrribute a πολιτεά to Draco and (b) that chapter 4 is not an interpolation. Assumption (a) depends upon Kenyon's text of 4.1: ἡ δὲ τάξις αὕτη [sc. τῆς πολιτείας: cp. 3.1: ἡ δὲ τάξις τῆς ἀρχαίας πολιτείας] in which αὕτη is Kenyon's emendation of αυτ + sign of abbreviation. Kenyon took the sign to be the abbreviation for -ης, Wilcken read the sign as *omicron* = ου: I confirmed this from autopsy in 1958, and it was reconfirmed by M. H. Chambers, "Notes on the text of the *Ath.Pol.*," *TAPA* 96 (1965) 31–39, at 33 and figure 1. Regarding (b), to prove that chapter 4 is an interpolation, there is no need to turn to the lack of historical value of its contents: reference to structure and tradition suffices. For the first, the placement of the chapter is incompatible with the ring structure of chapters 2, 3, and 5 (Keaney 1969[3]. 415 n. 20). For the second, the same lexicographer, Harpocration, whose text of the Ἀθπολ compels the conclusion that he used a version of 51.3 earlier than ours (Σ 19, s.v. Σιτοφύλακες) also shows that his version of 7.3 lacked the reference therein (καθάπερ διήρητο καὶ πρότερον) to chapter 4 (I 16 s.v. Ἱππάς; Π 45, s.v. Πεντακοσιομέδιμνον).

5. As we have at 16.1 and 7.

6. Compare the related function of the repetition of ἐξ ἧς at 27.1 and 34.2: Keaney 1984.162.

7. Her. *Ep*. 1: ἐξ ἀρχῆς ἐχρῶντο βασιλείᾳ.

16

δῆμος, πλῆθος, and πόλις

At 22.3, Aristotle says, θαρροῦντος ἤδη τοῦ δήμου (now that the people were confident), the Athenians used the law of ostracism for the first time. At 24.1, θαρρούσης ἤδη τῆς πόλεως (now that the city was confident), Aristeides advised the Athenians to seize the hegemony of the sea. At 27.1, Pericles προύτρεψεν τὴν πόλιν ἐπὶ τὴν ναυτικὴν δύναμιν, ἐξ ἧς συνέβη θαρρήσαντας τοὺς πολλοὺς ἅπασαν τὴν πολιτείαν μᾶλλον ἄγειν εἰς αὑτούς (turned the city in the direction of naval power, so that the common people grew confident and increasingly attracted to themselves complete control of the state). Shortly thereafter, Aristotle says that the δῆμος προῃρεῖτο τὴν πολιτείαν διοικεῖν αὐτός (the people chose to administer public affairs themselves). The first three passages belong to a pattern involving the interaction of political and military circumstances[1] and are linked by the verb θαρρεῖν, but this verb is applied to three different subjects, ὁ δῆμος, ἡ πόλις, οἱ πολλοί. In the last two passages, ὁ δῆμος and οἱ πολλοί seem to be equivalent: the question is, are they?

The same question can be asked of ὁ δῆμος and τὸ πλῆθος. At 2.1, the London papyrus reads στασιάσαι τούς τε γνωρίμους καὶ τὸ πλῆθος πολὺν χρόνον τὸν δῆμον (there was strife for a long time between the notables and the masses [the people]). πλῆθος and δῆμος cannot coexist, and it is generally (and rightly) agreed that τὸν δῆμον is a gloss on τὸ πλῆθος. Whether it is an attempt at an explanation or an emendation cannot be known, but its source is 5.1: ἀντέστη τοῖς γνωρίμοις ὁ δῆμος (the people rose against the notables). It is tempting to treat πλῆθος and δῆμος as synonymous, but, as we will see, that would be a mistake, for what Aristotle does here with these terms is one instance of a pattern.

In this chapter, I treat this vocabulary as follows: I. 1–7 πόλις and its nuances; I. 8: πόλις in paratexts; II δῆμος = assembly; III πλῆθος and assembly; IV δῆμος and πλῆθος/οἱ πολλοί in the same contexts.

I. πόλις

In his *Greek Index,* Sandys divides πόλις (singular) into four segments under three rubrics: (1) = ἀκρόπολις, (2) "the state/government" (3) "the citzens or citizenship."[2] These categories are too rough and leave little room for nuance: my division is as follows (doubtful and/or interesting cases are treated more fully):

1. = ἀκρόπολις (8.4, 24.3)
2. The physical city (not excluding the Acropolis): 1.1, 15.3, 22.4, 23.1.
3. The government exercising financial functions: 22.7 *(bis)*; 42.1, 4; 43.3; 44.1; 60.2 *(bis)*. This restricted meaning of πόλις is well brought out by 42.4: ἐκκλησίας ἐν τῷ θεάτρῳ γενομένης ἀποδειξάμενοι τῷ δήμῳ τὰ περὶ τὰς τάξεις καὶ λαβόντες ἀσπίδα καὶ δόρυ παρὰ τῆς πόλεως (in an assembly held in the theater [the ephebes] giving an exhibition of military maneuvers before the people and receiving shield and spear from the state). Here there is formal information about the place of assembly, the assembled people, and the source of the funds of the military equipment.[3]
4. = the franchise, citizenship: (26.4) μετέχειν τῆς πόλεως. This usage, also at 8.5, reflects the language of Pericles' decree: the same language is found in Nicomenes' citizenship-decree of 403/2 (Σ Aeschines 1.39).
5. Political life/activity: (26.1) of Cimon, πρὸς τὴν πόλιν ὀψὲ προσελθόντα (who had only recently turned to public affairs). Rhodes (326) cites parallels for the usage. None are from Aristotle, and again I assume that it is the language of his source.
6. [Matters connected with] the government. 3.6: the Areopagus διῴκει δὲ τὰ πλεῖστα καὶ τὰ μέγιστα τῶν ἐν τῇ πόλει; (administered most and the greatest of the city's affairs); 16.2: Peisistratus διῴκει . . . . τὰ περὶ τὴν πόλιν; 23.1: the Areopagus διῴκει τὴν πόλιν.[4]
7. The whole society under tyrannical control. 6.3: Solon τυραννεῖν τῆς πόλεως (tyrant over the city); 20.3: Isagoras and his friends κυρίους τῆς πόλεως (masters of the city); 32.3: the Four Hundred with the Ten αὐτοκράτορες ἦρχον τῆς πόλεως (powerful generals ruled the city); 34.2: Lysander κύριον τῆς πόλεως; 35.1: the Thirty κύριοι τῆς πόλεως; 35.1: the Thirty κατεῖχον τὴν πόλιν δι᾽ ἑαυτῶν (they gained control of the city); 35.4: the Thirty τὴν πόλιν ἐγκρατέστερον ἔσχον (they had a firmer hold on the city). The tyrannical connotation of κυρι- τῆς πόλεως is idiosyncratic to the *AP*: in the *Politics* it can be used (1304B9) in that way, but the phrase is not necessarily so restricted (1264B34).
8. The political community viewed in a nonfactional way. 24.1: θαρρούσης ἤδη τῆς πόλεως καὶ χρημάτων ἠθροισμένων πολλῶν, συνεβούλευεν ἀντιλαμβάνεσθαι τῆς ἡγεμονίας (when the city was by now confident and a lot of money had been collected, he [Aristeides] advised them to lay hold of the hegemony).

A paratext of the phrase θαρρούσης ἤδη τῆς πόλεως generates a highly complex set of theses. At 22.3, Aristotle says that θαρροῦντος ἤδη τοῦ δήμου they first applied the law on ostracism. The event mentioned just before this is the victory at Marathon, and from the date of that victory is dated the application of ostracism, two years later. Now, since Marathon is itself dated by an archon year, that victory is not brought in to establish a chronology: therefore, to mention it must have another purpose, and this can only be to explain the confidence of the δῆμος. A paratext at chapter 27 shows a similar process (27.1): Pericles turned τὴν πόλιν ἐπὶ τὴν ναυτικὴν δύναμιν, as a result of which [ἐξ ἧς] θαρρήσαντας τοὺς πολλούς. The processes had political results as well. The application of ostracism was one of the events in the course of which δημοτικωτέρα . . . ἐγένετο ἡ πολιτεία (22.1), and the reference to the confidence of οἱ πολλοί at 27.1 is followed by a sentence which begins with a reference to the sea battle at Salamis and ends with the statement that ὁ δῆμος . . . προηρεῖτο τὴν πολιτείαν διοικεῖν αὐτός (27.2). Thus, an action affecting the πόλις produces a result affecting οἱ πολλοί, and this ultimately affects ὁ δῆμος.

If we ask why this variety of terms, particularly the disjunction between πόλις and οἱ πολλοί/δῆμος, another paratext suggests the answer; 41.2: the seventh μεταβολή/κατάστασις, ἐν ᾗ πλεῖστα συνέβη τὴν πόλιν διὰ τοὺς δημαγωγοὺς ἁμαρτάνειν διὰ τὴν τῆς θαλάττης ἀρχήν (in which it happened that the city made the most mistakes because of the demagogues through rule of the sea). In this text, the factors contributing to the errors are two, demagogues and naval policy. The move toward ναυτικὴ δύναμις had advantageous political results for one segment of society, the δῆμος, but the naval policy was supported by all segments of society, the whole πόλις.

28.5: it is said explicitly of Nicias and Thucydides and implicitly of Theramenes that they were πολιτικοὺς καὶ τῇ πόλει πάσῃ πατρικῶς χρωμένους (their politial policy was directed toward the whole city in an ancestral way). I have suggested[5] that πατρικῶς connotes a nonfactional style of politics, and the phrase τῇ πάσῃ πόλει is the main paratext for the passages here discussed.

35.3: in the first phase of the regime of the Thirty, reaction to their policies was favorable: ἔχαιρεν ἡ πόλις. Favorable (if less emotional) reactions were attributed to (nonpolitical) segments of Athenian society by (the source of) Diod. 14.2: τοῖς ἐπιεικεστάτοις τῶν πολιτῶν εὐαρέστει τὰ γινόμενα (the best citizens were well pleased by what was taking place) and Xenophon, *Hell.* 2.3.12: ὅσοι συνῄδεσαν ἑαυτοῖς μὴ ὄντες τοιοῦτοι οὐδὲν ἤχθοντο (those who were conscious that they were not like [sc., the victims of the Thirty] were not at all displeased). Aristotle's intensification[6] of the reaction and its extension to the whole society is ironical, given the aftermath.

36.1: οὕτως δὲ τῆς πόλεως ὑποφερομένης. The verb is rare enough that its other occurrence in the work should provide a paratext: 25.1: for seventeen years after the Persian Wars the πολιτεία προεστώτων τῶν Ἀρεοπαγιτῶν endured καίπερ ὑποφερομένη κατὰ μικρόν. The connection between the two texts is not obvious and makes sense only when other paratexts are considered. The complete set is:

(a) 23.1: τότε μὲν οὖν μέχρι τούτου προῆλθεν ἡ πόλις ἅμα τῇ δημοκρατίᾳ *κατὰ μικρὸν αὐξανομένη* (up to this point there had been a gradual development and increase in the city and in the democracy)

(b) 25.1: *ὑποφερομένη κατὰ μικρόν* (though it gradually declined)

(c) 25.1: *αὐξανομένου* δὲ τοῦ πλήθους (masses increased)

(d) 36.1: οὕτως δὲ τῆς πόλεως ὑποφερομένης (when the city was declining in this way)

In (d) οὕτως can refer only to the end of chapter 35, at which Aristotle says that not less than 1500 individuals were put to death by the Thirty. This represents a decline in population and is thus linked to (a). The prefix αὐξ- links (c) to (a); and (a), together with the decline noted in (b), suggests that the rise in population of the πόλις was succeeded by the rise in (the power of) τὸ πλῆθος. This was coincident with the activity of Ephialtes leading to the downfall of the Areopagus.

It is significant that (b) and (d) link the Areopagus and Theramenes, for they are linked in another way by paratexts:

23.2: with Areopagite hegemony, ἐπολιτεύθησαν ᾿Αθηναῖοι καλῶς καὶ κατὰ τούτους τοὺς καιρούς (the city was well governed at this time)

33.2: after the four hundred were put down (αἰτιώτατοι δ᾿ ἐγένοντο τῆς καταλύσεως ᾿Αριστοκράτης καὶ Θηραμένης),. . . . δοκοῦσι δὲ καλῶς πολιτευθῆναι κατὰ τούτους τοὺς καιρούς. (the men most responsible for the overthrow were Aristocrates and Theramenes), . . . the Athenians seem to have been well governed at this time

II. δῆμος = ASSEMBLY

In the only substantial[7] discussion, Kaibel (52–53) observed that it is δῆμος and not πλῆθος which is used in the description of the contemporary constitution[8] and concluded that the basic component of πλῆθος is number or mass, that πλῆθος and οἱ πολλοί are synonymous and that δῆμος and πλῆθος are not synonymous. Kaibel did not argue this last point, nor did he discuss some problematic passages. The question deserves further examination, from two points of view.

The first: when δῆμος is specified in 42–69, it or part of it is equivalent to the assembly. This is clearest in 42.4, at which Aristotle says of the ephebes ἐκκλησίας ἐν τῷ θεάτρῳ γενομένης, ἀποδειξάμενοι τῷ δήμῳ τὰ περὶ τὰς τὰ περὶ τὰς τάξεις κτλ.[9] Nowhere in 42–69 does δῆμος denote or connote a δικαστήριον.[10] This part of my treatment will anticipate a suggestion to be made later, that the distinction between δῆμος and πλῆθος is one of actuality and potentiality, the former referring to a cohesive (and so acting) force, the latter to a potential force of that kind.

Here follows a list of passages in which the δῆμος is described as acting in assembly:

14.1: Peisistratus gets a bodyguard from the δῆμος, on the motion of Aristion.

18.5: κατέσκευασεν ὁ δῆμος ([the democracy instituted] a decision about carrying weapons during the Panathenaic procession).

22.3: θαρροῦντος ἤδη τοῦ δήμου, they applied (ἐχρήσαντο) the law on ostracism.

22.7: debate in the assembly (Plut., *vitThem* 4.1: παρελθὼν εἰς τὸν δῆμον) on the use of the revenue from the mines.[11]

25.2: the ἐπίθετα of the Areopagus were given τὰ μὲν τοῖς πεντακοσίοις, τὰ δὲ τῷ δήμῳ καὶ τοῖς δικαστηρίος (accretions. . . . some to the council of five hundred and some to the people and the jury courts). This looks forward to the ultimate takeover of some of the functions of the Council of Five Hundred at 41.2.[12]

25.4: the attack on the Areopagites was conducted in two phases, first before the Council of Five Hundred, πάλιν ἐν τῷ δήμῳ (and then in the assembly).

28.3: ὃς δοκεῖ μάλιστα διαφθεῖραι τὸν δῆμον ταῖς ὁρμαῖς (Kleon, it seems, more than anyone else corrupted the people by his wild impulses). That a reference to the assembly is meant is shown by the sequel: καὶ πρῶτος ἐπὶ τοῦ βήματος ἀνέκραγε κτλ.[13] (and was the first man, who, when on the platform, shouted).

29.2: τὸν δῆμον ἑλέσθαι κτλ. (the people shall elect).

34.1: ἀφείλετο τὴν πολιτείαν ὁ δῆμος διὰ τάχους (the people soon took away their control of the state). For the vote in assembly, cf. Thuc. 8.97.1: ἐκκλησίαν ξυνέλεγον (they gathered an assembly) .

34.3: καταπλαγεὶς ὁ δῆμος ἠναγκάσθη χειροτονεῖν τὴν ὀλιγαρχίαν (the people were intimidated and compelled to decide in favor of the oligarchy).

35.3: among the victims of the first reign of terror produced by the Thirty were τοὺς συκοφάντας καὶ τοὺς τῷ δήμῳ πρὸς χάριν ὁμιλοῦντας παρὰ τὸ βέλτιστον (malicious prosecutors and those who curried favor with the people contrary to what was best). It is impossible to take this as a reference to meetings of the assembly in the regime of the Thirty: there is no evidence that there were any nor what areas of competence would have remained to the people. The reference to συκοφάνται combined with a text of Xenophon (*Hell.* 2.3.12), shows that the people involved predated the Thirty and may have included some of those (28.4) οἱ μάλιστα βουλόμενοι θρασύνεσθαι καὶ χαρίζεσθαι τοῖς πολλοῖς πρὸς τὸ παραυτίκα βλέποντες (leaders whose chief desire has been to be outrageous and to gratify the masses, looking only to considerations of the moment).

III. πλῆθος AND ASSEMBLY

There are two passages in which πλῆθος is used in an assembly context. 34.1: when the Spartans were willing to come to terms, ἔνιοι μὲν ἐσπούδαζον, τὸ δὲ πλῆθος οὐχ ὑπήκουσεν ἐξαπατηθέντες ὑπὸ Κλεοφῶντος (some were eager to accept but the masses were not: they were deceived by Cleophon). ἔνιοι shows that πλῆθος means majority.[14] 32.1: the constitutional revisions of the Five Thousand were first produced, ἐπικυρωθέντων δὲ τούτων ὑπὸ τοῦ πλήθους (it was ratified by the masses). If πλῆθος here is not a majority (and we have no evidence for division), it will have been the term chosen by Aristotle to refer to a non-democratic assemblage.

IV. δῆμος AND πλῆθος

The next stage in the argument is to examine passages in which δῆμος and πλῆθος are found together, or texts in which it is not immediately clear why Aristotle has chosen one term in preference to the other.[15]

Two guidelines will be kept in mind. The first is the suggestion I made above, that the relationship between πλῆθος and δῆμος is one of potentiality and actuality. The second is a criterion argued by Kaibel (52), to the effect that "auch da wo πλῆθος ein politischer Begriff ist, fordert es stets im Sinne der Schriftstellers den Gegenbegriff einer geringerer Anzahl" (where πλῆθος is a political idea, it always requires in the mind of the author the corresponding idea of a smaller number). His examples are

2.1:	τὸ πλῆθος		opposed to	ὀλιγαρχικὴ πολιτεία
16.7:	"	"	"	Peisistratus
20.3:	"	"	"	the βουλή
28.3:	"	"	"	demagogues
32.1:	"	"	"	οἱ ἑκατόν
36.1:	"	"	"	the Thirty
41.2:	"	"	"	something like οἱ ἐπιεικέστεροι.

Kaibel draws particular attention to two passages. At 20.1, ἡττώμενος δὲ ταῖς ἑταιρείαις ὁ Κλεισθένης προσηγάγετο τὸν δῆμον, ἀποδιδοὺς τῷ πλήθει τὴν πολιτείαν (as Cleisthenes was getting the worse of the party struggle, he attached the people to his following, by proposing to give political power to the masses), the contrast is between the oligarchic clubs and the large population. At 9.2, ἡ εἰς τὸ δικαστήριον ἔφεσις ᾧ καὶ μάλιστά φασιν ἰσχυκέναι τὸ πλῆθος· κύριος γὰρ ὢν ὁ δῆμος τῆς ψήφου, κύριος γίγνεται τῆς πολιτείας (the right of appeal to a jury court—for when the people are masters of the vote they are masters of the state), the contrast is between the newly strengthened masses over against the once-strong aristocracy. With οἱ πολλοί the situation is similar: poor opposed to rich (2.3, 5.1, 24.3, 27.4) or a plurality (Mehrzahl) over against oligarchs (29.1, 36.1). This distinction is sharpest at 29.1: συμπεισθέντων τῶν πολλῶν διὰ τὸ νομίζειν βασιλέα μᾶλλον ἑαυτοῖς συμπολεμήσειν, ἐὰν δι' ὀλίγων ποιήσωνται τὴν πολιτείαν (the many were persuaded especially by the thought that the king would be more likely to fight . if they based the constitution upon a few men).

While it is hardly to be denied that the notion of number is (necessarily) present in each occurrence of τὸ πλῆθος/οἱ πολλοί, it is legitimate to ask if this fact, in general, is a sufficient explanation of why Aristotle chose these terms and, specifically, if the contrasts to which Kaibel points are actually those which Aristotle intended.[16] Two passages give pause. The first is at 24.3, at which Aristotle says that κατέστησαν δὲ καὶ τοῖς πολλοῖς εὐπορίαν τροφῆς (they provided ample maintenance for the common people). On one level, it is true to say that the poorer majority of the population will have benefitted from empire, but that is not the point here. The statement is followed by a list of recipients of public monies in their political functions (jurors, archers, council members, etc.), and this segment is summed up at 25.1: ἡ μὲν οὖν τροφὴ τῷ δήμῳ διὰ τούτων ἐγίγνετο (that is how maintenance for the people came into being). It will become clear why τοῖς πολλοῖς has been changed into τῷ δήμῳ.

In the second, at 27.4, Aristotle describes Pericles' action in providing jury pay as διδόναι τοῖς πολλοῖς τὰ αὑτῶν.[17] Kaibel uses this as an example of a contrast between rich and poor, but a more pointed contrast is suggested by the context: it is between οἱ πολλοί, the general population benefitted by jury pay, and οἱ δημόται, the restricted part of the population which belonged to Cimon's deme. This interpretation of the text is confirmed by a series of paratexts. These reveal that, with one exception,[18] every passage in which τὸ πλῆθος/οἱ πολλοί is found also contains an occurrence of ὁ δῆμος. It is not so much the number of times these terms are used as the way they are used which justifies recognizing in them a pattern.

The texts (some of which we have seen before) are as follows:

A1 (2.1): στασίασαι τούς τε γνωρίμους καὶ τὸ πλῆθος
A1a (2.3): πικρότατον ἦν τοῖς πολλοῖς
A2 (2.2): Solon πρῶτος ἐγένετο τοῦ δήμου προστάτης
B1 (5.1): τῶν πολλῶν δουλευόντων τοῖς ὀλίγοις (the many were enslaved to the few),
B2 ἀντέστη τοῖς γνωρίμοις ὁ δῆμος (the people rose against the notables)
C1 (9.1): μάλιστά φασιν ἰσχυκέναι τὸ πλῆθος (particularly contributed to the power of the masses)
C2 (9.1): κύριος γὰρ ὢν ὁ δῆμος τῆς ψήφου (for when the people are masters of the vote)
D2 (20.1): ἡττώμενος δὲ ταῖς ἑταιρείαις Κλεισθένης προσηγάγετο τὸν δῆμον (as Cleisthenes was getting the worse of the party struggle, he attached the people to his following,)
D1 (20.1): ἀποδιδοὺς τῷ πλήθει τὴν πολιτείαν (by proposing to give political power to the masses)
D2a (21.1): διὰ μὲν οὖν ταύτας τὰς αἰτίας ἐπίστευον ὁ δῆμος τῷ Κλεισθένει. (for these reasons the people placed their trust in Cleisthenes).
D1a (21.1): τότε δὲ τοῦ πλήθους προεστηκώς (then, as champion of the masses).
E1 (20.3): τῆς δὲ βουλῆς ἀντιστάσης καὶ συναθροισθέντος τοῦ πλήθους (the council resisted and the common people gathered in force)
E2 (20.3): ὁ δὲ δῆμος δύο μὲν ἡμέρας προσκαθεζόμενος (the people besieged them for two days).
F1 (22.1): τὸν Κλεισθένη στοχαζόμενον τοῦ πλήθους. . . .ἐτέθη καὶ

ὁ περὶ τοῦ ὀστρακισμοῦ νόμος (Cleisthenes [enacted other new laws] in his bid for popular support, among them the law about ostracism).

F2 (22.2): θαρροῦντος ἤδη τοῦ δήμου, τότε πρῶτον ἐχρήσαντο [i.e., functioning as δῆμος in assembly] τῷ νόμῳ τῷ περὶ τὸν ὀστρακισμόν (they used for the first time the law about ostracism)

G1 (24.3): κατέστησαν δὲ καὶ τοῖς πολλοῖς εὐπορίαν τροφῆς (they provided ample maintenance for the common people)

G2 (25.1): ἡ μὲν οὖν τροφὴ τῷ δήμῳ (maintenance for the people).

H (ch. 28): ὁ δῆμος is used exclusively for the one side of the rival factions: four terms are used for the other side (γνώριμοι, εὔποροι, ἐπιφανεῖς, ἕτεροι).

I (36.1): ἐπεὶ διεσπάρησαν οἱ λόγοι πρὸς τὸ πλῆθος (when his arguments gained currency among the masses)

I2 (36.1): φοβηθέντες μὴ προστάτης γενόμενος τοῦ δήμου (grew afraid that he might become champion of the people).

J (41.2): διαγεγένηται μέχρι τῆς νῦν ἀεὶ προσεπιλαμβάνουσα τῷ πλήθει τὴν ἐξουσίαν. (the constitution has continued to that in force today, continually increasing the power of the masses).

J2 (41.22): ἁπάντων γὰρ αὐτὸς αὐτὸν πεποίηκεν ὁ δῆμος κύριον. (the people have made themselves masters of everything).

Three general and preliminary observations are in order: (1) these sets of texts form small patterns and are part of a larger pattern; (2) each set involves stages in a process; (3) with the exception of one set, the first stage is represented by πλῆθος/πολλοί, the second by δῆμος.

We may begin with (3). The exceptions are D and Da: in both, δῆμος precedes πλῆθος. This is the only group in which there is a double set of correspondences. In D1a, τότε δὲ προεστηκώς refers to the same time as D1, ἀποδιδούς τῷ πλήθει τὴν πολιτείαν: that is, Cleisthenes' offer of πολιτεία was the means by which he attracted the δῆμος. D1 is introduced by ἡττώμενος δὲ ταῖς ἑταιρείαις. Now the first two parts of the complete sentence are, with minor changes, taken over from Herod. 5.66.2: ἑσσούμενος δὲ ὁ Κλεισθένης τὸν δῆμον προσεταιρίζεται (losing out, Cleisthenes attracted the people to his side). The last clause is Aristotle's addition and, with the addition, he has created a structure which views Cleisthenes and his reforms from two points of view, one antityrannical (from Herodotus), the other pro-πλῆθος. This double viewpoint explains how he has shaped chapter 20, with the first view enclosing the second, and it explains the contents of chapters 20 and (partly) 22. Thus, 20 is in a sense an introduction to 21 and 22, and μὲν οὖν of 21.1 rounds off the contents of that chapter. Within those contents the transition from πλῆθος to δῆμος has already been achieved with κατασχόντος τοῦ δήμου τὰ πράγματα and with Cleisthenes τοῦ δήμου προστάτης. Accordingly, δῆμος of ἐπίστευον ὁ δῆμος reflects the latter stage, πλῆθος of τότε τοῦ πλήθους προεστηκώς the earlier.[19]

In discussing (2) I shall use the symbols *a* = πλῆθος/πολλοί and its part of the process and *b* = δῆμος with its part of the process.

A. In the structure of chapter 2, *a/a*[1], in both forms (πλῆθος and οἱ πολλοί), provide a ring frame with *b* at its center. A situation *a* introduces the person who will resolve that situation in a particular guise, προστάτης τοῦ δήμου. This motif will be the subject of chapter 28 and, in this context, will be last used at I.

B. The same situation signalled by *b* produces a reaction by *a*. Here, *a* represents some kind of organized reaction.[20]

C. *A* sets up a result, *b* sets up a condition (κύριος τοῦ ψήφου) which, when fulfilled by a result dependent on another condition (κύριος τοῦ ψήφου), produces a different result (κύριος τῆς πολιτείας).

E. One action *b* leads to another action *a*. Aristotle has rewritten the version of Herodotus to produce the effect he wanted: 5.72.2: ἀντισταθείσης δὲ τῆς βουλῆς καὶ οὐ βουλομένης πείθεσθαι. . . . 'Αθηναίων δὲ οἱ λοιποὶ τὰ αὐτὰ φρονήσαντες ἐπολιόρκεον αὐτοὺς ἡμέρας δύο (the council resisting and unwilling to yield. . . . the rest of the Athenians, being of the same mind, besieged them for two days). In Aristotle's version, the δῆμος will include members of the βουλή along with rest of the πλῆθος.

F. Part *b* is one specific aspect of the general process sketched in D: F[1] corresponds to D.[1]

G. The actual situations of *a* and *b* differ only slightly. The first difference is that *a* has an economic nuance. Between *a* and *b* the components of *a* are listed (δικασταὶ μὲν γὰρ κτλ.) by function, and their functions are institutional. The second is that μὲν οὖν can connote the end of a process, but the process here consists only in spelling out the specfic institutional functionaries of the general πλῆθος.

I. has two links to A. In both (albeit in different ways), *a* is made up of a combination of πλῆθος/πολλοί. A has the first, and J the last, mention of προστάτης τοῦ δήμου.

J. brings partially to a close the process begun in A. The process is that whereby the πλῆθος/πολλοί first acts collectively during the προστασία of Solon, gains political power through institutional (especially dicastic) means, and finally solidifies that power with the last restoration of democratic government. As just noted, the process begins with A; its dicastic side first appears in C, it is l inked with the first occasion in which the δῆμος chooses to act in I; the ultimate convergence of the process and its dicastic aspect is in J. The text continues: ἁπάντων γὰρ αὐτὸς αὑτὸν πεποίηκεν ὁ δῆμος κύριον, καὶ πάντα διοικεῖται ψηφίσμασιν καὶ δικαστηρίοις, ἐν οἷς ὁ δῆμός ἐστιν ὁ κρατῶν. καὶ γὰρ αἱ τῆς βουλῆς κρίσεις εἰς τὸν δῆμον ἐλήλυθασιν. One of the perfect tenses, πεποίηκεν, shows that the process, as goal-directed, is complete. The other perfect tense, διαγεγένηται, shows that the result of the process continued to be felt μέχρι τῆς νῦν, and in this way the process has come full circle: τῷ πλήθει shows that the original process, πλῆθος → δῆμος, has reversed itself and become δῆμος → πλῆθος. The dicastic aspect of the process keeps pace, for the reference to judgments of the βουλή is an introduction to chapter 45.

NOTES

1. Cf. Keaney 1984.

2. With uncharacteristic brevity, Kaibel (55) is satisfied to define πόλις as "das politische Gemeinwesen."

3. Both Harpocration Π 59 = s.v. Περίπολος and Σ Aeschines 2.167 have παρὰ τοῦ δήμου instead of the παρὰ τῆς πόλεως of the London papyrus: I assume that this is a slip, caused by τῷ δήμῳ.

4. Cp. 14.3: Πεισίστρατος. . . . διῴκει τὰ κοινὰ πολιτικῶς μᾶλλον ἢ τυραννικῶς. This usage is almost indistinguishable from the "nonfactional" nuance of (8) below.

5. Chapter 14 "Aristotle and Theramenes."

6. There is also paronomasia: τοὺς τῷ δήμῳ πρὸς χάριν ὁμιλοῦντας. . . . ἔχαιρεν ἡ πόλις. . . .τοῦ βελτίστου χάριν (those who curried favor with the people. . . . the city was pleased. . . . from good motives).

7. Cf. also Rhodes 88–89.

8. οἱ πολλοί also is not found in D.

9. Cf. also 42.2 (συλλεγέντες), 43.3 (συνάγωσιν), and 44.2 (συναγάγωσιν).

10. On 46.2, cf. Rhodes 549.

11. In the phrase, συμβουλευόντων τινῶν τῷ δήμῳ διανείμασθαι τὸ ἀργύριον (some men proposed that the money should be distributed to the people), there is a consensus that τῷ δήμῳ is indirect object of διανείμασθαι. It is not clear why it should not rather be taken, solely or ἀπὸ κοινοῦ, with συμβουλευόντων.

12. Cf. Keaney 1963.135.

13. Cp. the references in Theopompus 115 F 92 to Cleon's activity in the ἐκκλησία.

14. For the divided reaction to the proposals, cf. Diod. 13.53.1.

15. That the two terms are not mutually convertible is shown by *Pol.* 3.1275B7–8: ἐνίαις γὰρ οὐκ ἔστι δῆμος, οὐδ᾽ ἐκκλησίαν νομίζουσιν ἀλλὰ συγκλήτους (in some constitutions there is no body comprising the people, nor a recognized assembly, but only an occasional rally): here, πλῆθος could not be substituted for δῆμος.

16. At 16.7, οὐδὲν δὲ τὸ πλῆθος οὐδὲ ἐν τοῖς ἄλλοις παρηνώχλει κατὰ τὴν ἀρχήν, ἀλλ᾽ ἀεὶ παρεσκεύαζεν εἰρήνην καὶ ἐτήρει τὴν ἡσυχίαν (gave the masses no trouble in other respects during his rule but always kept the peace and saw that all was quiet). I think that no particular *contrast* is intended but that πλῆθος simply refers to the population: close to this is the support of Peisistratus (16.9): ἐβούλοντο γὰρ καὶ τῶν γνωρίμων καὶ τῶν δημοτικῶν οἱ πολλοί (he had many supporters both among the notables and among the ordinary people).

17. Here, οἱ πολλοί is not followed by ὁ δῆμος, and this fact suggests that its use is not part of this pattern. The contrast to τοῖς πολλοῖς which Aristotle intended is strongly marked: it is τῶν δημοτῶν πολλούς.

18. This is at 28.4: οἱ μάλιστα βουλόμενοι θρασύνεσθαι καὶ χαρίζεσθαι τοῖς πολλοῖς (whose chief desire has been to be outrageous and to gratify the masses). The para-text is at 35.3, of the Thirty who τοὺς τῷ δήμῳ πρὸς χάριν ὁμιλοῦντας. . . .ἀνῄρουν, (they eliminated those who curried favor with the people), and it is not clear why τῷ δήμῳ was not used at 28.4. A subtext, Isoc., *Panath.*: ὅταν μὲν θαρρῶσι, τούτους μάλιστα τιμῶντας, τοὺς πρὸς χάριν λέγοντας (whenever they are confident, they elect to office especially those who speak to gratify), does not help. It may be that the text was influenced by 28.3: τὸ πλῆθος ὕστερον μισεῖν, the objects of hatred in this case including Cleophon.

19. For the structure of these chapters, cf. chapter 8, "Vertical Structure: Ring Composition," and Keaney 1969.417–21.

20. This is a detail invented by Aristotle: there is no trace of it in Plutarch, *vitSol*.

17

The Dating Formula

In the historical part of the *AP*, Aristotle has frequent recourse to a dating formula, the elements of which are three, usually in this order: (A) a year (cardinal or ordinal number), (B) reference to a preceding event (usually μετὰ xxx) and (C) reference to an archon (ἐπὶ δεῖνα ἄρχοντος). Following is a complete list of instances of Aristotle's use of this formula and its variations: N = number, Y = year, (Y) = ἔτει implied); [μετὰ-] means that the μετά-phrase is in initial position. Passages to receive special attention are marked with an *.

After Solon

1. 13.1 Y N   cardinal
   ἐπὶ μὲν ἔτη τέτταρα
2. 13.1* N (Y)   ordinal
   τῷ δὲ πέμπτῳ μετὰ τὴν Σόλωνος
   ἀρχήν
3. 13.1* N (Y)   ordinal
   καὶ πάλιν ἔτει πέμπτῳ
4. 13.2 N   cardinal
   ἔτη δύο καὶ δύο μῆνας [μετὰ δὲ
   ταῦτα]

Peisistratus

5. 14.1 Y N   ordinal
   ἔτει δευτέρῳ καὶ τριακοστῷ μετὰ   archon
   . . . θέσιν
6. 14.3 N Y   ordinal
   ἕκτῳ ἔτει μετὰ–κατάστασιν   archon
7. 14.4* Y N   ordinal
   ἔτει δὲ δωδεκάτῳ μετὰ ταῦτα
8. 15.1* Y N   ordinal
   ἔτει μάλιστα ἑβδόμῳ [μετὰ δὲ
   ταῦτα] μετὰ–κάθοδον
9. 17.1* Y N   cardinal
   ἔτη τριάκοντα καὶ τρία ἑὸς
   δέοντα εἴκοσι
10. 19.2* Y N   ordinal

Peisistratids
ἔτει δὲ τετάρτῳ μάλιστα μετὰ-θάνατον

11. 19.6* Y N   cardinal
ἔτη μάλιστα ἑπτακαίδεκα. . . .   archon
ἑνὸς δεῖ πεντήκοντα

Democracy
12. 21.1 Y N   ordinal
ἔτει τετάρτῳ μετὰ–κατάλυσιν   archon
13. 22.2* Y N   ordinal
ἔτει πέμπτῳ μετὰ–κατάστασιν   archon
14. 22.3* Y N   ordinal
ἔτει δὲ μετὰ ταῦτα δωδεκάτῳ   archon
15. 22.3* Y N   cardinal
ἔτη δυο μετὰ τὴν νίκην   archon
16. 22.5* (N) Y   ordinal
εὐθὺς δὲ τῷ ὑστέρῳ ἔτει   archon
17. 22.6* Y N   cardinal
ἐπὶ μὲν οὖν ἔτη γ'
18. 22.6* N Y   ordinal
τῷ τετάρτῳ ἔτει [μετὰ δὲ ταῦτα]   archon
19. 22.7* Y N   ordinal
ἔτει δὲ τρίτῳ μετὰ ταῦτα   archon
20. 22.8* N Y   ordinal
τετάρτῳ δ' ἔτει   archon
21. 23.5 Y N   ordinal
ἔτει τρίτῳ μετὰ–ναυμαχίαν   archon
22. 25.1–2* Y N   cardinal
ἔτη δ' ἑπτακαίδεκα μάλιστα μετὰ   archon
τὰ Μηδικά
23. 26.2* N Y   ordinal
ἕκτῳ ἔτει μετὰ–θάνατον   [archon]
24. 26.3 Y N   ordinal
ἔτει δὲ πέμπτῳ μετὰ ταῦτα   archon
25. 26.3* (Y) N   ordinal
καὶ τρίτῳ μετὰ τοῦτον   archon
26. 27.2* N Y   ordinal
ἑνὸς δεῖ πεντηκοστῷ ἔτει [μετὰ   archon
δὲ–ναυμαχίαν]

The Four Hundred
27. 32.2* Y N   cardinal
ἔτεσιν δ' ὕστερον. . . .   archon
μάλιστα ἑκατόν
28. 33.1*N   cardinal
μῆνας. . . .μῆνας   archon
29. 34.1 Y N   ordinal   (406/5)
ἔτει δ' ἑβδόμῳ μετὰ–κατάλυσιν   archon

Democracy

30. 34.2 (N) Y	(ordinal)	(405/4)
τῷ γὰρ ὕστερον ἔτει		archon
31. 35.1*	(404/3)	archon
32. 39.1*		archon
33. 40.4 Y N	ordinal	
ἔτει τρίτῳ μετὰ–ἐξοίκησιν		archon
34. 41.1*		archon

Variations from the original formula are most precisely discussed from different approaches, and it will be found that, occasionally, variations from the original themselves are involved in the creation of new patterns, as in the first set of passages in II below.

I

(A) AB are lacking at 35.1, 39.1, and 41.1. In the first, the text sums up by ring frame a process which began at 34.2:

τῷ γὰρ ὕστερον ἔτει ἐπ᾽ ᾽Αλεξίου ἄρχοντος ἠτύχησαν τὴν ἐν Αἰγὸς ποταμοῖς ναυμαχίαν, ἐξ ἧς συνέβη κύριον γενομένον τῆς πόλεως

in the following year, the archonship of Alexias, they lost the battle of Aegospotami, and as a result of that [Lysander] became master of the city, and

Λύσανδρον καταστῆσαι τοὺς τριάκοντα τροπῷ τοιῷδε. . . . οἱ μὲν οὖν τριάκοντα τοῦτον τὸν τρόπον κατέστησαν ἐπὶ Πυθοδώρου ἄρχοντος (35.1)[1]

set up the Thirty in the following manner. . . . in this way the Thirty were established, in the archonship of Pythodorus

The reason why Aristotle delayed the archon date to chapter 35 may be one of, or a combination of, three factors, historical, stylistic, and thematic. Historically, it is unclear exactly when the Thirty were established.[1] It is possible that this took place before Pythodorus[2] was selected as archon. If this uncertainty was in Aristotle's sources, he may have delayed mentioning that archon until after he mentioned the establishment. One result of this delay, on the structural level, was to enable him to make a discrete segment of this process.

When Aristotle refers to the second of successive years, his formula is τῷ ὕστερον/ὑστέρῳ ἔτει (cp. 22.5). Uniquely, in these chapters, there are three successive years marked. He had used the phrase for the second and perhaps thought that a repetition for the third year would have been stylistically otiose.

I suggest also that, with the help of the closed structure, Aristotle wanted to make a direct thematic link without chronological interruption between the event of 405/4, the battle of Aegospotami, and the installation of the Thirty. A causal link is suggested by the language, ἐξ ἧς,[3] and a chronological tightness by the structure and the repetition of language.

39.1: Chapter 39 begins: ἐγένοντο δ᾽ αἱ διαλύσεις ἐπ᾽ Εὐκλείδου ἄρχοντος. Elements A and B can be used only when there is reference to two different areas of time, one backward, the other forward. Here, there is only a single referent, an event already described: ἐφ' ὧν συνέβη καὶ τὰς διαλύσεις γενέσθαι (38.3). As in 34/5, this segment is marked off by a ring frame: γενομένων δὲ τούτων τῶν διαλύσεων (40.1).

41.1: The situation in 41.1 is similar: ταῦτα μὲν οὖν ἐν τοῖς ὕστερον συνέβη γενέσθαι καιροῖς, τότε δὲ κύριος ὁ δῆμος γενόμενος τῶν πραγμάτων ἐνεστήσατο τὴν νῦν οὖσαν πολιτείαν ἐπὶ Πυθοδώρου μὲν ἄρχοντος. ([the final reconciliation] took placed subsequently. Meanwhile the people took control of affairs and set up the present constitution, in the archonship of Pythodorus). There is a back reference (τότε δὲ)[4] to the series of events beginning at 39.3.

II

17.1: Πεισίστρατος. . . . ἀπέθανε νοσήσας ἐπὶ Φιλονέω ἄρχοντος, ἀφ' οὗ μὲν κατέστη τὸ πρῶτον τύραννος ἔτη τριάκοντα καὶ τρία βιώσας, ἃ δ' ἐν τῇ ἀρχῇ διέμεινεν ἑνὸς δέοντα εἴκοσι. (Peisistratus. . . . died from an illness, in the archonship of Philoneos: he had lived thirty-three years from his first seizure of the tyranny, spending nineteen of those years in power). C, a version of B (ἀφ' οὗ), A/cardinal.

19.6: παρέδωκαν. . . . ἐπὶ Ἁρπακτίδου ἄρχοντος, κατασχόντες τὴν τυραννίδα μετὰ τὴν τοῦ πατρός τελευτὴν ἔτη μάλιστα ἑπτακαίδεκα, τὰ δὲ σύμπανα σὺν οἷς ὁ πατὴρ ἦρξεν ἑνὸς δεῖ πεντήκοντα ([the Peisistratids] handed over [the Acropolis to the Athenians] in the archonship of Harpactides: the Peisistratids had held the tyranny for about seventeen years after their father's death, and the total length of the tyranny, including their father's rule, was thirty-six yerars: CBA/cardinal.

32.2: ἡ μὲν οὖν ὀλιγαρχία τοῦτον κατέστη τὸν τρόπον ἐπὶ Καλλίου μὲν ἄρχοντος, ἔτεσιν δ' ὕστερον τῆς τῶν τυράννων ἐκβολῆς μάλιστα ἑκατόν (that is how the oligarchy was set up, in the archonship of Callias, about a hundred years after the expulsion of the tyrants): CB (ὕστερον) A/ cardinal.

The placement of C in 17 may have initially been influenced by the importance of the archon date: this is not simply an item of information but part of a chronologically based argument. The repetition of the CBA order suggests that the passages are to be taken together. At 19.6, B (μετὰ τὴν τοῦ πατρὸς τελευτήν) provides one link to 17, and, at 32.2, a link to 19 is again contained in B (ὕστερον τῆς τῶν τυράννων ἐκβολῆς).

22: No less than eight instances of the formula are in chapter 22, and an overview of its structure may provide a first explanation for what anomalies exist. The chapter states a thesis in its first sentence: δημοτικωτέρα πολὺ τῆς Σόλωνος ἐγένετο ἡ πολιτεία (the constitution became much more democratic than that of Solon); describes a condition to which Cleisthenes responded: καὶ γὰρ συνέβη τοὺς μὲν Σόλωνος νόμους ἀφανίσαι τὴν τυραννίδα διὰ τὸ μὴ χρῆσθαι, καινοὺς δ' ἄλλους νόμους θεῖναι τὸν Κλεισθένην (many of Solon's laws had ben consigned to oblivion by the tyranny, through not being used, and Cleisthenes enacted other new laws); and proceeds with a list of measures. Here, καὶ γὰρ is used to set out the way in which the πολιτεία became δημοτικωτέρα,[5] by attributing a group of laws to Cleisthenes but switching the focus from Cleisthenes to the Athenians, for it is the Athenians who implement all of these measures.[6] The formula:

22.2: A/ordinal BC
22.3: ABA/ordinal C
22.3: A/cardinal B
22.5: A/ὑστέρῳ C
22.6: A/cardinal
22.6: BA
22.7: ABC (ἐπί omitted)
22.8: AC (" ").[7]

It is easy to see that a rigid application of the formula eight times in a concentrated space would have been stylistically intolerable: at the same time, it is clear that the formula is the element basic to this chapter, but with variations, and never used in the same way more than once.

The most striking set of variations comes at 22.3, in which B is (uniquely) within A, there is (uniquely) a combination of an ordinal and a cardinal number and two versions of B. The purpose is clear: it is partly to advert to the specific application of the general theme of legislation announced at the beginning of the chapter and partly to draw attention to the first instance of a psychological theme, the θάρσος of the *demos*.[8]

III

Thrice C is missing from the full formula:

14.4: ἔτει δὲ δωδεκάτῳ μετὰ ταῦτα περιελαυνόμενος ὁ Μεγακλῆς
15.1: μετὰ δὲ ταῦτα ὡς ἐξέπεσε τὸ δεύτερον ἔτει μάλιστα ἑβδόμῳ μετὰ τὴν κάθοδον
19.2: ἔτει δὲ τετάρτῳ μάλιστα μετὰ τὸν Ἱππάρχου θάνατον.

Of 15.1 Rhodes (206) comments: "The sentence is grammatical nonsense, with no main verb, and some have corrected it. . . . more probably we should accept that the author has failed to work out his long sentence." I suspect, with others, that there is textual corruption, but that it is more deeply rooted than has been assumed. With one exception, Aristotle does not repeat elements of his chronological pattern as this text does (μετὰ ταῦτα, μετὰ τὴν κάθοδον). The exception, 22.3, is not a parallel, for there the repetition is a rhetorical contrivance. I think that something has dropped out here, and that may have included an archon date. I have no explanation for the omission of C in the other passages.

IV

I end with mostly *seriatim* comments on the remainder.

13.1: C is replaced by οὐ κατέστησαν ἄρχοντα.
13.1: B is replaced by πάλιν and C by ἀναρχίαν.
25.2: A (cardinal), B and delayed C.

The delay is because Aristotle is talking about two processes, one of the gradual decline of the council of the Areopagus (ὑποφερομένη κατὰ μικρόν), the other of Ephialtes' attacks. It is not known for how many years these attacks went on, but the culmination (πρῶτον, ἔπειτα) of the process was in a specific year and is so dated.

26.2: normal AB and C is worked into the narrative (καὶ πρῶτος ἦρξεν ἐξ αὐτῶν Μνησιθείδης). The same is true of 33.1 in which B is lacking (a full calendar year had not intervened) and the version of C is ἦρξεν ἐξ αὐτῶν Μνησίλοχος.
26.3: an unusual form of B, μετὰ τοῦτον, with reference to the archon of two years before who had just been mentioned.[9]
27.2: order BAC. The version of B is μετὰ δὲ τὴν ἐν Σαλαμῖνι ναυμαχίαν, and the purpose of the emphatic order is to contrast Athens' success in that war with her failure in the Peloponnesian war and specifically with 29.1: μετὰ τὴν ἐν Σικελίᾳ γενομένην συμφοράν.

NOTES

1. Details at Rhodes 436–37.
2. On the structure, cf. chapter 6, "Vertical Structure: Ring Composition."
3. Cf. Keaney 1984.162
4. Cp. 21.1.
5. There is a precise parallel at 27.1: δημοτικωτέραν ἔτι συνέβη γενέσθαι τῶν πολιτείαν· καὶ γὰρ κτλ. (the constitution now became still more democratic).
6. ἐποίησαν, ᾑροῦντο, ἐχρήσαντο, ἐκυάμευσαν, ὠστράκιζον, ὥρισαν. So in 27, Pericles initiates activity (παρείλετο, προύτρεψεν), and the *demos* προηρεῖτο τὴν πολιτείαν διοικεῖν αὐτός.
7. Although the formula in the phrase ἄρχοντος Ἀθήνησι δεῖνα is regular in such late sources as Dionysius of Halicarnassus, Pausanias and the Marmor Parium, earlier instances of the phrase without ἐπί are quite rare: Herod. 8.51.1: Καλλιάδεω ἄρχοντος Ἀθηναίοισι (Herod. never uses the ἐπί- formula); Lysias F 129 Sauppe (*apud* Harpocration L 15 = s.v. Λέχαιον, . . . τὸ Λέχαιον ἕαλω Μνασίππου ἄρχοντος (perhaps not verbatim: Harp. always uses ἐπί when citing Atthidographers (Δ 50 = s.v. Διαψήφισις, Π 101 = s.v. Προπύλαια, S 55 = s.v. Συμμορίαι); [Dem.] 49.30: οὗτος ὁ χρόνος ἦν Ἀλκισθένους ἄρχοντος; Demetrios of Phaleron F 149 W [Diog. Laert. 1.22]: πρῶτος σοφὸς ὠνομάσθη ἄρχοντος Ἀθήνησι Δαμασίου, καθ' ὃν καὶ οἱ ἑπτὰ σοφοὶ ἐκλήθησαν (the καθ- clause in Diogenes' rewriting may have forced out an original ἐπί. Cp. F 150 W: ἐπὶ Καλλίου); Philochorus F 31: Κέβριδος ἄρχοντος (from Hesychius, not verbatim), F 66: τοῦ γὰρ Ἀναξικράτους

ἄρχοντος (not verbatim, according to Jacoby); Plutarch *vitThes* 36.1: Φαίδωνος ἄρχοντος (the genuine works of Plutarch contain only one example of the ἐπί- formula, *vitDemos* 24.2); and Athenaios 5.217E: ἄρχοντος Ἐπαμείνονος, ἐφ' οὗ τελευτᾷ (in which the ἐφ- clause may have affected an original ἐπί). One could restore ἐπί in the text of 27, but I suspect that the omission is due to the desire for variation.

8. Cf. 24.1, 27.1 and Keaney 1984.162.

9. μετὰ τοῦτον is equivalent to μετὰ τοῦτον ἄρχοντα. Compare the Atthidographic formula for each year: name, demotic, ἐπὶ τούτου, narrative.

18
Chapter 45: ἡ βουλή

Chapter 45 raises question of three kinds: internal structure, contextual structure, and theme. These are interrelated, but distinctions are necessary because each rubric has its own contribution to the correct understanding of the chapter. By contextual structure, I refer to the question of why the chapter is placed here vis-à-vis chapters 42–69. By theme, I understand the relationship of the contents of the chapter to the contents of the ᾿Αθπολ as a whole.

I. *INTERNAL STRUCTURE*

At first glance, the outer limits of the chapter seem to be clear: in chiastic form, 45.1: ἡ δὲ βουλὴ (A) πρότερον μὲν ἦν κυρία (B) seem to be balanced by 45.4: τούτων μὲν οὖν ἄκυρός (B¹) ἐστιν ἡ βουλή (A¹). This balance is effected by the linguistic contrast of κυρία and ἄκυρος. On the other hand, the anecdote of 45.1 has its own structure and is set within a structure similar to, but more elaborate than, the outer frame:

45.1: ἡ δὲ βουλὴ πρότερον μὲν ἦν κυρία καὶ (formerly the council had full powers)

A: χρήμασιν ζημιῶσαι καὶ (to impose fines,)

B: δῆσαι καὶ (to imprison and)

C: ἀποκτεῖναι. (to put to death.) καὶ Λυσίμαχον αὐτῆς ἀγαγούσης ὡς τὸν δήμιον καθήμενον ἤδη μέλλοντα ἀποθνῄσκειν Εὐμηλίδης ὁ ᾿Αλωπεκῆθεν ἀφείλετο οὐ φάσκων δεῖν ἄνευ δικαστηρίου γνώσεως οὐδένα τῶν πολιτῶν ἀποθνῄσκειν· καὶ κρίσεως ἐν δικαστηρίῳ γενομένης, ὁ μὲν Λυσίμαχος ἀπέφυγεν, καὶ ἐπωνυμίαν ἔσχεν ὁ ἀπὸ τοῦ τυπάνου, (when it had taken Lysimachus to the executioner, and he was sitting waiting for the death sentence to be carried out, Eumelides of Alopece took him away, saying that no citizen ought to be put to death except by the sentence of a jury court. A trial was held in court: Lysimachus was acquitted, and came to be known as the man who returned from the garotte,) ὁ δὲ δῆμος ἀφείλετο τῆς βουλῆς (the people then took away from the council)

C¹: τὸ θανατοῦν καὶ (the right to execute and)

B¹: δεῖν καὶ (imprison and)

Α¹: χρήμασι ζημιοῦν, (fine,) καὶ νόμον ἔθετο, ἄν τινος ἀδικεῖν ἡ βουλὴ καταγνῷ ἢ ζημιώσῃ, τὰς καταγνώσεις καὶ τὰς ἐπιζημιώσεις εἰσάγειν τοὺς θεσμοθέτας εἰς τὸ δικαστήριον, καὶ ὅ τι ἂν οἱ δικασταὶ ψηφίσωνται, τοῦτο κύριον εἶναι. (and enacted a law that, if the council convicted a man of wrongdoing or wanted to punish him, its convictions or punishments should be brought before the jury court by the *thesmothetae*, and whatever the jurors voted should be final.)

The chiastic structure at the beginning and end, the balanced clauses in the middle, the central chiasmus (δικαστηρίου γνώσεως/κρίσεως–ἐν δικαστηρίῳ), the wordplay (ἀποθνήσκειν ending two clauses, the two different meanings of ἀφείλετο)—all these show that Aristotle spent considerable care in the construction of this passage.

This anecdote is tied to the beginning of the ring frame but does not take up all the intervening space, nor does the end of the anecdote coincide with the grammatical end of the sentence/paragraph: this goes on to say that the adverse decisions of the βουλή are referred by the θεσμοθέται to a court, and, whatever the court decides, τοῦτο κύριον εἶναι. The reference to a function of the θεσμοθέται would more naturally be expected in the chapter devoted to those officials where, in fact, it is found (59.4): thus, what is unusual is the repetition, and to this we shall return. In terms of the internal structure, it can be said that there is a slight rounding-off with the repetition of κύριον, and this takes us to the next point.

II. THEMATIC STRUCTURE

If, because of κυρία–κύριον, 45.1 is a clearly defined segment, it remains to ask what relation it has to the rest of the chapter. Now 45 as a whole does not so much state as illustrate a theme, that authority over certain functions once held by the βουλή has passed to a court. Thus, thematically, 45.1 looks forward to the rest of the chapter as well as backward to the passages in which the theme comes up. The first of these is 25.2: ἅπαντα περιεῖλε [sc., Ephialtes] τὰ ἐπίθετα δι' ὧν ἦν ἡ τῆς πολιτείας φυλακὴ καὶ τὰ μὲν τοῖς πεντακοσίοις, τὰ δὲ τῷ δήμῳ καὶ τοῖς δικαστηρίοις ἀπέδωκεν (he took away from the council [of the Areopagus] all the accretions which gave it its guardianship of the constitution, giving some to the Council of Five Hundred and some to the people and the jury courts). Two points are immediately to be made: (1) the Council of Five Hundred is distinguished from the *demos* and the courts; (2) there is much debate about which powers were taken over by assembly, courts, and council, a debate which need not concern us here.

Clues to Aristotle's intention are provided by the language of some paratexts. The first is one phrase of 26.2—ἡ τῆς πολιτείας *φυλακή*—which recalls Solon's action toward the Areopagus (8.4)—τὴν δὲ τῶν Ἀρεοπαγιτῶν ἔταξεν ἐπὶ τὸ νομοφυλακεῖν, ὥσπερ ὑπῆρχεν καὶ πρότερον ἐπίσκοπος οὖσα τῆς πολιτείας (appointed the Council of the Areopagus to guard the laws, just as previously it had been overseer of the constitution). The back-reference is to 3.6, and both 9.4 and 3.6 include among the duties of this body κολάζειν καὶ ζημιοῦν κυρίως/κυρία οὖσα (having full power to chastise and punish). The theme of κυρι- is next taken up in 41.2: ἐνδεκάτη. . . . ἀφ' ἧς διαγεγένηται μέχρι τῆς νῦν, ἀεὶ προσεπιλαμβάνουσα τῷ πλήθει τὴν ἐξουσίαν. ἁπάντων γὰρ αὐτὸς αὑτὸν πεποίηκεν ὁ δῆμος κύριον, καὶ πάντα διοικεῖται ψηφίσμασιν καὶ δικαστήριοις, ἐν οἷς ὁ δῆμός ἐστιν ὁ κρατῶν. καὶ γὰρ αἱ τῆς βουλῆς κρίσεις εἰς τὸν δῆμον ἐληλύθασιν (eleventh, from which the constitution has continued to that in force today, continually increasing the power of the masses. The people have made themselves masters of everything, and control all things by means of decrees and jury courts, in which the sovereign power resides with the people; even the jurisdiction of the council has been transferred to the people). In the structure of chapter 41, this last sentence (καὶ γὰρ . . . ἐληλύθασιν) is added to and thus extends the outer ring of an A/B/B¹/A¹ frame. The extension is to provide for further development of the theme of 41, and the development comes in chapter 45.

III. *CONTEXTUAL STRUCTURE*

More properly speaking, the development of one part of the ring comes in chapter 45, that part which concerns the judicial functions of the βουλή. There is another part which is structurally developed—ψηφίσμασιν καὶ δικαστηρίοις—assembly and courts. After a necessary chapter (42) in which eligibility for citizenship is defined, a structure implicit in assembly courts begins: the first office defined is the βουλή. The first subdivision of that body is the prytanizing tribe. The first duty of the subdivision is to convene council and assembly: (43.3) καὶ ὅσα δεῖ χρηματίζειν τὴν βουλὴν . . . οὗτοι προγράφουσι. . . . προγράφουσι δὲ καὶ τὰς ἐκκλησίας οὗτοι (they prescribe what business the council is to deal with. . . . likewise they prescribe the meetings of the assembly). The only officials mentioned in 45 in connection with the judicial functions of the council are the *thesmothetai*, the first statement made about the *thesmothetai* in their chapter (59.1) is πρῶτον μὲν τοῦ προγράψαι τὰ δικαστήριά εἰσι κύριοι (they have the power, first, to prescribe the days on which the jury courts are to sit), the last archontic official mentioned is the *thesmothetes* (66.1); and the last segment of the work is devoted to the *dikasteria*.

The preceding may be sufficient to explain why the βουλή is discussed here, but one or two things more can be said. There are three anomalous features about the content of chapter 45: the first is the repetition of the statement about the *thesmothetae* in 59.4, the second is the repetition of the statement about the *dokimasia* of the archons in 55.2. The more natural context for each statement is the later one. Since 45 gives us no more *information* on these matters than is found in 55 and 59, the reason for the anomalous content of 45 is thematic. What Aristotle has done is to take material from its normal context and use it to illustrate the theme of κῦρος and its transference to the *demos/ dikasterion*. He applies this process of transference to three different organs (archons, Areopagus, council) in three different ways, but what is common to all three is that each loses a power, and this power is judicial (3.5; 26.2). The final anomaly in the content is the anecdote. This is the only instance of an anecdote in D, and its uniqueness underscores the thematic importance of its moral.

As we saw at the beginning of this chapter, the first structural principle informing 45 is the chiastic link between 45.1 and 45.4. We have also seen that 45.1 has its own structure, and this would seem to leave 45.2 and 45.3 in midair. Again, Aristotle solved this problem by a unique application of a familiar structure. 45.2 begins κρίνει δὲ τὰς ἀρχὰς ἡ βουλὴ τὰς πλείστας, καὶ μάλισθ᾿ ὅσαι χρήματα διαχειρίζουσιν (the council has jurisdiction over most officials, especially those who handle money). The sentence begins with the verb, κριν-, the nominal form of which, κρίσις, was the focal point of the transition, in one matter, of jurisdiction from the council to the law court. The specific point of the anecdote is articulated and generalized in the next clause: ἡ οὐ κυρία δ᾿ ἡ κρίσις, ἀλλ᾿ ἐφέσιμος εἰς τὸ δικαστήριον (its judgment is not final but referrable to the jury court). The point is then applied to two more instances, and these are joined in chiastic order:

45.2: ἔφεσις (A) δὲ καὶ τούτοις (B) . . .
45.3: νῦν δὲ τούτοις (B¹) ἔφεσίς (A¹) ἐστιν εἰς τὸ δικαστήριον.

19

The Other πολιτεῖαι

In an earlier chapter, I remarked that, irrespective of opinions on the authorship of the *AP* itself, few now would hold that Aristotle was responsible for all of the remaining one hundred and fifty-seven *politeiai*. The controlling assumption here is that the sheer size of the collection precludes single authorship. Since we know nothing of the absolute size of any of the other *politeiai*,[1] and nothing of the way or ways in which they were produced, this assumption should share the same fate as others discarded in our first chapter.

An obvious way to assess authorship is to compare to the *AP* what evidence from the other *politeiai* can be compared. The major categories within which I have been analyzing the contents of the Ἀθπολ are structure, subtext/source, paratext/repetition, and context. Even a cursory review of the fragments shows the difficulties inherent in attempting any large comparison between that work and their contents, but the task is not totally impossible, and some fruitful results can be teased out.

I. STRUCTURE

With minor exceptions, it may be assumed that the combination of N(arrative) and D(escription) was operative in the πολιτεῖαι, but the difficulties here are both general and specific. In general, the largest single category of fragments concerned foundation stories, and Plutarch seems perfectly justified to have characterized the works as κτίσεις. This is, however, precisely the part of the *AP* which has not been preserved.[2] This interest in origins reflects the needs of the later scholars who used the *politeiai* (e.g., commentators on classical poets) and the peculiar tastes of the excerptor, Heracleides Lembos, but it is not easy to see what "political" relevance such origin stories had or what credence Aristotle placed in many of them. For the latter, it would be interesting to know if he drew the kind of functional borderline between history and prehistory as did Herodotus (1.5.3). I suggest that he did, at least by the criterion of credibility. The suggestion is possible only because, ocasionally but rarely, an item from a πολιτεία is known to us through the phenomenon of double transmission. By this I mean that the same event is known through two channels. In the *Constitution of Ceus* (F 511 R), we are told by one source (Σ Theocr. 5.53) that Aristotle said (ὥς φησιν Ἀριστοτέλης), that Aristaios was taught the production of olive and honey by the nymphs who had raised him. A similar story in Heraclides 27 begins "they say": φασιν. The verb with its anonymous subject showed that Aristotle was recounting a story people told, and that his account of it did not entail belief in it. So also, in the *Constitution of Tenedos* (F 593 R), Stephanos of Byzantium reports Aristotle's account (φησίν) of the punishment in the law on adultery, the first victim of which was the legislator's son. The same story in Heracleides 24 is again introduced by the generalizing φασίν. There are frequent examples of cautionary λέγεται[3] and φασί[4] used to introduce accounts either implausible in themselves or suspicious for some reason now unclear. These accounts tend to be mythical or prehistorical, but one from the archaic age will interest us in the next section.

From the former point of view, it would not be a mistake to question the "political" relevance of origin stories if we had only the fragments to rely on. Not one of these attaches political significance to any such story, As it happens, however, the *AP* has one prehistoric figure with whom not one but two political phenomena are connected. This is Ion who, when he came to Attica, was the first polemarch (3.2); and, when he and his fellows settled in, the population was divided into four tribes and four tribe kings (41.2). These socio-political innovations, the tribal system, the four kings, and the office of polemarch, lasted down to and beyond Aristotle's time. That the fragments of the *politeiai* may not be useful guideposts in this regard is suggested by the fact that the lexicographer Harpocration[5] cites Aristotle on Ion, and Heracleides included that part of the text in his excerpts; but neither noted the political application.

II. SUBTEXT/SOURCE

According to Plutarch (F 538 R), Aristotle reported (ἱστόρηκε) that the social institution at Sparta known as the *krypteia* was one of the political devices (πολιτεύματα) of the lawgiver Lykurgus. Heracleides' version (10) is: λέγεται δὲ καὶ τὴν κρυπτὴν εἰσηγήσασθαι (he is said to have introduced the *krypteia*). The reason for Aristotle's skepticism in this particular case is, again, unknown: it does, however, bespeak an attitude which seems especially to have affected the Λακπολ but is observable in other works as well, The attitude is Aristotle's willingness, with the availability of new source material, to change his mind or to question secondary sources he had used previously. From this point of view, since any statement Aristotle made in the earlier[6] books of the *Politics* on matters prior to the fourth century must have been based on secondary sources, it is legitimate to treat those statements, as well as these and similar sources, as subtexts. I discuss three sets of texts in this connection.

For the *AP*, we have already seen in chapter 3 above the most notable change: in *Pol.* 2 and 3, Aristotle believed that Solon made no change in the appointment of magistrates, while in 8.1 and 47.1 we learn that a Solonian law established sortition.[7]

For the second set, one of the historians whom Aristotle used in *Pol.* 7 for the early history of Italy was Antiochus of Syracuse: it is he who lies behind the reference to οἱ λόγιοι τῶν ἐκεῖ οἰκούντων (the chroniclers of the settlers there) of 1329B8. It is acknowledged that Aristotle followed Antiochus so closely, even in error,[8] that Jacoby is justified in printing 1329B5–22 as one of the texts in his collection of historians of Magna Graecia (577 F 13). By the time Aristotle came to compose the πολιτεῖαι of individual cities, he thought himself able to correct Antiochus. The latter's version (555 F 10) of the settlement of Croton identified Myscellus as its founder: for Aristotle, that person was Croton.[9]

A small phrase from Heracleides may serve as a transition to the final set of passages. We saw earlier that ἐξ ἀρχῆς was used at the beginning of several, perhaps of the majority, of πολιτεῖαι. In sharp contrast, the beginning[10] of the Λακπολ may have been something like Her. 9: τὴν Λακεδαιμονίων πολιτείαν τινὲς Λυκούργῳ προσάπτουσι πᾶσαν (some attribute the whole constitution of the Lacedaemonians to Lykurgus). This programmatic statement is absolutely unique in Heracleides' excerpts and was surely intended by Aristotle to underscore a new approach he was taking toward early Spartan history. In *Pol.* 2 and 7, he was concerned to criticize the traditional Lycurgan constitution of Sparta and those, like Thibron, who eulogized it. Now, he questioned the tradition itself, and there are small bits of evidence showing the results of this new approach.[11]

III. PARATEXT/REPETITION AND CONTEXT

With rare exceptions, fragments come unaccompanied by paratexts or context, and this might be the time to treat some similarities between the *AP* and other *politeiai,* although the evidence continues to be ambiguous and the results necessarily inconclusive.[12]

Some years ago, I suggested that the received punctuation of a fragment of the ΛακΠολ (F 538 R = Plut. *vitLyc* 28.7):[13] Ἀριστοτέλης δὲ μάλιστά φησι καὶ τοὺς ἐφόρους ὅταν εἰς τὴν ἀρχὴν καταστῶσι πρῶτον, τοῖς εἵλωσι καταγγέλλειν πόλεμον be changed to ἀρχήν, πρῶτον (Aristotle says that the ephors, when established in office, first declare war on the Helots). The change makes the declaration the first of a series of official announcements[14] and has a precise parallel in the announcement of the archon at Athens who (56.2): εὐθὺς εἰσελθὼν πρῶτον μὲν κηρύττει. . . . ἔπειτα [as soon as he has entered upon his office, first makes a proclamation. . . . next).

The parallelism here is double, of content and of context: the latter because we can be fairly confident that the passage on Sparta was found in the descriptive part of that πολιτεία. The number of fragments which can be assigned to D is depressingly small, and we have nothing like chapter 45, which thematically bridges N and D. There are some further parallels, of language and of theme, but we cannot take them too far. Thus, the language of Her. 14, quoted in note 3, is that the *AP* uses of Solon at 7.1: πολιτείαν δὲ κατέστησε (established a constitution), but this kind of language is determined by the constitutional content of the series.[15] We have one instance of αὔξησις: this affected the ruling family of Corinth[16] but nothing suggests that other elements of that pattern (κατὰ μικρόν, προάγειν/προελθεῖν) attended the increase. There are occurrences of πρῶτος, but none show the patterned use we observed in *AP* 27 and 28.[17] δοκεῖν is found, but only once in a political context, and that from the *AP:*[18] the Herodotean word δόκιμος is used of Pheidon of Argos (Her. 39) and we cannot tell if it had ironic implications; the verb εὐδοκιμεῖν is found once, but of the fabulist Aesop (Her. 33).

In general the evidence of the fragments is fragile but at least in one instance affords a strong basis of comparison. This is Her. 19, from the Κορινθίων πολιτεία: Περίανδρος δὲ [1] πρῶτος μετέστησε τὴν ἀρχὴν [2] δορυφόρους ἔχων καὶ [3] οὐκ ἐπιτρέπων ἐν ἄστει ζῆν, [4] ἔτι δὲ κτῆσιν ὅλως καὶ τρυφὴν περιαιρῶν, [5] μέτριος δὲ ἦν ἐν ἄλλοις, [6] τῷ τε μηδένα τέλος πράσσεσθαι ἀρκεῖσθαί τε τοῖς ἀπὸ τῆς ἀγορᾶς καὶ τῶν λιμένων, [7] καὶ τῷ μήτε ἄδικος μήτε ὑβριστής εἶναι (Periandros was [1] the first to change the constitution [2] by virtue of his having a bodyguard and [3] not allowing people to live in the city, and also [4] by entirely outlawing the possession of slaves and luxuries. But he was [5] moderate in other respects; [6] in not levying a tax on anyone, in being satisfied with a tax on goods from the market and the harbor, and [7] in being neither unjust nor overbearing). The parallels, not only in content but also in structure, with the career of Peisistratus are clear.

It will be recalled that Aristotle's account was, like the *AP* itself, divided into a narrative segment and a descriptive segment. So here (1) and (2) are paralleled by Peisistratus' first accession to power, assisted by bodygards (14.1). Near the beginning of the second segment, Aristotle said of Peisistratus that ἔν τε γὰρ τοῖς ἄλλοις φιλάνθρωπος ἦν κτλ (in general he was humane etc.), and this is paralleled by (5).[19] There followed (16.2–4) remarks on the tyrant's economic policies and his financial self-interest, just as in (6). The beginning of the final part summed up social: δημοτικὸν εἶναι τῷ ἤθει καὶ φιλάν-θρωπον (his democratic and humane manner) and legal: (ἐβούλετο πάντα διοικεῖν κατὰ τοὺς νόμους (he was willing to administer everything according to the laws) aspects of his character, and these are briefly encapsulated in the epithets applied to Periandros, μήτε ἄδικος μήτε ὑβριστής.[20]

It is possible to take the comparison one step further. In an earlier analysis, we saw that Aristotle's portrait of Peisistratus and his regime was not intended to be read in isolation but that he was to be contrasted with Solon as the two practitioners of the politics of personality and of institutions. The final remark of Heracleides suggests that Periandros was a practitioner of both, for, like Solon,[21] βουλὴν δὲ ἐπ᾽ ἐσχάτων κατέστησεν, οἳ οὐκ ἐφίεσαν δαπανᾶν πλέον ἢ κατὰ τὰς προσόδους (at the last,[22] he established a council, which did not allow spending beyond one's income).

These parallels, which unfortunately cannot be established for other πολι-τεῖαι, lead to the suggestion that the kinds of structured patterns informing, as I have argued, the Ἀθπολ may have been found in other works also. If so, the convenience for a person faced with composing a large number of these works is obvious. I will close by suggesting two other processes which may have facilitated composition. The first is the possibility that the *politeiai* were dictated. I have only one piece of evidence for this: it is the frequency of the collocation μὲν οὖν in framing ring composition. This is a feature of Aristotle's lecture style,[23] and, while lecturing is not the same as dictation, they are related.[24]

The second process: in working with subtexts we have perforce been limited to written sources. In his biological researches, we know that Aristotle used written sources, autopsy, and information orally imparted. For the πολιτεῖαι, autopsy will have come mainly from his travels between the first and second stays at Athens. For oral information, I cite some further texts from Heracleides:

Crete (15): διαιτῶνται δὲ Κρῆτες πάντες καθήμενοι θρόνοις. ἄρχονται δὲ τῶν παρατιθεμένων ἀπὸ τῶν ξένων, μετὰ δὲ τοὺς ξένους τῷ ἄρχοντι διδόασι δ' μοίρας (all the Kretans sit upon chairs [to eat]. They begin by serving food to the guests. After the guests, they allot four portions to the ruler). καθόλου δὲ πολλὴ φιλανθρωπία τοῖς ξένοις ἐστὶν ἐν Κρήτῃ καὶ εἰς προεδρίαν καλοῦνται (in Crete there is generally much hospitality to strangers, to whom they assign seats of dignity).

Etruria (44): πάντες δὲ ὑπὸ τῷ ἱματίῳ μετὰ τῶν γυναικῶν κατάκεινται[25] κἂν παρῶσί τινες καὶ τοὺς καταλύοντας ξένους φιλοῦσιν (The Etruscans all lie down beneath the same himation with their wives, even if some [guests] are present, and they treat kindly the strangers who stay [with them]).

Phasis (46): φιλόξενοι δ'εἰσὶν ὥστε τοὺς ναυαγοὺς ἐφοδιάζειν καὶ γ' μνᾶς διδόντας ἀποπλεῖν (the people of Phasis are hospitable so that they furnish victims of shipwreck with supplies, give them three minas, and send them off).

Lucania (48); οἱ δὲ Λευκανοὶ φιλόξενοι καὶ δίκαιοι (the Lucanians are hospitable and just).

Aphytis (72): φασὶ δέ ποτε ξένον πριάμενον οἶνον μὴ ἀναλαβεῖν ἐπείξαντος αὐτὸν τοῦ πλοῦ, καταλιπεῖν δὲ αὐτὸν ἐν τῇ ἀποστάσει οὐδενὶ παραδόντα, ὕστερον δὲ κατ' ἄλλην ἐμπορίαν εὑρεῖν τοῦτον ἄθικτον (they say that once a stranger, who bought wine, did not take it along, since his voyage was urgent, but left [the wine] in the storehouse without entrusting it to anyone: later, when he came [there] on another trip, he found the wine untouched).

Natives of a place may boast about local hospitality. It is equally likely that hospitality impressed its recipients, and I suggest that some of these were (students and?) acquaintances of Aristotle.

NOTES

1. The Λακεδαιμονίων πολιτεία was probably second in length. This is arguable not so much from the consideration that the number of fragments is second to that of

Athens as from three other facts: Sparta was the second-most interesting *polis* in Greek antiquity, Heracleides gave the second-most space and second position to it in his *Excerpts*, and at least six other writers had written specifically on it before Aristotle. Four of these are mentioned in the *Politics*, two as private individuals, Lysander and Pausanias (5.1301B19–20), and two as writers, Tyrtaeus 5.1306B39f.: δῆλον δὲ τοῦτο ἐκ τῆς Τυρταίου ποιήσεως τῆς καλοιμένης Εὐνομίας (this is clear from the poem of Tyrtaeus entitled *Eunomia*), and Thibron 7.1333B18–20: οὕτω καὶ Θίβρων ἀγάμενος φαίνετα τὸν τῶν Λακώνων νομοθέτην, καὶ τῶν ἄλλων ἕκαστος τῶν γραφόντων περὶ τῆς πολιτείας αὐτῶν (so the writer Thibron is clearly an admirer of the Laconian lawgiver, and so too is each of the others who write about the Spartan constitution). Crete may have held third place, again because of its interest to political theorists and because Heracleides devoted third place to it in order and space, but a Κρητῶν πολιτεία is not attested outside of Heracleides.

2. How much space Aristotle expended on the early history of Athens cannot be known. On the basis of earlier research, Rhodes (65) calculates that the beginning would have taken up between four and six pages of Kenyon's *OCT*.

3. *Excc.* 22, 26, 30, 64, 65, 70, 71. Skepticism about early political traditions may have extended to Crete: Herod's excerpt begins τὴν Κρητικὴν πολιτείαν λέγεται πρῶτος καταστῆσαι Μίνως (Minos is said to have been the first to establish the Cretan constitution).

4. 24, 25, 37, 46, 53, 55, 66, 72, 74. Note that the appeartance of Peisistratus before the homicide court (16.8), discussed in chapter 10, is introduced in the *Politics* by φασί (1315B20),

5. A 194 = s.v. ᾿Απόλλων πατρῷος ὁ Πύθιος.

6. My assumptions are that books 7, 8, and 2 are roughly contemporary, 3 later; and 4, 5, and 6 last. See, most recently, J. M. Rist, *The Mind of Aristotle: A Study in Philosophical Growth* (Toronto 1989) 146–59.

7. For some *alleged* discrepancies between the *Politics* and the *AP*, see Keaney 1980[1].

8. This is the ethnically false equation of the Opici and Ausones. Cp. 555 F 7: ᾿Αντίοχος μὲν οὖν φησι τὴν χώραν ταύτην ᾿Οπικοὺς οἰκῆσαι, τούτους δὲ καὶ Αὔσονας καλεῖσθαι (Antiochus says that the Opici settled this land, and these were also called Ausones) with 1329B18–20: ᾤκουν δὲ τὸ μὲν πρὸς τὴν Τυρρηνίαν ᾿Οπικοὶ καὶ πρότερον καὶ νῦν καλούμενοι τὴν ἐπωνυμίαν Αὔσονες (on the Tyrrhenian side dwelt the Opicians, called Ausonians both in ancient and modern times).

9. Herod 68: Κρότωνα ἐξ ἀρχῆς Κρότων ᾤκισεν (in the beginning Croton settled Croton), from the Κροτωνιατῶν πολιτεία.

10. It must be noted that there is no certainty that this was the beginning. I hazard the claim on two grounds: (1) the unique quality of the statement; (2) the fact that the account of Lycurgus is not continuous but (a) begins with our statement, is interrupted by (b) a detail about the poet Alcman, and reverts to (c) an extended account of Lycurgus' constitution. The difficulty with this is that the intervening material is chronologically out of place, and originally (c) may have followed without this interruption.

11. E.g., the attribution of the ephorate to King Theopompus (6. 1318A27) rather than to Lycurgus. This evidence is treated at Keaney 1980[1]. 52–53.

12. The longest fragment which, it is safe to assume, preserves the *ipsissima uerba* of its author is in Athenaios 576AB = F 549 R). From the Μασσαλιωτῶν πολιτεία, it is written in an archaic style and shows enough features alien to Aristotle's diction that it cannot in the first instance have been written by him. (Cf. Keaney 1980[2].) Several features suggest that it was from the early Ionian historian, Hecataeus. This is not an argument that Aristotle did not compose the *Constitution of Marseilles:* it means only

that he incorporated a single source more fully there than was his habit to do when, as with the *AP*, he was working with a plurality of sources.

13. Keaney 1971[1]. The suggestion has since been confirmed by a computer-assisted word search.

14. For other announcements by the ephors on the same occasion, cf. F 539 = Plut. *vitCleom* 9.2: εἰς τὴν ἀρχὴν εἰσιόντες; *Mor.* 550B: εὐθὺς εἰς τὴν ἀρχήν.

15. Cf. also, of Rhegion, Her. 55: πολιτείαν δὲ κατεστήσαντο ἀριστοκρατικήν (they established an aristocratic constitution).

16. Her. 19: the sons of Bacchis, οἳ τὸ γένος οὕτως ηὔξησαν ὥστε Βακχιάδας ἀντὶ Ἡρακλειδῶν καλεῖσθαι τοὺς ἀπ'αὐτῶν (who so strenghtened their family that those descended from them were called Bacchiadal instead of Heracleidal].

17. Her. 10; 14; 37.

18. Her. 1: ἀπὸ δὲ Κοδριδῶν οὐκέτι βασιλεῖς ᾑροῦντο διὰ τὸ δοκεῖν τρυφᾶ καὶ μαλακοὺς γεγονέναι (after the Codridae, kings were no longer chosen, since they seemed to be effeminate and soft). On this, cf. Keaney 1963[1].139–41 and Rhodes 78.

19. For μετρ-, compare 16.1: διώκει δ'ὁ Πεισίστρατος. . . . τὰ περὶ τὴν πόλιν μετρίως κτλ. (Peisistratos managed the city's affairs moderately).

20. Items (3) and (4) do not fit neatly into this reconstruction. On the model of the *AP*, they should follow (5) (cp. 16.3: μήτε ἐν τῷ ἄστει διατρίβωσιν). If the reconstruction is correct, Heracleides has distorted the order, as he did elsewhere (in his excerpting of the *AP*, his paragraph 7 should follow 4). Although we happen to know the subtext for (3): Ephorus 70 F 179 *apud* Diog. Laert. 1.98, οὐκ εἶα ἐν ἄστει ζῆν τοὺς βουλομένους (he did not allow those who so desired to live in the city), that throws no light on the problem.

21. 8.4: βουλὴν δ' ἐποίησε.

22. The meaning of the phrase is unclear: cf. E. Will, *Korinthiaka* (Paris 1955) 512 with note 3.

23. E.g., *Pol.* 5.1301A19; 01B5; 02B31 al.

24. It may be relevant that Aristotle uses εἴρηται in his back references (*AP* 11.1; 16.2; 55.3).

25. An exaggerated and erotically oriented version of this in Theopompus 115 F 204 served as Aristotle's subtext.

Bibliography

Chambers: M. H. Chambers, ed. *Aristoteles* ΑΘΗΝΑΙΩΝ ΠΟΛΙΤΕΙΑ (Leipzig 1986).

Day-Chambers: J. Day and M. Chambers, *Aristotle's History of Athenian Democracy* (Berkeley and Los Angeles 1962).

Düring: I. Düring, *Aristotle in the Ancient Biographical Tradition* = *Studia Graeca et Latina Gothoburgensia* 5 (Göteborg 1957).

D(ilts): M. R. Dilts, *Heraclidis Lembi Excerpta Politiarum* = *Greek, Roman and Byzantine Monograph* 5 (Durham 1971).

FHG: C. Müller, *Fragmenta Historicorum Graecorum* 3 (Paris 1849).

Hignett: C. Hignett. *A History of the Athenian Constitution* (Oxford 1952).

J(acoby): F. Jacoby, *Die Fragmente der griechischen Historiker* (Berlin 1923–58; Leiden 1957–).

Jacoby: F. Jacoby, *Atthis: The Local Chronicles of Ancient Athens* (Oxford 1949).

Jaeger: W. W. Jaeger, *Aristotle: Fundamentals of the History of his Development,*[2] Tr. R. Robinson (Oxford 1948).

Kaibel: G. Kaibel, *Stil und Text der* ΠΟΛΙΤΕΙΑ ΑΘΗΝΑΙΩΝ *des Aristoteles* (Berlin 1893).

Keaney 1963[1]: Keaney, J. J., "The Structure of Aristotle's *Athenaion Politeia,*" *HSCP* 67 (1963) 115–46.

Keaney 1963[2]: "Two Notes on the Tradition of Aristotle's Writings," *AJP* 84 (1963) 52–63.

Keaney 1969[1]: "The Alleged Alphabetization of Aristotle's *Politeiai,*" *CP* 64 (1969) 213–18.

Keaney 1969[2]: "Ring-composition in Aristotle's *Athenaion Politeia,*" *AJP* 90 (1969) 406–23.

Keaney 1970[1]: "The Text of Androtion F 6 and the Origin of Ostracism," *Historia* 19 (1970) 1–11.

Keaney 1970[2]: The Date of Aristotle's *Athenaion Politeia,*" *Historia* 19 (1970) 323–36.

Keaney 1974: "Theophrastus on Greek Judicial Procedure," *TAPA* 104 (1974) 179–94.

Keaney 1976: "Androtion F 6 Again," *Historia* 25 (1976) 480–81.

Keaney 1979[1]: "Two Textual Notes on Aristotle, I: *Ath. pol.* 58.3; II: F 538 Rose (Plutarch, *Lycurgus* 28.7)": *LCM* (1979) 17.

Keaney 1979[2]: "A Source/Model of Aristotle's Portrait of Theramenes," *CJ* 75 (1979) 40–41.

Keaney 1980[1]: "Hignett's *HAC* and the Authorship of the *Athenaion politeia,*" *LCM* 5 (1980) 51–56.

Keaney 1980[2]: "Hecataeus as a Source of Aristotle F 49 Rose," *LCM* 5 (1980) 87–88.

Keaney 1981: "Aristotle's *Politics* 2.12.1274a22–b28," *AJAH* 6 (1980) 97–100.

Keaney 1982: Review of P. J. Rhodes, *A Commentary on the Aristotelian* Athenaion
     Politeia (Oxford 1981), *AJP* 103 (1982) 161–63.
Keaney 1984: "A Narrative Pattern in Aristotle's *Athenaion Politeia*," *Greek, Roman*
     and Byzantine Monographs 10, 161–63.
Keaney-Connor: —and W. R. Connor, "Theophrastus on the End of Ostracism," *AJP*
     90 (1969) 313–19.
Keaney-Raubitschek: —and A. E. Raubitschek, "A Late Byzantine Account of Ostra-
     cism," *AJP* 93 (1972) 87–91.
Keaney-Szegedy-Maszak: —with A. Szegedy-Maszak, "Theophrastus *De eligendis*
     magistratibus," *TAPA* 106 (1976) 227–40.
Levi: M. A. Levi, *Commento storico alla* Respublica Atheniensium *di Aristotele* (Mil-
     ano 1968).
Moraux: P. Moraux, *Les listes anciennes des ouvrages d' Aristote* (Louvain 1961).
Newman: W. L. Newman, *The politics of Aristotle with an Introduction, Two Prefatory*
     Essays and Notes Critical and Explanatory, 1–4 (Oxford 1887–1902).
Rhodes: P. J. Rhodes, *A Commentary on the Aristotelian* Athenaion Politeia (Oxford
     1981).
Rhodes: P. J. Rhodes, tr. *Aristotle*, The Athenian Constitution (Harmondsworth-Balti-
     more 1984).
R(ose): V. Rose, *Aristotelis qui ferebantur librorum Fragmenta* (Leipzig 1886).
Sandys: J. E. Sandys, *Aristotle's* Constitution of Athens, 2nd. ed. (London 1912).
Saunders: T. J. Saunders, *Plato*, The Laws (Harmondsworth-Baltimore 1970).
Saunders: *Aristotle*, The Politics, tr. by T. A. Sinclair, revised and re-presented by T.
     J. Saunders (Harmondsworth-Baltimore 1981).
Weil: R. Weil, *Aristote e l'histoire; Essai sur la* "Politique" (Paris 1960).
W(ehrli): F. Wehrli, *Die Schule des Aristoteles* 1: *Dikaiarkhos* (Basel 1967), 9: *Phainas*
     (Basel 1969).

General Index

Index locorum